Malcolm Brocklehurst was born in Torquay, England. For many years he worked in the aerospace industry – in the late 1960s as a development engineer on Concorde. As a consultant in the European aircraft industry, he travelled widely, working in Bremen, Hamburg, Madrid, and Toulouse, where he became interested in the mysteries of Rennes-le-Château, the Knights Templar, the Freemasons, and the Holy Grail. He lives in Cleveleys, Lancashire, and sometimes writes under the pseudonym of Majinka.

The Secret History of Christianity

Malcolm Brocklehurst

Magpie Books, London

Constable & Robinson Ltd
3 The Lanchesters
162 Fulham Palace Road
London W6 9ER

This edition published by Magpie Books,
an imprint of Constable & Robinson Ltd 2008

A copy of the British Library Cataloguing in Publication Data
is available from the British Library

ISBN 978-1-84529-763-3

Printed and bound in the European Union

1 3 5 7 9 10 8 6 4 2

Acknowledgments

I would like to acknowledge Robert Feather for his work on cracking codes and his theory of the source of the treasures of the Essenes in his book *The Copper Scroll Decoded*.

I am grateful to Glenn McQuire for constructive pointers about Masonic history, to Peter Messerbender for his help on the Tunic Crosses located in Cornwall, and to Alan Scott for providing information relating to the parchments found at Rennes-le-Château.

Thank you to Christina Spieler for providing the data on the alchemist's medallion held in the Viennese Kunsthistorisches Museum, and to Sylvia Leach for her research at Rennes-le-Château.

My thanks to all the staff at Cleveleys Library, and particularly to Brenda, for all their help with my research, and to all the members of all denominations of the Cleveleys Writers' Group, which meets at the library, for their support and criticisms. Particular thanks are due to David Pitman for his editing of my first draft.

Finally, I would like to thank my wife Mary, for her patience and fortitude as a "computer widow" for the last few years, and all my friends and colleagues, who have listened and commented and made criticisms, for their support – their input has been invaluable.

Dedication

"The awakening of any individual is a cosmic event."
Clark Emery

With that Gnostic statement, I dedicate this book to all peoples of whatever creed or colour, in the hope that they will grasp the thorn bush of truth; if the thorns then prick you in the search for truth, don't blame the thorn bush, but give thanks for the rose that grows on it.
"Majinka" Brocklehurst

"When I use a word," Humpty Dumpty said in rather a scornful tone, "it means just what I choose it to mean – neither more nor less."

"The question is," said Alice, "whether you can make words mean so many different things."
Lewis Carroll

Meditate, and read on.

Contents

Paintings and other images referred to in the text can be seen on-line at www.cleveleyswriters.co.uk

Introduction

The purpose of this book is to get the reader to think, and to understand the enormous confidence trick that has been played on the faithful in the name of the major religions. As well as being an examination of Christianity, it seeks to understand what happened to the Templars and their lost treasure, and probes further back, to the Pharaohs and their wealth. There are many mysterious links between the Templars, the Holy Grail, and the Church. I encourage readers to ask questions of their religions, so that some of the mythology that cloaks all religions may be swept away, and Christians may live in harmony with Muslims, free of dogma that is either outdated or, in some cases, deliberately misleading, intended to subjugate those who do not have access to modern scientific knowledge. I also call on theologians to criticize this book, thereby initiating a process whereby the truth may be revealed.

I was christened a Protestant and throughout my life I have strived to respect all my fellow human beings, irrespective of colour or creed. I have found, however, that misleading dogma associated with Christianity, Judaism, and Islam acts as an obstacle to free thought, which, in turn, fuels bigotry, preventing people of one faith from understanding the faiths of others, thereby preventing them from caring for their fellow human beings. If I ask myself, "What is a Jew and what is an Arab?" a further question presents itself: "If a person is a Jew, does he or she belong to a religion or a race?" Given that there are Russian, American, British, and German Jews – in fact, Jews of many different nationalities – then the answer must be that to be Jewish is to be an adherent of the Jewish religion. Following the same line of thought, one may ask the question, "To which race do the Israelites belong?" The answer is, of course, the Semitic race, however when I refer to the Catholic Encyclopedia I find that "Arabia" is the cradle of Islam and, in all probability, the home of the Semitic race. According to the same source, the term "Semite" was first proposed by Ludwig Schlözer to describe languages related to Hebrew. Via Eichhorn's *Repertorium* the name eventually came into general use and has now been widely adopted, except that modern science uses it in a somewhat wider sense to include all those peoples who are either demonstrably of Semitic origin, or who appear in history as completely enveloped by the Semitic cultures. In ancient times the whole of western Asia, with the exception of the peninsula of Asia Minor, was Semitic. The Semitic race that came out of Arabia eventually split into the two mainstream religions of Judaism and Islam and consequently there are two statements that are equally true: The Jewish state of Israel is, in fact, an Arabic nation, with a Jewish religion; and the Arabic nations are Semitic, with an Islamic faith.

Business is Business

The maxim "Business is business, my boy" was not lost on the early Catholic Church. Pope Leo X (1513–21) will always be remembered for his profound statement: "It has served us well, this myth of Christ." He was referring, of course, to one of the greatest confidence tricks the world has ever known; one which has become a multi-million-dollar business which has fed on the fears of the poor, and on the masses who have been kept in ignorance of the truth. For two thousand years the Church of Rome has run one of the finest corporate empires the world has ever seen. The directors of this business empire have held the power of life and death over its shareholders and they have tampered with the books on a scale which would be considered fraudulent in the corporate world. On the positive side, the Church has played a role in the moral education of humanity, but that applies to all the religious doctrines of the world. The "Fat Cats" who control the business conglomerates of the twenty-first century are amateurs compared with one of the finest business minds in history; I am referring to the Roman Emperor Constantine, who founded a business empire which has survived and increased its profits year on year for the last 1,700 years. To build this business empire, Constantine, who had the power of the Roman legions to back him, was either a very lucky or a very astute businessman.

From about AD 310 Constantine and Maxentius were locked in a power struggle for the imperial crown of Rome. The power struggle was decided when it came to a head in AD 312. Maxentius was defeated and killed by the army of Constantine at the battle of Milvian Bridge, but before the battle Constantine is alleged to have had a vision from the sun god Sol Invictus. Legend has it that Sol Invictus displayed a huge illuminated cross in the sky with the words "*In hoc signo vinces*" ("By this sign you will conquer") emblazoned across it. Probably the sun was particularly hot that day and Constantine was suffering from a form of heat stroke, because the symbol of the cross had little to do with Sol Invictus. It is more likely that the shining sun caused Constantine to hallucinate and to think that the sign of the sun god was the sign by which he would conquer, consequently he would have had halos inscribed on the shields of his troops, and not the sign of the cross.

Later, in AD 331, the historian Eusebius of Caesarea rewrote the history books and created a different legend: that it was the sign of the cross coupled with the letters "*Chi Rho*" that was emblazoned on the shields of Constantine's troops as they went into battle. No matter which legend you believe, it is a fact that Constantine was victorious and, after the battle of Milvian Bridge, the Roman Senate had a triumphal arch erected in the Roman Coliseum. An inscription on the arch proclaimed that victory was won by "Prompting of the Deity" – but the Deity described as the miracle worker was Sol Invictus and not Jesus Christ. Despite persecution, Christianity had survived for over three centuries before Constantine, but to really take hold and expand, it needed a boost.

There were large numbers of Christians living throughout the Roman Empire; consequently Constantine looked to harness the Christian "vote" to strengthen his claim to be head of state. Constantine thus gave Christianity the impetus it required to become a worldwide religion. When Constantine came to power, the Roman Empire was already in decline. He has always been regarded as a tolerant ruler, and history has regarded him as the cornerstone of the Christian faith for the legitimacy which he lent to it. He was sufficiently astute to realize that an empire in decline had either to wage war and conquer new lands or to create growth by expanding trade throughout the existing empire. He opted for the latter, and the first stage was to unite the pagans throughout the empire under one party, one leader, and one religion. Constantine thus set out to establish himself as a father figure who would be the saviour or messiah of the people and who would also provide a focus for the primitive beliefs of the pagan masses. He must have had some very astute advisers because they hit on the idea of centralizing the popular religions of the day by situating their "business centres" in the heart of Byzantium, which was renamed Constantinople in honour of the emperor.

By moving his capital from Rome to Constantinople, Constantine put the Holy Church at the crossroads between Asia Minor and the emerging European provinces. With Constantine established as a godlike father figure, work began to consolidate all the religions in the empire under a single umbrella. Constantine devised a marketing campaign directed at the pagan tribes of the far-flung Roman Empire by prescribing a policy of "Our god is far better than your god." To accomplish this Constantine combined the feast days of the Christian religion with the popular Sol Invictus. The religious cult of Sol Invictus had originated in Syria and had found its way into Roman life via the conquered Syrians. The cult had monotheistic

attributes that made it an ideal base from which
Constantine could launch his policy of one religion, one
party, and one leader. Under this umbrella of state protection, the early Christians flourished and gradually adapted
their religion to accommodate the Sol Invictus cult.

In AD 321 Constantine issued an edict proclaiming that
the law courts should close on the day set aside for worship
of the sun god; that day was to be "sun day." Up to that time
the Christians had accepted the Jewish Sabbath, which
begins on Friday evening and ends on Saturday evening, as
their day of rest. Now in AD 321 they adopted the new "sun
day" as their Sabbath, or holy day. It was around this time
that the crowned head with its halo of light began to appear
in Christian churches. Constantine had successfully merged
two of the major religions of the Roman Empire.

Now he embarked on phase two of his plan to bring as
many of the elements of other pagan cults under the
single umbrella of Christianity as possible. The new
composite faith had the added attraction of promising
eternal life to converts. The cult of the Egyptian goddess
Isis was another religious faith that had spread through
economic contact to most regions of the Middle East.
Such contact enabled Romans, Jews, and Greeks of the
first century to have access to Egyptian religious ideals,
which explains why shrines to Isis have been found in
many Roman towns and cities. Due to the co-existence of
Christianity and the worship of Isis within the Roman
world prior to Constantine's creation of a single faith,
there are similarities between artists' portrayals of the
Virgin Mary and baby Jesus, on the one hand, and Isis
cradling her child Horus, on the other.

Another religion, similar to the worship of Isis, which
had originated in Persia was also flourishing in the Roman
Empire at this time; this was the cult of Mithras, which
conveniently had many of the attributes of Christianity.

The priests of Mithras were referred to as "Magi," as are the wise men referred to in the Gospels who visit Jesus at his birth in Bethlehem – another case of cross-pollination between legends. The Christians of Constantine's era interpreted the Magi's anticipation of the coming of Jesus as confirmation of their own faith and consequently they welcomed the worshippers of Mithras into the Christian worship of Jesus the Saviour.

Further standardization was to follow: previously, Jesus's birthday had been celebrated on 6 January, but for the pagans 25 December was symbolically significant as it marked the "*Natalis Invictus*," the "rebirth" of the sun when the days – in the northern hemisphere, at least – begin to lengthen again, consequently celebrations of the birth of Jesus were shifted to 25 December. Mithras's birth was celebrated on the same day so there was no trouble conflating the births of Jesus and of Mithras. Other fables originating in the cult of Mithras have been adopted into the Christian calendar; for example, Mithras was said to have had shepherds present at his birth when he, too, was born in a manger.

The Indian cult of the Redeemer Krishna also contributed to the merging of Roman religious traditions, contributing belief in a "virgin birth" to Christian dogma. In folklore relating to the birth of Krishna, the Redeemer, Vishnu the Sun God impregnates the Virgin Jasoda who had been chosen to be his mother. The shepherds come to adore the new-born Krishna, but the jealous Rajahs order the killing of all male children born on the same night as Krishna. Doesn't all this sound familiar?

The legends of one cult appear to have been integrated with the legends of another cult to be retold as the story of the birth of Jesus Christ. Gradually the myths and legends were told and retold, until they had merged into a story which came to be accepted as fact by the early Christian Church – but what that Church needed was a messiah, or leader.

With Constantine blending the best of all the cults into one faith or religion, the religious zeal of the times led the masses to believe in Constantine as the father of the state, and, as such, he was regarded as the Messiah of the people. This belief eventually led to the acceptance by the early Christians of the concept of God the Father, but the matter of the Messiah Jesus was pushed to one side until Constantine convened the Council of Nicaea in AD 325.

The purpose of the Council of Nicaea was to unite the various factions and rival elements within the Christian church in sharing a common belief with a catholic, i.e., universal, dogma. Prior to the meeting of the council, Constantine and his advisers had been playing at creating god, but eventually the questions asked by the masses could no longer be answered by the political leaders of the day. The Bishops of the Christian church were convened and met in council at Nicaea with a mandate from Constantine to determine the exact role of Jesus in the Christian religion.

Eventually, after many days of indecisive debate, Constantine ordered the Bishops to vote to define the role of Jesus. The vote was not unanimous, but by a democratic process Jesus was accepted as being divine, the Son of God, and, as such, God himself. This was almost certainly the only election in history when "God" was a candidate in a democratic election, and from that moment Christianity was up and running as a business empire.

The Council of Nicaea was merely the beginning of two thousand years of dogma that have elevated early legends and myths into the fundamental articles of faith of the Christian Church, and led to its business centre – namely, the Catholic Church – attaining heights undreamt of by the early Christians. With the conclusion of the Council of Nicaea, it was time for the newly legitimized Christian faith to consolidate the respectable position that it had achieved within the Roman state. It was also a time for the Roman Christian sect to seek revenge on the pagan Roman sects which had persecuted them for the past three centuries. The pagan flesh that was now fed to the lions in the coliseum was as nourishing as the Christian flesh they had savoured for over three hundred years.

The Council of Nicaea had consolidated the Christian beliefs of the third century, which had been adapted to take in the best of other religions, and had begun the process of creating a centralized business with the Roman state as its body and Constantinople as its heart.

The Gospels which form the basis of the Christian faith have been heavily edited. As they were written during a time of Roman occupation and the suppression of subversive organizations, some of the stories concerning Jesus included coded information for "those with ears to hear." All leaders need foot soldiers, and Jesus was no exception, but to boost recruitment he had to unite the die-hard Jewish traditionalists and the Gentiles. Unification would have put an end to the sectarianism, but that would have caused resentment in the die-hard communities, and would also have had to be carried out in secret to avoid the watchful eyes of the Roman authorities. Instead, Jesus advocated the Essene practice of baptism to "welcome" Gentiles into the Jewish faith. Such baptismal ceremonies were conducted on the shore of the Sea of Galilee and entailed Gentiles wading into the sea while Jesus walked out over the water on some form of jetty to perform the baptism ceremony; hence Jesus was said to have "walked on the water" and "fished," or pulled the Gentiles from the water. Thus he instructed his disciples to became "fishers of men," one of many coded phrases in the Gospels.

Although the first Gospels were written thirty to sixty years after the crucifixion, the words of Jesus are quoted with a certainty that cannot be accurate. Yet the early

Church accepted the Gospels as a factual account of the words of Jesus.

Consider, too, the questions that have been asked of priests and the answers that have been given over the last two thousand years; the dogma of the Church can be no more than the interpretation placed on certain questions at particular points in time. Today, if one asked the question, "How can a virgin conceive and give birth?" The answer, if given at all, would be entirely different to that given by ignorant clerics in the past whose deliberations have passed down into the Church's dogma, with often embarrassing results. As later generations of priests attempted to substantiate the dogma with current thinking, error compounded error until the truth finally disappeared in the fanatical or otherwise warped thinking of priests long since dead.

To return, however, to the accusation that the Church has deliberately edited the Gospels to suit its dogma; prior to the First Ecumenical Council of the Catholic Church, held at Nicaea in AD 325 and the Hebrew Council of Jamnia in AD 90, there was only an Old Testament. At the Council of Jamnia a selection of manuscripts had been added, but only Matthew, Mark, Luke, and John survived the Council of Nicaea. It was in AD 331, six years after the Council of Nicaea that Bishop Eusebius of Caesarea, "The Father of Ecclesiastical History," was commissioned by Constantine to produce fifty scriptures, or Bibles, on the best parchment; it was then that the first editing occurred. The Bibles were for use in the churches of Constantinople, the new capital of the Roman Empire. Why were fifty copies needed? Had all the old copies suddenly become unusable or worn out? If so, why would someone of the emperor's status place what was really just an order for new books? It would be reasonable to assume that the old scriptures were now obsolete and new editions were required in the churches to reflect current thinking.

It has long been accepted that the Gospel of Mark was the first to be written because the writers of the Gospels of Luke and Matthew actually copied whole sections of text from the Gospel of Mark. It has also been known for centuries that the last twelve verses of the final chapter of the Gospel of Mark were added by an unknown cleric during some editorial process. Given that the additional verses give the first account in any of the Gospels of the Resurrection, this was an enormously significant editorial intervention. The stories of the Resurrection that appear in the other Gospels are pirated information that was added to the Gospel of Mark after the original draft text was submitted to the early Church.

Originally, when the Apostles went forth from Jerusalem to spread "the Word," it is the Apostle Mark who is traditionally credited with the establishment of Christianity in Egypt, which became known as the Coptic Church. The Coptic Church still exists today outside of any influence from the Church of Rome and believes in Jesus the man and not in Jesus the God who rose from the dead. It was this belief which was held to be heretical by the Council of Chalcedon in AD 451 and became known as the monophysite heresy. We now know the reason why those twelve verses were added to Mark's Gospel. The Doubting Thomas story is a further example of the scandalous additions that have been made to the Gospels by scribes who were ignorant of the historical facts of life in Roman times. In the fable of Doubting Thomas, there is a risen Jesus who bears the "nail holes" from the crucifixion in his hands and feet, yet if we are to believe the time scale for the trial, execution, and resurrection of Jesus as presented in the Gospels, we must also take into account the fact that the Romans strictly observed the religious laws of the Jews. It was Jewish law that a crucified body should not be allowed to remain on a cross on the Jewish Sabbath. Therefore,

Jesus's crucifixion must have resulted in death on the day of his crucifixion at some point before sunset. In addition, the eve of the Passover made that particular Sabbath doubly sacred.

The Romans used two basic methods of crucifixion: fast, and slow. Both methods resulted in the death of the victim, but which one was used depended on what message the authorities wanted to send out. If the slow method was used, the victim would be nailed to the cross with a small saddle or horn between his legs to support his crotch. The victim was then left to suffer for days before dying of shock and exposure. For the fast method, the victim's feet were placed on a small platform and his wrists tied to the crossbar. The victim was then left with the certain knowledge that death was only a couple of hours away when the executioner came to perform the coup de grâce. The executioner used a club called a *crucifragium* to break the legs of the condemned person. With the body thus deprived of its support, it would sag until its entire weight was suspended on the thongs attaching the wrists to the cross. The circulation became strangled and death from suffocation and heart failure usually occurred within the hour. According to the Gospel of John, the executioner broke the legs of the two thieves who were executed alongside Jesus. This indicates that due to the impending Sabbath and the Passover, all the executions carried out on that day were in accordance with the fast-track method. The Gospel states that the executioner was astonished when he came to Jesus to find him already dead. If that circumstantial evidence were to be presented to a court today, a jury would have to conclude that Jesus was tied, rather than nailed, to the cross, and that Thomas could not have been invited to put his fingers into the wounds in the hands of Jesus.

In the Beginning

A tiny grain of truth surrounds the birth of Jesus: it happened, of that there is no doubt, but it is the virgin birth, the conception aided by heaven that is questionable. Through the ages, writers have catered for the intellect of their readers, therefore when St Paul wrote his epistles to a public that had an established religion and faith he wrote, "Jesus was born of the flesh," and he meant that statement literally.

When the Gospels of Matthew and Luke came to be written for the early church, it was at least sixty years after the birth of Jesus. Luke, a converted Syrian Gentile from Antioch, with a perfect command of Greek, was a physician and a disciple of Paul. He accompanied Paul on his second journey from Troas to Philippi around AD 49 (Acts 16:10–37), and again towards the end of Paul's third journey around AD 58. Luke was again with Paul when he was imprisoned in Caesarea, and he was with him on his adventurous trip from Caesarea to Rome and during Paul's first period of captivity in a Roman prison (Col. 4:14). According to the Vatican's Biblical Commission of June 1912, Luke was written before the Acts of the Apostles and before the destruction of Jerusalem in AD 70. That claim is substantiated by the fact that the Acts conclude with a description of Paul's ministry at the end of his first period of captivity in Rome in AD 63. The Gospels were written around the time of the establishment of the Pauline doctrine and had to tell of a happening that would make the Christian God better and bigger than anything that the Gentiles and pagans already worshipped. Consequently the myth of the virgin birth was introduced in the two original Gospels. Roman pagans had long held Isis in high esteem as one of their favourite deities; therefore, when Jesus was voted a God at the Council of Nicaea, a niche was required for his mother, the Virgin Mary, and thus hyperdulia (worship of the Virgin Mary) began. This eventually led the Council of Ephesus in AD 431 to proclaim Mary "Deipara" as Mother of God. Hyperdulia was included in the religious package offered to the pagans and the Virgin Mary, Mother of God, quickly assumed the mantle and titles long worn by the ancient Egyptian Goddess Isis, such as "Redemptress" and "Star of the Sea." It was largely expediency that led the Roman pagans to utilize the shrines of Isis. Thus the first statues of the Virgin Mary were existing statues of Isis, with perhaps a new coat of paint.

It was during this same period in the fourth century that John Chrysostom, the Patriarch of Constantinople, issued to the early Church the incredible edict that Mary had experienced "perpetual virginity"; his thesis was that Mary's hymen had remained intact throughout conception and had remained intact after the birth of Jesus. In this way, another layer was added to the accretion of absurdity. Today's Church remains burdened with John Chrysostom's theory of perpetual virginity, ratified as dogma by the Lateran council two hundred and fifty years after it was put forward.

It was not until the sixteenth century that Mary was elevated to a higher position in the Catholic Church. The elevation took place at the Council of Trent, which was convened on 13 December, 1546, to discuss and take action on the challenge to Catholic doctrine posed by the Protestant movement. It was at this council that the bishops proclaimed Mary free of all sin, which led to the doctrine of immaculate conception. Three centuries later, Pope Pius IX promoted the theory of immaculate conception as an article of faith, and, in 1958, a Mariological Congress was held at Lourdes where it was proposed that Mary be proclaimed *causa efficiens*, or "the agent or cause that produces." The significance of this would have been that without the intercession and mediation of Mary the Redemptress "no Grace could fall from God above" on the faithful gathered below.

The proposition failed to gather sufficient votes on that occasion, but in 1964 Pope Paul VI elevated Mary to *Mater Ecclesiae*, or "Mother of the Church," and Mary automatically became *causa efficiens*. Now the faithful can speak to God only through the "Redemptress." Isis had come a long way from being an Egyptian deity to recognition as the mother of the Christian God, an elevation due to the 1870 edict that proclaimed the infallibility of the Pope. It distresses Protestants, and bemuses non-believers, that while glorious, gilded statues of the Virgin Mary abound in Catholic churches, statues of Jesus seem almost neglected.

But had it not been for a scribe's error, this worship of the Virgin Mary would not have come about. The factual evidence which led to the eventual elevation of Mary began three centuries before the birth of Christ when Ptolemy Philadelphus of Egypt ordered the Old Testament to be translated from Hebrew into Greek for the Jewish population of Alexandria. The Jews no longer read or spoke Hebrew so a translation was commissioned, which has become known as the Septuagint, either because it took seventy days to complete, or because it was translated by seventy scribes. The translation progressed satisfactorily until a scribe came to Isaiah 7:14, where a problem arose. The Hebrew reads, "Behold a young girl shall conceive and bear a son, and shall call his name Emmanuel." Rabbis had long accepted that the verses were symbolic, a prophecy about the future of Israel. However, the Scribes had to translate the word for "young girl" into Greek which has only one word for virgin, *parthenos*, meaning a female whose hymen was intact and had had no sexual experience. The Jews, however, considered a young girl to be of marriageable age at about fourteen, and if a groom had been found, it was acceptable that she should not retain her virginity after that age; if she did, it was considered an insult to God. Therefore the Hebrew language had two words for "young girl," *almah* and *bethula*, and the latter translates directly into Greek as *parthenos*, or "virgin." The Hebrew scripture of Isaiah used the Hebrew word *almah* which means a woman of any age who has not had children. So as there was no Greek equivalent for the Hebrew *almah* the scribes had no option but to use the Greek *parthenos*. Hence the Bible now reads, "Behold a virgin shall conceive and bear a son, and shall call his name Emmanuel."

Three-and-a-half centuries after Ptolemy Philadelphus of Egypt ordered the Old Testament to be translated from Hebrew into Greek for the Jewish population of Alexandria, the writers of the Gospels of Matthew and Luke must have foraged in ancient Greek scripts for prophecies that could supplement the facts of the birth of Christ and naturally they read the Greek Septuagint which contained the word *parthenos*. The writer of the Gospel of Matthew must have been amazed to find a prophecy that supplemented the rumours of the Christian faithful that a virgin had conceived, and that God was responsible for her condition. The other two Gospels of Mark and John were written by Jews who had no need to resort to the Greek, but relied on the existing Hebrew scriptures for reference. Therefore neither John nor Mark made the same mistake when they came to Isaiah, but accepted the Hebrew word *almah*, meaning a woman of any age who has not yet had a child.

The fact that many stories were still circulating in the early Church as to the true parentage of Jesus suggests that Mary may well have been impregnated by a person other than her betrothed, Joseph. If Joseph had been responsible, the Jews of the day would have accepted Mary as an unmarried *almah*, but rumours had persisted, leading Matthew and Luke to offer the explanation that "God must have done it." In our less credulous age, we know that God couldn't have "done it," yet Joseph admits that Jesus was not his child. In the next chapter, we will examine references in the Bible which suggest the identity of Jesus's biological father.

Scandalous Times

In his book *The Jesus Scroll*, Donovan Joyce claims that the real father of Jesus can be deduced from the scriptures – all that is required is some detective work. In Galatians 1:18–19, Paul writes, "after three years I went up to Jerusalem to see Peter, and I abode with him for fifteen days. But of the other disciples I saw none, save James, the Lord's Brother." Now Matthew 10:3 clearly states that James was the son of Alpheus and as brothers must have a common father or be stepbrothers, then Jesus's real father was Alpheus.

Mark 15:40 states that "there were also women looking on afar off: among whom was Mary Magdalene, and Mary the mother of James the less and of Joses, and Salome." James the less, who was present at the crucifixion, was so called because he was younger than James, the other disciple named in the Gospels. According to the *Catholic Encyclopedia*, James the less was the son of Alpheus (Clopas, or Cleophas) and of a certain Mary. Mark 6:3 reads, "Is not this the carpenter, the son of Mary, the brother of James, and Joses, and of Juda, and Simon and are not his sisters here with us? And they were offended at him."

However, the plot thickens with another clue to be found

in descriptions of the crucifixion. To quote John 19:25, "Now there stood by the cross of Jesus, his mother and his mother's sister, Mary the wife of Cleophas (Alpheus), and the Mary Magdalene." This implies that of the four females present at the execution of Jesus there were two sisters, both named Mary. Did the writers or editors assume that the readers were gullible enough to believe that sisters had been given the same name? The claim is ridiculous, but both Matthew and Mark name three females as being present at the execution, namely Mary Magdalene, Mary the mother of James the younger (or lesser) and Joses, and the mother of Zebedee's children. Was John mistaken or has an error occurred in editing and translating? If the Gospel of John has been altered, either deliberately or in error, it is possible that his account originally read, "Now there stood by the cross of Jesus, his mother Mary the wife of Cleophas (Alpheus), and his mother's sister (Salome), and the Mary Magdalene." If that is correct, then Alpheus, the brother of Joseph, was the real father of Jesus.

Times may change, but human behaviour tends to remain constant and it is possible that Mary, although betrothed to Joseph, had sexual relations with his brother Alpheus. When Mary found herself pregnant, she would have faced a dilemma because she was betrothed to Joseph and the Jewish laws were strict. Although the couple were not married, their betrothal was considered sacred and binding, with dire consequences for either party if he or she committed "adultery" after the betrothal. All devout Jews observed the law of Mishna and Joseph was a devout Jew, therefore breaking the law would have been abhorrent to him. Under the law of Mishra, there were three counts which would have compelled Joseph to divorce Mary: adultery; leprosy or any venereal disease; or any form of clandestine intercourse.

When Mary informed Joseph that she was pregnant, she

may have realized that Joseph would have to decide between the law and his feelings for her. So, being pregnant and knowing that Joseph was not the father, how could Mary tell Joseph of her problem in such a way that he would forgive her? One options might be to make the unanswerable claim that God was the father. In those far-off, biblical times, fairy tales and mythology were still the norm, and most people believed in them. In the twenty-first century, we tend to be more sceptical about the idea of God impregnating a virgin.

Joseph's mind appears to have been troubled with the news of Mary's pregnancy. His immediate reaction is described by Matthew: "Then Joseph her husband, being a just man and not willing to make her a public example decided to divorce her." Anyone knows that sleep does not come easily to a troubled mind, and so it was with Joseph, who had the problem of Mary's pregnancy on his mind when he went to bed. He awoke from a troubled sleep in which he thought that a divine voice had spoken to him, confirming that "God had done it." As Joseph did not publicly divorce Mary, he must have believed her, but at this point in the story, he disappears into the background – he is barely mentioned again, except, briefly, on two occasions: Jesus's circumcision and later, when Jesus is lecturing in the temple at the age of twelve. The story of Jesus lecturing in the temple appears only in the Gospel of Luke, and, as the historian Josephus relates a similar story about himself, there is a persistent rumour that Luke's Gospel was influenced by his contemporary and mentor Josephus. If that is true, it obviously casts doubt on the story of Jesus teaching in the temple.

As Joseph didn't publicly divorce Mary, but disappears from the Gospels when Jesus is twelve years old, it is possible that Joseph died, leaving Mary as a widow. In those circumstances, the logical and practical thing for Mary to do would have been to contact the father of Jesus to continue and consolidate their relationship, but it is also likely that during those twelve years, Alpheus would have married and had children. Some of those children were followers of Jesus and his brother Joses, for example, to quote Mark 2:14, "And as he passed by, he saw Levi the son of Alpheus sitting at the receipt of custom, and said unto him, Follow me. And he arose and followed him." So Levi is named as the son of Alpheus, and, if Alpheus was the natural father of Jesus, Matthew and James were brothers.

The Gospels also name James as the son of Mary and Alpheus and name Mary as the mother of James the less and Joses: "Is not this the carpenter's son? Is not his mother called Mary? and his brethren, James, and Joses, and Simon, and Judas?" (Matthew 13:55); "And when the Sabbath was past, Mary Magdalene, and Mary the mother of James, and Salome, had bought sweet spices, that they might come and anoint him" (Mark 16:1).

Matthew 13:55–56 tells us that Jesus had at least four brothers and two sisters, so unless we assume that Mary "slept around," in which case she would have been branded a harlot, it can be assumed that their father was also the father of Jesus. The four brothers are named as James, Joses, Simon, and Judas, but who was the father of Jesus's brothers and sisters? He is named as Alpheus, therefore unless we believe that God worked for a while as a carpenter, we must assume that Matthew's reference to Jesus being the son of a carpenter refers to the trade of the man who impregnated Mary. If Jesus had the brothers and sisters named above, they, too, would have been the children of a carpenter, however, there is no mention in the Gospels of Joseph ever being a carpenter. In Mark 6:3, we read, "Is this not the carpenter, the brother of James and Joses and of Judas and Simon?" So while Mark states that Jesus was a carpenter, Matthew claims that he was the son of a carpenter.

The third-century theologian Origen drew attention to inconsistencies and omissions in the Gospels. He stated that the accepted tradition in the early church that Jesus had followed his father's trade was not mentioned in the Gospels. Therefore the passage quoted in Mark 6:3 must have been inserted after the third century, when Origen made his observations. Why would the scriptures have been edited to include the passage in Mark 6:3? Could it have been to draw attention away from the vocation of Jesus's real father? But then the Gospels do state that the father of Jesus was a carpenter, and also that Jesus was the son of a carpenter.

So who was Mary? The Bible tells us very little of her parentage, with only a reference in Luke 3:23: "And Jesus himself began to be about thirty years of age, being (as was supposed) the son of Joseph, which was the son of Heli." However, an apocryphal Gospel, the Protoevangelium of James, dating from the end of the second century, although unauthenticated and unreliable, names Mary's parents as Ann and Joachim. The *Catholic Encyclopedia*, too, names Joachim, which means "Yahweh prepares," as the father of the Virgin Mary, and in the Talmud, Mary is named as the daughter of Heli. The name Joachim is a variant of the name Eliachim or Heli, and the theologians or ancient editors of the Gospels substituted the name of Yahweh for the name of Eli or Elohim. The Gospel of James states that because of the fervent prayers of Joachim and Anna, they were blessed with the birth of Mary. Joachim is reputed to belong to the royal family line of David, and Anna to the priestly family of Aaron, which provides the basis for outlining the lineal descent of Jesus, indicating that he had a royal and priestly pedigree.

King of the Jews versus Prophet

Who was the historical King of the Jews: Jesus or John? To answer that question requires a brief look at Jewish history around 1000 BC, as well as an understanding of what it took to inaugurate and maintain the priesthood for the ecclesiastical leadership in Israel. King David originated the inauguration by dividing the Israeli priesthood into twenty-four courses, or family divisions. This practice remained in place for the next four hundred years, until Persia overran Israel and deported the leading civic leaders, the priests, and their families to Babylon. After seventy years, the Persians let the descendants of the deported courses, or families, return to Israel. Once back in Jerusalem, the courses resumed their priestly duties. However, four of the returning courses could not prove their family genealogical line, and those four families were barred from holding priestly office. One of the four barred courses was that of Abijah.

In Luke 1:5 we read that, "There was in the days of Herod, the king of Judea, a certain priest named Zechariah, of the course of Abijah: and his wife was of the daughters of Aaron, and her name was Elisabeth." Miriam is known to the Christian world as the Virgin Mary, the mother of

Jesus. Miriam and Elisabeth were cousins and Elisabeth's son was destined to become John the Baptist. So, according to the Bible, a member of an excluded course had infiltrated the priesthood of the temple in Jerusalem.

This would have been disturbing to early theologians, who may well have edited the Gospels so as to disguise the true course of John the Baptist. Or an error may have been made due to ignorance of Jewish history because the courses of Joarib and Abijah were very closely related, but if that were the case, then the editors were incorrectly briefed; they should have been restricted to merely checking the grammar of the translations, rather than performing a technical edit when they lacked the necessary knowledge. However, if there was no error and the editors of the Gospels were attempting deliberately to conceal the true course of John the Baptist and his cousin Jesus, then it is highly probable that the course of Joarib was deliberately edited to read Abijah.

John the Baptist and Jesus were both entitled, through family connections on their mothers' sides, to be candidates for the position of high priest. Consequently, both could claim to be "Priestly Messiahs," but Jesus alone, because of his Royal David lineage and his membership of the course of Joarib on his father's side, was capable of being a "Royal Messiah." In other words, Jesus was eligible to control spiritual and secular matters while wielding the sword of state, while John was eligible only to control spiritual matters.

That same division of power is evident in more recent history. The Holy Roman Emperor Charlemagne claimed descent through the Merovingians from Mary Magdalene and Jesus. In AD 800 Charlemagne was crowned emperor by Pope Leo III while he knelt in Saint Peter's in Rome. From that time the Emperor claimed to be the supreme temporal ruler of Christendom by royal descent from David while delegating spiritual matters to the Pope, who, as the vicar of God on earth, catered for the souls of Charlemagne's subjects. From 1438 until 1806, with one exception, every Holy Roman Emperor was from the house of Hapsburg. The Emperor Charlemagne considered the delegation of spiritual matters to the Pope to be legal because Jesus had had dual roles as both a Priestly and Royal Messiah, through having descended from both priestly and royal courses.

John and Jesus were Hasmoneans, of the royal line of David and of the course of Joarib. John was older than Jesus by six months, making him the Messiah, or leader, albeit in only a spiritual sense. The story of the wise men, therefore, seeking out the "King of the Jews," as related in the Gospel of Matthew, is, in fact, the story of the search for John, not Jesus.

When the news of the birth of a "King of the Jews" reached the ears of Herod, his own objective of establishing a royal bloodline to the throne of Israel, was threatened. History records that Herod ordered the killing of all male infants in Bethlehem under the age of two, the so-called "Massacre of the Innocents." That Herod murdered Zechariah is well known, but did he murder in a fit of temper and without establishing the location of the heir to the throne? After the murder of Zechariah, Elisabeth fled into the desert as a widow with her eighteen-month-old son John. It is recorded that she died eighteen days later. Also recorded in the Gospels is the fact that Joseph took Mary and the baby Jesus and fled into Egypt to escape the wrath of Herod. It would appear that both were under a similar threat.

So, at the age of eighteen months, John had been orphaned, but he was to rescued by a group of ultra-orthodox Jews called the Essenes, who inhabited part of the Nile Delta near Alexandria. The Essenes, who were an offshoot of an earlier esoteric healing sect of Judaism known as the Therapeutae, were a holy sect which offered shelter and an education to orphans, who, on maturity, would augment their ranks. Within the Essenes there were many sub-groups, such as the Nazarenes and the Ossaeans. The northern Nazarenes were known as the B'nai-Amen, or "Children of God," while the southern Ossaeans based at Qumran were known as the B'nai-Zadok, or "Children of Zadok." It is important to establish in which community of Essenes John, and Jesus, grew up and were educated.

It is widely accepted that John the Baptist was an Essene from Qumran. This is substantiated by Qumran's location on the Dead Sea, only five miles from the River Jordan, where John performed his baptisms. John was said to live in the desert to the south-west of the River Jordan, exactly where Qumran was located. Another piece of circum- stantial evidence which points to John being an Essene from Qumran is the fact that the Essenes were vegetarians and John's diet of "locust" was, in fact, a fruit similar to a carob, and not an insect as might be supposed. Finally, the Qumran Essenes practised baptism and were often called "Baptists."

Having been taken into Egypt by Mary and Joseph to escape Herod, Jesus probably received his early training in a community of Essenes, or Theraputae, living on Lake Mareotis, as described by Philo, a Jewish philosopher who lived around two thousand years ago. When Herod's son, also King Herod, died, the royal family of Jesus returned to northern Israel to a community of Nazoreans near Mount Carmel, the headquarters of the Essene movement today. In those days, there was no town called Nazareth, only a co-operative village of Essenes known as the Nazarenes.

Some of the disciples of Jesus the Nazarene were Zealots or Sicarii associated with other offshoots from the mainstream doctrines of the Essenes. The title "Jesus of Nazareth" is interesting because, at the time of Jesus's birth, the village of Nazareth did not exist. There is no mention in any Roman records, maps, or letters of a town or village named Nazareth. If we take it that the original reference was to "Jesus the Nazarene," that firmly establishes him as a member of the northern Nazorean sect that was an offshoot of the Essenes.

The infant John the Baptist escaped Herod and was hidden away from the world for approximately thirty years until he walked out of the desert to begin his ministry. But what was his ministry? Was he revealing himself to claim his inheritance as the next Priestly Messiah of the Jews?

Jesus, too, had disappeared for a time, having escaped to Egypt. If both John and Jesus grew up thinking that Herod had killed the other, each would have assumed that he was the true inheritor of the title of Priestly Messiah. Were the Essenes investing in the long-term political future when they assumed the role of educational mentors of two young Hasmonean heirs to the throne of Israel? If so, it is highly probable that their aim was eventually to usurp the temple priests by establishing John as the Priestly Messiah and Jesus as the Royal Messiah, and establishing Essene control of the temple under royal patronage. Possibly the Essenes and the Therapeutae employed the principle of the Jesuits 1,500 years later who claimed that given a child until the age of seven, they would give back a man who would be theirs for life.

It would have been a typically hot, dry, and dusty day when John the Baptist wandered out of the desert to begin to assemble a band of followers. On the banks of the river Jordan, he baptized his new disciples, symbolically washing away prior allegiances and sins. Was this symbolic cleansing performed as an exercise to bond together an "army" of followers? Luke 3:14 tells us that soldiers came to hear him and were also recruited. Was John, in fact, proclaiming to the crowds that they should "prepare ye a way for the Lord; make his path straight" for himself to assume the mantle of Messiah, King of the Jews?

Matthew 3:13–15 describes the confrontation between Jesus and John as a stand-off, with each inviting the other to join him. Jesus would surely have seen only a limited future in the leadership of a seemingly half-crazed wild man coming out of the desert. However, Jesus bided his time and agreed to join John. Symbolically, he accepted his baptism and affiliated himself with John's "party," but we can only speculate as to whether he was made John's second-in-command. Immediately after Jesus and John joined forces, Jesus disappeared into the wilderness to contemplate the future, where he was subjected to the temptations described in the Gospels. The specific temptations are simply an attempt by theologians to describe and interpret what occurred in the mind of Jesus – unless, of course, one believes that the "Goat of Menzies" actually materialized out of the desert dust.

The Temptations

We can only speculate as to the thoughts of Jesus in the wilderness, but if we consider Jesus as a man, rather than as the son of God, interesting possibilities present themselves which may lead us to the truth, though to Christians, indoctrinated by two thousand years of dogma, such speculation may seem heretical. Suppose, however, that Jesus considered – and it is quite likely that he would have done – what would be best for Israel. Would he have felt that Israel would be best served by a Priest King, or Messiah, who seemed half-crazed and unsuited to lead a rebellion against Rome?

He would have had to confront the temptation to usurp John and take over the role of Priestly Messiah in addition to that of Royal Messiah – a profound exercise in soul-searching, no doubt. Could he do the unthinkable and betray his cousin to assume both roles? To do so he could certainly have placated his conscience with the thought that he would be doing it for the sake of the country.

The Gospel writers offer scenarios pitched at the level of their early readers, rather than early twenty-first century readers. If one attempts to create a scenario to fit the facts and brush aside the accretion of myth and legend, then it is

possible that when Jesus emerged from the wilderness he
ordered one of his followers to inform the authorities of the
true goal of John's ministry. That would certainly square
with the accounts of the Gospel writers who describe John's
arrest at the end of Jesus's forty days of meditation. John had
been baptizing people openly for some time, so it seems
strange that he should have been arrested just as Jesus
returned from the wilderness.

Following John's arrest and his execution by Herod
Antipas, Jesus became both Priestly and Royal Messiah. He
led his followers into the desert and held what today might
be termed a political rally. Presumably this was attended
not only by Jesus's followers, but by John's too. John's
followers would have been left without a leader and most
of them would have welcomed the opportunity to discuss
the future of their group and its leadership. One obvious
option was to combine the two factions into a single,
coherent force and what better way to do that than to eat
and drink together while outlining a common strategy?
Mark 6:34 describes the feeding of the multitude as
follows: "And Jesus, when he came out, saw much people,
and was moved with compassion toward them, because
they were as sheep not having a shepherd, and he began to
teach them many things."

There is a suggestion in that pronouncement that Jesus was
to become a shepherd, or leader, and guardian, for his own
followers, as well as those of John. At that moment, Jesus's
mission gathered momentum, possibly because he had
succumbed to the temptations to which he had been subjected during his forty days of meditation, and eliminated his
rival.

Egypt and the Essenes

Egypt exerted a strong influence on the early development of Judah. Many biblical characters, from Abraham through to Jesus, had links with Egypt, especially those who were resident in Egypt for long periods, where they would have been influenced by the religious culture of the country. It is likely that Jesus's formative years were spent in Egypt and influenced by the Essenes, but where did the Essenes come from?

In 1947, what came to be known as the Dead Sea Scrolls were found at Qumran, and later, in 1952, a copper scroll was found in Cave Three in the same location. At Manchester University, under the guidance of John Allegro, the copper scroll was carefully unrolled and deciphered. It had been written in code almost two thousand years beforehand and revealed the hiding places of ancient treasures. In *The Copper Scroll Decoded*, Robert Feather tracks down those hiding places with remarkable ingenuity and exemplary detective work. Since the discovery of the copper scroll some of the sites have been re-excavated, but they have not yielded any new treasures (though treasures may well once have been hidden in such sites, and since been looted). However, on one site, the

Temple Mount, evidence of Templar excavations made in the twelfth century have been discovered. The Essenes of Qumran had been the final keepers of these treasures – but what was the source of their wealth?

The wealthiest nation in biblical history was undoubtedly Egypt. At that time the vast majority of Egypt's wealth was in the hands of the pharaohs. Abraham and Abram in the Bible are, in fact, the same person. Genesis 17:5 tells us that Abram was renamed Abraham, "the father of many nations," and in Genesis 17:15 Abram's wife, Sarahi, is renamed Sarah. The Old Testament names three patriarchs: Abraham, Jacob, and Joseph, each favoured by the pharaohs. We must assume that each of these patriarchs built up a collection of treasured artefacts. If Abraham, Jacob, and Joseph were the source of the treasures described in the copper scroll, we need to establish how they gained that wealth and how it came to be in the hands of the Essenes.

Genesis 12:10 describes Abram and his beautiful wife Sarah travelling down into Egypt. We are told that they left the city of Ur in southern Babylon around 1500 BC and travelled to Canaan before continuing on to Egypt. The Bible also relates how Abraham encountered the pharaoh and conspired with Sarah to pass her off as his sister. He told Sarah that this was to protect his life as he could be killed if the pharaoh coveted Sarah. Abraham, as the head of his wandering clan, held most of his clan's wealth in the herds that he owned, but after the pharaoh had slept with Sarah, Abraham went out of Egypt "rich in cattle, in silver, and in gold." The first source of some of the treasure therefore has to be Abraham, who could be regarded as one of the first pimps in recorded history. Throughout Abraham's life he was a monotheist, a believer in a single god, and he may well have passed this belief on to the pharaoh, who would eventually become his mentor.

The second source of the Essene's wealth was most probably Jacob, the grandson of Abraham and the father of Joseph, who returned from Canaan to Mesopotamia to find a wife. In searching for a wife, Jacob managed to find two, with two handmaidens thrown in for good measure. He left Mesopotamia with Leah, Rachel, and their two handmaidens and began to procreate with all four. Over the next few years, being a virile man, he fathered twelve sons and a daughter. His eleventh son, Joseph, was sold into slavery in Egypt.

In his middle age, Jacob was encouraged to emigrate with his family to Egypt where he became a respected friend of the pharaoh and, in his old age, he changed his name to Israel. The pharaoh held Jacob in such high esteem that when Jacob died his body was embalmed in the traditional manner and he was mourned as a national figure by the Egyptian court for seventy days, something which would only have been done for a close associate of the pharaoh.

Joseph, the great-grandson of Abraham, who had been sold into slavery in Egypt by his brothers, is the third and probably the richest of the three sources of the Essene's wealth. In his youth, Joseph gained a reputation as an interpreter of dreams. Most famously, he interpreted the pharaoh's dreams concerning seven lean cows devouring seven fat cows, and seven full ears of corn being devoured by seven thin ears of corn. Joseph told the pharaoh that his dreams meant that there would be seven years of good harvests in Egypt, followed by seven bad years. The pharaoh (probably Amenhotep IV) was so pleased with Joseph that he appointed him as Vizier, the second most powerful position in Egypt. Joseph kept the position of Vizier for at least the seven years of plenty and the following seven years of famine. At the end of those fourteen years, Joseph must have been one of the richest

men in Egypt. There is more to the story, however, and
before we name the guardian of this accumulated wealth, it
is necessary to take a look at the families of the pharaohs
Amenhotep I and Amenhotep IV.

Did Abraham's monotheistic belief take root in the mind
of his close friend the pharaoh, and, if it did, was it handed
down to the children and grandchildren of Amenhotep I?
Something of that nature must have influenced the thinking
of Amenhotep IV because, when he came to the throne,
he implemented a monotheistic belief, abolishing the
numerous Egyptian cults and creating an official religion
for Egypt with one god, Aten. To bring about this change
in Egyptian culture, Amenhotep systematically destroyed
cults and banished their priesthoods. It was a slow process,
but gradually he replaced the Egyptian pantheon of gods
with Aten, who was symbolized by a solar disc.

The solar disc merely symbolized a god who was
unimaginable. Amenhotep did not intend the solar disc of
Aten to become an idol, rather the disc with its extending rays
was meant to act as a guide to a Supreme Being, which should
be sought in the hearts of the worshippers. Amenhotep later
built a city and temple to the north of Thebes, calling it
Akhetaten, meaning "the horizons of Aten." Pharaoh
Amenhotep IV also took the title Akhenaton, which means
"he who serves on behalf of Aten." The assumption that
Amenhotep IV was the pharaoh during Joseph's time is
based on the fact that after the sudden death of Amenhotep
IV, Joseph, who was Vizier to the pharaoh, fell from favour
at the court. Why would a regime get rid of Joseph who was
without question a successful administrator of proven
genius? Why was Joseph demoted when he was a national
hero who had saved Egypt from the famine? Was he
dismissed by the priesthood which Amenhotep IV had
abolished? The answer must lie in his association with his
deceased mentor and the new religion.

With the sudden death of Amenhotep in 1332 BC the dispossessed priests would have taken the opportunity to regain power, making Egypt once again polytheistic and idol-worshipping. But when Smenkhkara, the young brother of Amenhotep, tried to assume the throne he was murdered, because he would probably have maintained the status quo. After his death, the priests would have been desperate to have a pharaoh that they could manipulate, and their choice was the young Tutankhamen. At the age of only eleven, he inherited the throne in a country which was involved in a cultural and spiritual struggle between idolatry and monotheism. The Vizier Ay, who for many years had ruled Egypt, went back to Akhetaten for one last time and brought Tutankhamen back to Thebes. But Ay's strategy to reinstate the old priesthood could not change Tutankhamen who had grown up in the royal palace at Akhetaten, immersed in the principles of monotheism – his indoctrination by his father would have been difficult to overcome. As Tutankhamen and his wife Ankhesenpaten established themselves on the thrones of Egypt, Tutankhamen started to agitate for a return to a monotheistic culture, but he had little hope of success unless he could rid himself of his Vizier Ay. Tutankhamen's throne has the Aten disc prominently displayed, standing as eternal testimony to his continued adherence to the one true god, Aten.

But Tutankhamen was apparently outwitted and murdered at the age of only twenty-one. There is circumstantial evidence for this in the results of a series of forensic tests carried out for a television programme, which points to the ambitious Vizier Ay as the perpetrator of the crime. After Tutankhamen's murder, Ay forced Ankhesenpaten to marry him so he could gain the throne, but her religious upbringing made her abhor any return to polytheism. Eventually Ankhesenpaten died, possibly as a result of a plot hatched by Ay.

A final piece of circumstantial evidence for Akhenaton IV being the pharaoh during Joseph's lifetime is to be found at the Temple of Seti I at Abydos, where a list of the pharaohs of Egypt is inscribed. Two names, however, are missing from the list. Someone, or a group of people, in ancient Egypt has attempted to obliterate forever the memory of Akhenaton and Tutankhamen, an enormous task of which probably only the priesthood would have been capable.

Later, at the time of the enslavement of the Hebrews, a new pharaoh ruled over Egypt, who was not a contemporary of Joseph. It is recorded that this pharaoh proclaimed to his people that the "children of Israel are more and mightier" than the Egyptians (Exodus 1:8–11). With that proclamation, the pharaoh set taskmasters to oppress the Israelites and force them into slavery with a forced labour program to build cities for the pharaoh at Pithom and Raamses. The descendants of Jacob's family were still followers of the religion of Aten but were now outcasts, and were enslaved and set to work for the Egyptians, something which they endured for the next one hundred and fifty years, under successive pharaohs. During this time they were sustained by their belief in an omnipotent god, Aten or Jehovah (a rose by any other name is still a rose) who would one day manifest himself to rescue them from slavery. During those one hundred and fifty years the priests of Aten disappeared or went underground, but the philosophy of one God and Akhenaton's ideals did not become obsolete; they lived on, as did the accumulated wealth of the temples of Aten. With some of that wealth the Aten priesthood paid for their escape, but they hid those treasures which were too bulky or numerous to be easily transported.

It is likely that Abraham, Jacob, and Joseph were the sources of the accumulated treasure troves encrypted on the copper scroll, and we know that the priests of Aten became the custodians of the treasures from the Great Temple and the Treasury at Akhetaten. There is circumstantial evidence that the copper scroll was in the safekeeping of the Qumran Essenes; by association, therefore, the priests of Aten (or Jehovah) were, in fact, the Qumran Essenes.

The Egyptian Essenes, or priests of Aten, were writers and philosophers, responsible for translating the old Jewish Scriptures into the Greek Septuagint. It was during the inscription of the Septuagint that theological changes were made which deviated from the accepted Jewish texts. While making the translations, the Essenes were guilty of a remarkable marketing exercise for Aten, because the Septuagint translations of the words of the early Jewish prophets became the Bible, forming the foundation for the Old Testament texts.

As these Essene writings supported the doctrines of the priests of Aten (for Aten, we should now read Jehovah), what we read in the Bible today is the ideology of monotheism as originated by the Pharaoh Akhenaton IV. This ideology was refined by the Essenes to become the reference documents used by the early scribes when they recorded the Old Testament. Quotations recorded in the New Testament also have their origin in corrupted translations of the Jewish Scriptures. The representation of God as the sun, represented by the solar disc of Aten, was meant to act as a guide to the Supreme Being that should be sought in the hearts of the worshippers. Consequently, in every Christian church today, sun-like halos are to be found adorning altar pieces, and the monstrance, used in Catholic churches to display the consecrated host, or wafers, has the appearance of a sunburst.

Neither of the historians Josephus, who lived in Judea, or Philo of Alexandria, writing in the first century, mentions the Christians, however they did describe a religion with

doctrines and moral attitudes similar to Christianity, which
they called Essenism. In the first century there were, in fact,
both Jewish and Christian Essenes, and it was only when the
Christian Essenes became part of the Roman Empire that
they became known solely as Christians. Even Eusebius, an
ecclesiastical writer of the fourth century, asserts in his
History of the Church that the Therapeutae (Essenes) were
Christians, and that their writings were the forerunners of the
Christian Gospels. The Essenes left us their doctrines in the
form of the Dead Sea Scrolls; these include the incarnation,
atonement, and trinity, all of which are included in the rituals
of Christianity. Both the Essenes and the early Christians
also believed in baptism and that all members should share
their knowledge and possessions; all property belonging to
initiates became the property of the community.

The Essene Community was led by a council of twelve
with a central committee of three priests with overall jurisdiction. Similarly, the early Christian church in Jerusalem
was controlled by a "committee" of the twelve Apostles.
This committee of twelve was maintained even after the
hanging of Judas, which indicates that the committee of the
Apostles had positions to be filled when vacancies
occurred. In common with the Essene community, three
disciples, namely Peter, James, and John, led the committee
of the Apostles. Both the early Christians and the Essene
community believed in a Messiah, with Jesus as the
Christian candidate and the Essenes with a "Teacher of
Righteousness."

Further similarities are to be found in the common
terminology of the Christian and Essene doctrines. Jesus
preached, "Blessed are the meek for they shall inherit the
earth," while the Essenes preached that the community of
Essenes were the poor and the meek, who were also
preparing themselves to inherit the earth.

Jesus and the Magdalene

The early Church maintained that Jesus was not married, but how can we know that? It is not something that is spelled out, one way or another, in any of the scriptures. All male Jews possessing the mental ability to work, and particularly those trained as rabbis or religious teachers, were obliged by the very nature of their priestly function to marry. Despite all the editing of the Gospels by the early Church, traces remain to indicate that Jesus was married.

The Gospels tell us that Peter, a prominent disciple of Jesus, was married. Surely if Peter's marital status is confirmed, so too should that of the main character in the whole story, Jesus? If Jesus was celibate, as some traditions maintain, then a state of celibacy should also have been recorded. Jesus certainly did not preach celibacy. The matter is not referred to in the Gospel of Matthew, so it is necessary to take into account Jewish customs of the first century. Contemporary Jewish law laid down a strict code of practice by which Jews were supposed to lead their lives. Luke tells of Jesus and his disciples wandering about the country in the company of women, which would have been a scandalous state of affairs under Jewish law unless the groups of women were wives or relatives. In Judaism, being a single man was seen as almost sinful in the eyes of Jehovah, consequently a father was obliged to find a wife for his son. It can be assumed, therefore, that Jesus's father would have attempted to fulfil his obligations towards his sons, and find them wives. Matthew 13:55–56 tells us that Jesus had at least four brothers and two sisters. Boys were regarded as having attained maturity between the ages of thirteen and sixteen, but a girl was of marriageable age at thirteen. Many scholars believe that Jesus married Mary Magdalene and that marriage would have taken place at the customary age of sixteen, meaning that any issue would have been about sixteen when Jesus began his ministry – this has relevance as far as Barabbas is concerned.

The Bible tells of a wedding in a small town called Cana, which was situated in the heartland of the Hasmonean following. Early Gospel texts give the spelling as Kana, which gives us a clue as to the local industry of that town. Kana was located on the shores of Galilee and was the source of "kaneth," a type of reed that grew in the area. These reeds were extremely straight and strong, making excellent shafts for spears (of relevance, as will become clear later, to the crucifixion). In the early fifteenth century a copy of a manuscript entitled *The Life of Mary Magdalene* by Raban Maar, the Archbishop of Mayence between AD 776 and AD 856, was found at Oxford University. The manuscript asserts that Mary Magdalene's mother was of the tribe of Benjamin and related to the Royal Hasmonean House of Israel through the House of Bethany. The Gospel of Matthew also informs us that Jesus was of the Judaic House of David and a descendant of King Solomon, thus by marrying into the House of Benjamin, Jesus would be joining two royal bloodlines. Therefore a marriage between Jesus and Mary Magdalene would have resulted in a new bloodline for their royal heirs. Any child born of this potent political union would have had the potential to make a legitimate claim to the throne and restore the historical lineage of kings as it had been in the time of Solomon. Any offspring from the royal union would also have been seen as a sign of hope during the Roman occupation because the bonding of the two royal households would have fulfilled many Hebrew prophecies, uniting a country of so many political factions. Politically, the Zealots would have used any coalition or alliance against the Romans to help free Israel. With all of this in mind, is it possible that the wedding at Cana was that of Jesus and Mary Magdalene? John 2:1–5 tells us:

> And the third day there was a marriage in Cana of Galilee; and the mother of Jesus was there:
> and both Jesus was called, and his disciples, to the marriage.
> And when they wanted wine, the mother of Jesus saith unto him, They have no wine.
> Jesus saith unto her, Woman, what have I to do with thee? mine hour is not yet come.
> His mother saith unto the servants, Whatsoever he saith unto you, do it.

Ignorance of contemporary Jewish customs is apparent in the editorial mutilation of the original texts by the editors of the four Gospels. As Fida Hassnain points out in *A Search for the Historical Jesus*, the only person with the authority to give orders to servants at a wedding feast was the bridegroom, or his mother. So it appears that the brief mention of the wedding at Cana was left in the Gospels to inform readers of a miracle attributed to Jesus, though with the identity of the bride and groom obscured. It seems that as Mary, the mother of Jesus, orders the procurement of additional wine, she was the host. It is unlikely that a guest would order more wine at a large wedding, particularly when one considers the large volume of wine involved.

John 2:6 tells us: "And there were set there six water pots of stone, after the manner of the purifying of the Jews, containing two or three firkins apiece." So how much additional wine was Jesus providing? If we take a mean average and assume that each pot held two-and-a-half firkins, then multiply that by six, Jesus was providing an additional fifteen firkins of wine. A firkin is the equivalent of nine gallons, so Jesus is providing another 135 gallons of wine, or 1,080 pints (511 litres), or approximately 682 bottles of wine. When we consider that this miracle provided extra wine, in addition to that supplied by the caterers, we can assume that there were well over a thousand, or perhaps even fifteen hundred wedding guests, hardly the quiet, village affair implied by the Gospels. Rather, it suggests the wedding celebration of a prominent, possibly royal, couple. In the days before calendars, Jews referred to days in relationship to religious festivals, such as the Passover, for example.

John 2:2 states, "And both Jesus was called, and his disciples, to the marriage."

Was Jesus called to remind him of the date and as a warning not to wander off too far? The messenger who calls Jesus to the wedding is named as Nathanael of Cana: "There were together Simon Peter, and Thomas called Didymus, and Nathanael of Cana in Galilee, and the sons of Zebedee, and two other of his disciples" (John 21:2). In John 1:48–49 we read:

> Nathanael saith unto him, Whence knowest thou me? Jesus answered and said unto him,
> Before that Philip called thee, when thou was under the fig tree, I saw thee.
> Nathanael answered and saith unto him, Rabbi, thou art the Son of God; thou art the King of Israel.

Jesus knew the Hasmonean town of Cana and it is likely

that the relatives of Jesus and the family of Mary Magdalene both lived there. Although Nathanael did not at first recognize Jesus; Jesus recognized Nathanael, suggesting that Jesus had been away from Cana for some time.

The Gospel of Luke tells us that some time after the wedding at Cana, Jesus visited Martha and her sister Mary Magdalene. If we read the Gospels in the light of known contemporary Jewish customs, that visit seems to confirm that Jesus was married, and that Mary Magdalene was his wife, and Martha his sister-in-law. Evidence from the Gospels is found in the following passage from Luke 10:38–42:

> Now it came to pass, as they went, that he entered into a certain village, and a certain woman named Martha received him into her house
> And she had a sister called Mary, which also sat at Jesus's feet, and heard his word.
> But Martha was cumbered about much serving, and came to him, and said, Lord, dost thou not care that my sister hath left me to serve alone? Bid her therefore that she help me.
> And Jesus answered and said unto her, Martha, Martha, thou art careful and troubled about many things.
> But one thing is needful and Mary hath chosen that good part, which shall not be taken away from her.

Mary Magdalene, by remaining in the house while her husband is away, is shown behaving as a good wife according to the Jewish customs of the time. The returning husband would have been welcomed home by other members of the household, while the dutiful wife would have met him only in the sanctity of their own home. Also according to Jewish custom, only a wife would sit at her husband's feet, all of which points to Mary Magdalene being the wife of Jesus. In addition, there is a telling episode in the Gospel of John which seems to confirm that Jesus was married to Mary Magdalene, the sister of Martha (John 11:1–5 and 28–29):

> Now a certain man was sick, named Lazarus, of Bethany, the town of Mary and her sister Martha.
> (It was that Mary which anointed the Lord with ointment, and wiped his feet with her hair, whose brother Lazarus was sick.)
> Therefore his sisters sent unto him, saying, Lord, behold, he whom thou lovest is sick.
> When Jesus heard that, he said, This sickness is not unto death, but for the glory of God, that the Son of God might be glorified thereby.
> Now Jesus loved Martha, and her sister, and Lazarus.
>
> And when she had so said, she went her way, and called Mary her sister secretly, saying, The Master is come, and calleth for thee.
> As soon as she heard that, she arose quickly, and came unto him.

When Jesus returns to the house of Martha, Mary Magdalene behaves impeccably as a good Jewish wife and remains in the house while he is welcomed home by other members of the household. Although no mention is made of Mary actually being in mourning for her brother-in-law, it seems likely she was "sitting shiva," the position adopted by a Jewish woman during mourning. Married women were not allowed to pause or break away from their mourning position unless called by their husbands. While the Gospel of John seems to confirm the marital status of Jesus, the raising of Lazarus from the dead seems to confirm His links to the Essenes (John 11:38–39 and 43–44):

> Jesus therefore again groaning in himself cometh to the grave. It was a cave, and a stone lay upon it.
> Jesus said, Take ye away the stone. Martha, the sister of him that was dead, saith unto him, Lord, by this time he stinketh: for he hath been dead four days.

And when he thus had spoken, he cried with a loud voice,
Lazarus, come forth.
And he that was dead came forth, bound hand and foot with
graveclothes; and his face was bound about with a napkin.
Jesus saith unto them, Loose him, and let him go.

According to the historian Flavius Josephus, when a Jewish
man became an initiate of the Essenes, a solemn and
symbolic ritual took place, reminiscent of a third-degree
Masonic ritual. The Essenes also had symbolic excommunication rituals which were implemented if a member
became a dissident from their holy order. This ritual took
the form of wrapping the dissident in a burial shroud and
entombing him for four days to complete the excommunication. Therefore, when Jesus came to the cave of the
entombed Lazarus and bade him come forth, the evidence
suggests that Jesus was "raising" Lazarus from his excommunicated state and not literally "raising the dead."

A final piece of circumstantial evidence that Jesus was
married is to be found in the Gospel of Mark 14:3: "And
being in Bethany in the house of Simon the leper, as he sat
at meat, there came a woman having an alabaster box of
ointment of spikenard very precious; and she break the box,
and poured it on his head." All cultures have rituals relating
to royalty, and Jewish culture was no exception. Ritualistic
anointment with spikenard was allowed under Jewish law
only for the dead or for royalty; in fact, the possession of
spikenard was forbidden unless the user was a high
priestess or wife of a royal person. As Jesus was certainly
not dead, we must accept that, either physically or symbolically, He was regarded as the King of the Jews. This fact
is emphasized as the woman with the alabaster jar anoints
Him in a symbolic union with herself which signifies the
king's royal status as the "Anointed One," and reaffirms
Jesus as the Hebrew Messiah.

In AD 591, Pope Gregory I, delivered a sermon in Rome

in which he declared that Mary Magdalene was the same person as the sinner in Luke's Gospel. In the same sermon, Pope Gregory also identified the sinner who was the sister of Lazarus as the Mary who anointed Jesus with spikenard (John 11:2 and 12:3). Thus the Roman Catholic Church of the sixth century maintained that the two women named Mary were one and the same woman, and so began fifteen hundred years of character assassination in which Mary Magdalene was labelled a prostitute. It was only at the Second Vatican Council (1962–65), that her place in the church was officially affirmed as "Apostle to the Apostles." That recognition was confirmed in the new Catholic missal of 1969 and reiterated by Pope John Paul II in his 1988 encyclical *Dignitatum Mulieris*. The Catholic Church issued a retraction and humbly and very quietly admitted its error, but by then much damage had already been done to Christian belief and to feminism within the Church.

How important was Mary Magdalene in the life of Jesus? There are several clues which provide evidence of the status of Mary Magdalene. In the various Gospels seven "lists" are to be found which indicate a hierarchy of women who were companions of Jesus. Mary Magdalene is listed at the top of six of those lists, preceding even Mary the mother of Jesus. These clues were the way in which the writers of the Gospels identified the true status of Mary Magdalene as the wife of the king of the Jews. Mary Magdalene was also adept in the use of aromatic oils and fragrances, as shown by her use of spikenard. Religious artwork throughout the Christian era has often shown Mary Magdalene carrying an alabaster jar.

Jesus, His Family, and the Middle Years

There is much circumstantial evidence that Jesus was married, but did he father any children? In other words, did Jesus and Mary Magdalene have a family? One of the clearest clues pointing to the birth of their first child is derived from the Gospel of John 4:45–46:

> Then when he was come into Galilee, the Galileans received him, having seen all the things that he did at Jerusalem at the feast, for they also went unto the feast.
> So Jesus came again into Cana of Galilee, where he made the water wine. And there was a certain nobleman, whose son was sick at Capernaum.

And in John 10:22 we read that Jesus was in Jerusalem for the feast of the dedication (i.e., Hanukkah), and it was winter. So ten months after the feast of the Passover which had preceded the wedding at Cana, Jesus was once again in Cana. According to Jewish custom, the marriageable age for a man was about sixteen. Could it be that while Jesus was away from home Mary Magdalene, also a teenager, had given birth ten months after their wedding to their first child – a child named Jesus bar Abbas? It seems likely that Mary

Magdalene gave birth to at least one child, and quite possibly three, and that her first-born child is actually referred to in all four Gospels.

When Mary Magdalene anointed Jesus on the Saturday evening before what was to become Palm Sunday, both Jesus and Mary were performing a symbolic ceremony to inform all present that the King of the Jews was about to stake his claim to the throne of David. When Jesus attempted to cleanse the temple, it was an act of sedition punishable in only one way, by crucifixion. The resulting uprising failed and Jesus escaped from the temple guards and the Romans, but it would be fair to assume that there would have been some casualties, and some revolutionaries taken prisoner, in the mêlée. In Mark 15:7 we read: "And there was one named Barabbas, which lay bound with them that had made insurrection with him, who had committed murder in the insurrection," and in Luke 23:18–19: "And they cried out all at once, saying, away with this man, and release unto us Barabbas; who for a certain sedition made in the city, and for murder, was cast into prison." Unless we assume that there were two separate revolts or acts of sedition on that Passover feast, we must assume that Barabbas was a member of Jesus's group, but who was Barabbas? *Bar* means "son of" and *abbas*, the master. Was Barabbas, therefore, the son of the master, Jesus, and Mary Magdalene? Writing in the fourth century, the early Christian writer Jerome, claims that in the lost Gospel of the Hebrews, the title Barabbas was written as bar Abbas and was preceded by the name Jesus. So, just as Jesus may have been termed Jesus the Rabbi, his son might have been known as Jesus bar Abbas, the son of the master, or rabbi. Without access to the original source material, however, it is impossible to establish the truth or otherwise of this assertion.

Jesus's Mission: The Coup

With John the Baptist having been eliminated by Herod, the thirty years of training that the Essenes had invested in Jesus were about to bear fruit; He was to make a bid for the throne of David, a coup against the authority of Rome. Failure to seize the throne would result in death by crucifixion, the outcome recorded by the Gospels. A number of religious scholars argue that the revolt in the temple was specifically directed against the Sadducees who administered the profitable temple rituals, organized the lucrative sales of sacrificial livestock, and ran the money-changing facilities in the temple. All of this was controlled by the High Priest, Joseph Caiaphas. When Jesus instigated the riot in the temple, Caiaphas's lucrative temple businesses were threatened and Caiaphas and the Sanhedrin condemned Jesus for blasphemy. Jesus was then taken before Pontius Pilate, the Roman prefect of Judea, because the Sanhedrin lacked the powers to sentence someone to death. Pilate sentenced Jesus to death for sedition, not for offences against the Sanhedrin.

It is important to examine the order of events in the week preceding the crucifixion as recorded in the four Gospels, and to ask why the Gospel of John differs in its chronology with respect to the temple riots.

Around 1790, the Gospels of Matthew, Mark, and Luke became known as the Synoptic Gospels because they share the same content, style, and order of events, at odds with the Gospel of John. All the Gospels were written many years after the crucifixion, but the Gospel of Mark is considered to have been the original Gospel from which Matthew and Luke copied whole sections of text. The writer of the Gospel of Mark probably had some earlier texts on which to base his account, and all the writers of the Synoptic Gospels would also have heard the folk tales of local storytellers, who had been embellishing and distorting the story for the past fifty years.

Why were the Gospels written, who was their intended audience, and, most importantly, who wrote them? The Synoptic Gospels were certainly not written for a Jewish audience, but they were intended to convey information to different audiences. It seems clear that Mark, Matthew, and Luke shared the same pacificist, non-political slant in their writing. The writer of the Gospel of John seems to have had recourse to different folk memories to the writers of the other Gospels.

Luke was Greek and a medical doctor, whose Gospel gives an account of Jesus ministering to a prominent Roman citizen who lived in the Palestinian capital of Caesarea. According to Clement of Alexandria, the Gospel of Mark was written in Rome by Mark, a contemporary of Paul. If true, that would explain the Pauline theological approach in the Gospel of Mark. Clement also claims that the Gospel of Mark was written for a Greek and Roman audience, therefore Jesus is presented as a pacifist rather than a political opponent of Rome, and His crucixion is blamed on the Jews. Such an approach was necessary if the message of the Gospel was to have any impact on the Roman world.

The Gospel of John was written in the second half of the first century for wealthy Greek citizens of the Roman Empire who had turned away from pagan gods and adopted

Christianity. To the Greeks any reference to a Jewish Messiah would have been offensive, so John removed these references. Thus the Gospel of John focuses more on the later part of Jesus's life, in and around Jerusalem and Judea, and does not mention his birth or any association with the line of David. John describes Jesus as a divine being, who came to be regarded as part of the Holy Trinity, transforming Jesus into a god. The Gospels of Matthew, Mark, and Luke state that the temple uprising was on Palm Sunday, however, while the same account is given in the Gospel of John, its position in the chronology is different (John 2:13–15):

> And the Jews' passover was at hand, and Jesus went up to Jerusalem,
> and found in the temple those that sold oxen and sheep and doves, and the changers of money sitting,
> and when he had made a scourge of small cords, he drove them all out of the temple, and the sheep, and the oxen; and poured out the changers' money, and overthrew the tables

All four Gospels agree that the temple riot occurred around the time of a Passover, but John's account places the riot at an earlier time in Jesus's life, which is surely incorrect. At the time of the temple uprising, Jesus bar Abbas, the putative son of Jesus, was already a young man; Jesus was crucified at some point in his early to mid-thirties, so the Gospel of John must be incorrect in placing the temple riot so early in Jesus's life.

What happened on what came to be known as Palm Sunday and during the week before the Passover, when thousands of Jews crowded into Jerusalem? Any coup or revolution aims to seize the principal communication centres and perhaps this is what Jesus was doing in instigating a riot in the temple. The Jewish revolutionaries would have aimed to infiltrate personnel into key areas under cover of a crowd. To attract a large crowd, Jesus knowingly fulfilled a prophecy that the Messiah would present himself riding on an ass. In doing so, He got crowds out onto the streets, thereby providing cover for the revolutionaries. Then, with the revolutionaries in place in the temple, Jesus signalled the beginning of the revolt by overturning the moneylenders' tables. This is one of very few instances in the Gospels in which Jesus is portrayed as acting violently. One other such instance occurs in Luke 22:36 when Jesus tells his followers to arm themselves: "Then said he unto them, But now, he that hath a purse, let him take it, and likewise his scrip, and he that hath no sword, let him sell his garment, and buy one."

Perhaps Jesus overturned the tables of the moneylenders in the temple deliberately, knowing that people in the crowd would scramble and fight for the money tipped onto the floor, thereby causing a diversion which would make it harder for the temple guards to restore order. This account sees Jesus as the leader of a hard core of revolutionaries, deliberately staging a riot. The Gospels do not indicate how many followers Jesus had in the temple, but a Hebrew copy of a document attributed to Josephus gives a figure of two thousand, and the Roman procurator Sossianus Hierocles gives a figure of nine hundred.

If this assumption of a deliberately staged disturbance is correct, Jesus must have hoped that the revolt would spread. Perhaps the depiction of a display of temper on the spur of the moment by Jesus in the Gospels was, in fact, intended as an uprising against Roman authority. How many troops did Pilate have at his disposal? Although reinforcements were due to arrive in a few days' time, on Palm Sunday itself, he had only five hundred soldiers, plus a small body of guards under the control of the Sanhedrin.

As far as Jesus was concerned, the revolt, if that is what it was, would have seemed to have got off to a good start, but He had become too popular, and his staged entrance on an ass had generated far bigger crowds than anyone could have anticipated therefore the temple yard would have been filled with over a thousand people. The arrival of a disciplined force of five hundred seasoned Roman soldiers into this mèlée, would have made short work of the revolutionaries, as well as creating panic. Some prisoners would have been taken among the wounded and the dying, and perhaps one of these was Jesus bar Abbas, while Jesus and his disciples managed to escape.

Jesus and his disciples would have fled Jerusalem, to be joined later by the the remnants of his followers, straggling after them in small groups. Jesus, as leader, would have questioned each survivor in order to determine who had been injured, who killed, and who had been taken prisoner. By nightfall it must have been apparent that Jesus bar Abbas was either dead or had been taken prisoner.

The Roman legal system worked swiftly. A criminal was usually tried immediately, and, if guilty, the sentence imposed was quickly enacted. Yet the Gospels tell us that at the time of the trial of Jesus, Barabbas was still alive, five days later. Did Pilate keep him alive for so long in order to use him as a bargaining chip so that he could capture the leader of the uprising rather than His son?

After the temple riot, Jesus and his followers retreated to Bethany, where, probably in the house of his brother-in-law Lazarus, they must have spent hours debating the best policy for Jesus, His family, and most importantly, Israel. Jesus could have escaped Pilate's forces, but ne could not abandon his son, Jesus bar Abbas, so a plan was devised. First, a safe house would have to be found in Jerusalem, as described in Mark 14:13–14:

> And he sent forth two of his disciples, and saith unto them, Go ye into the city, and there shall meet you a man bearing a pitcher of water, follow him.
> And wheresoever he shall go in, say ye to the goodman of the house, The Master saith,

> Where is the guest chamber, where I shall eat the Passover with
> my disciples?

This passage reveals that Jesus expected to eat the Passover
on the Thursday before going to his execution on the Friday
(this would have been abhorrent to an orthodox Jew, but not
to an Essene as Essene celebrations of the Passover began on
the Wednesday night). The plan, which was intended to save
Jesus from crucifixion, would have to begin at 6 p.m. on the
Wednesday, and end with the "execution" which would
begin at about midday on the Friday. Two disciples were sent
to Jerusalem to meet a stranger carrying a pitcher of water. It
was customary or women to carry water, rather than men,
unless they belonged to a male-oriented house or commune.
Both the Essenes and the associated Nazoreans were male-
oriented communes, so it seems likely that the safe house was
to be provided by the Essenes. The two disciples would also
have been able to identify the water carrier by his white
robes, the customary dress of the Essenes. This suggests that
the Essenes provided the venue for the Last Supper.

Although there is no mention of Joseph of Arimathea
before the events preceding the crucifixion, Jesus must
have had the backing of some influential and wealthy men
to be able to feed and arm a large group. Did these influential men negotiate with Pilate on behalf of Jesus during the
five days preceding the Passover? There is no evidence of
such negotiation, but why otherwise would a militant Jesus
have surrendered as meekly as we have been led to believe?
Knowing that the penalty for insurrection was a slow and
excruciating death by crucifixion, Jesus and his followers
would no doubt have contemplated a fight to the death with
the Romans, rather than meekly surrendering – but then
Jesus bar Abbas would have been crucified anyway. Would
Jesus, the King of the Jews, have surrendered so meekly,
were it not to save his son?

The Put-Up Job

For nearly two thousand years there have been rumours, derived from various apocryphal writings from the third to the fifth centuries, that a few years after the crucifixion, Pilate converted to Christianity and that his wife, Claudia Procula, who was a Jewish proselyte at the time of Jesus's death, later became a Christian. Certainly, the Russian Orthodox Church celebrates a day in honour of Claudia Procula, who was canonized as Saint Procula, and the early Coptic Church of Greece did so, too. The early Coptic Church of Egypt and Ethiopia once held Pontius Pilate in such high regard that they canonized him and dedicated a holy day to his memory. Eusebius, in the fourth century, notes that according to Greek historians, Pilate "wearied with misfortunes," committed suicide. But other traditions assert that Pilate converted to Christianity and was condemned to death by the Roman Senate, which is why the Coptic Church of Egypt and Ethiopia revered Pilate as a martyr and for many years celebrated 25 June as the feast day of Saint Pontius Pilate and Saint Procula (the Russian Orthodox Church celebrates Saint Procula day on 28 October). Is there something known to these Churches that has been suppressed by the mainstream Church? Did

Pilate collude in a plot to save the life of Jesus? If so, he had three possible motives: while appearing to do the bidding of the Emperor, Pilate may have been corrupt, and open to being bribed; he may simply have been buying time; or it could be that the businessman Joseph of Arimathea knew Pilate socially, and had converted him to Jesus's cause and lobbied him on behalf of Jesus.

Pilate may have been a secret disciple, corrupt, or merely politically astute – having calculated that with his limited military resources he would have been hard pushed to suppress what might have developed into a full-scale rebellion throughout Judea. Perhaps Pilate, having nipped the rebellion and captured Jesus bar Abbas, the leader's son, wanted the leader himself, thereby deferring to the future, the problem of Jesus bar Abbas and his claim to the Hasmonean throne.

Whether Pilate accepted a bribe or not he had to be seen to have executed a revolutionary. Perhaps men negotiating on behalf of Jesus succeeded in getting Pilate to accept Jesus the Rabbi in exchange for Jesus bar Abbas; they might also have paid some money in case Pilate needed to bribe anyone else involved, but was there a plan to save the life of Jesus the Rabbi? For such a plan to succeed, it had to be timed very carefully, and done with Pilate's connivance.

If Jesus and his disciples sat down to the Last Supper in the safe house on the Essene Passover, it would have been on the Wednesday, forty-eight hours prior to the Jewish Orthodox Passover as described in the Synoptic Gospels. According to the time scale of those Gospels, Jesus's arrest and crucifixion would have had to take place within six hours, which is clearly absurd, even allowing for Roman efficiency. The Synoptic Gospels state that following His arrest, Jesus was escorted through the city to the house of Caiaphas to be interrogated. The Sanhedrin was not allowed to convene during the hours of darkness, so Jesus's trial would have to have taken place at dawn. Even allowing for first light at 4 a.m., the trial over, the accusers would have had to get Pilate out of bed at 6 a.m., then Jesus had to be taken before Antipas for his judgement before finally returning to Pilate to be sentenced and released to the Roman soldiers for scourging and robing in mockery as King of the Jews. Thereafter, Jesus had to drag His cross all the way to Golgotha. It is impossible for all this to have taken place before 9 a.m., however organized the Sanhedrin might have been.

Perhaps the improbable time scale of the Synoptic Gospels is the result of its authors, or editors, attempting to eliminate all references which might tie events to the Essene Passover. Instead, they placed the emphasis on the Orthodox Passover, celebrated on Friday evening at the commencement of the Sabbath, but this would have meant that the crucifixion took place on the Sabbath, which could not have been the case. The Gospel of John, on the other hand, gives the time of Jesus's interrogation by Pilate and his offer to release Jesus, as noon (John 19:14–16):

> And it was the preparation of the Passover, and about the sixth hour, and he saith unto the Jews, Behold your King!
> But they cried out, Away with him, away with him, crucify him. Pilate saith unto them, Shall I crucify your King? The chief priests answered, we have no king but Caesar.
> Then delivered he him therefore unto them to be crucified. And they took Jesus, and led him away.

This time scale in the Gospel of John allows twelve hours for the trial to take place on the Thursday, and has Pilate delivering Jesus up for crucifixion at about noon on the Friday. In terms of Roman law, Pilate could impose the death penalty for murder, insurrection, or treason. As Jesus had not been charged with murder, he must have been found guilty of insurrection or treason. In the scriptures it is stated clearly that the insurrection was to restore the throne to the Hasmonean King of the Jews. Pilate ordered an inscription, in Greek, Hebrew, and Latin, reading "JESUS OF NAZARETH, THE KING OF THE JEWS" to be placed on the cross, but the priests were offended by this and asked Pilate to amend the inscription to read, "Jesus of Nazareth I am the King of the Jews." Pilate dismissed the request, responding, "What I have writ, I have writ"; it seems clear that Jesus was being executed for insurrection.

Pilate had to be seen to do his duty and implement the law to safeguard the interests of Tiberius Caesar, but he could still earn his bribe. A public execution was required to show that Jesus had indeed been executed, but it would have been quite possible for Pilate to use security concerns as a justification for removing witnesses and followers to a point from which they could witness the event without actually being close by. It would then have been possible for some manipulation of the event to take place. The main problem confronted by Jesus and his followers was to somehow create the illusion that He had been executed, but for Him to survive the ordeal. Illusions are, obviously, easier to create when the audience is further away, so the execution site had to be carefully chosen to keep any observers at a distance.

Coincidentally, the execution site chosen by Pilate happened to be adjacent to a garden owned by Joseph of Arimathea, a member of the Sanhedrin and known to be a secret disciple of Jesus, all of which hints at some collusion. Presumably Joseph of Arimathea's garden and tomb were used to inter Jesus's body with Joseph's consent. In case Tiberius Caesar got wind of the plot, Pilate had two other men crucified with Jesus. Admittedly, this is speculative, crafted around the facts as given in the Gospels, which, themselves, were second- or even third-hand accounts of what had been seen to take place.

Under Jewish law, the male next-of-kin of the deceased, in this case Joseph, automatically became the legal guardian of the family of the deceased. Joseph of Arimathea therefore had a legal obligation to intercede and negotiate with Pilate. As a wealthy man and a social peer of Pilate, Joseph of Arimathea would have been able to suggest to Pilate that it might be wise to move the execution of the heir to the Hasmonean throne to a more private place. Joseph could have made the point that had Jesus been crucified in the usual place of execution, his followers may well have initiated another insurrection. Together, Joseph and Pilate would have decided on a place of execution with walls or hedges to hold back the public. The chosen site should also have a cave or some other hiding place nearby to conceal people who could offer medical help to Jesus following his ordeal. Golgotha fulfilled all these requirements, having a garden nearby which contained an unused tomb, supposedly for Joseph of Arimathea's eventual use. The Gospels claim that the garden and tomb were adjacent to a place of public execution and consequently littered with human bones, in which case why would Joseph of Arimathea have constructed a tomb for his own use in such a place?

For Jesus to survive His "crucifixion," he had to give witnesses the illusion of death on the cross, but before that moment He leaves the care of His mother after His death to His beloved disciples (John 19:26–27):

> When Jesus therefore saw his mother, and the disciple standing by, whom he loved, he saith unto his mother, Woman, behold thy son!
> Then saith he to the disciple, Behold thy mother! And from that hour that disciple took her unto his own home.

In doing so, Jesus named His next of kin, who, under Jewish law, would look after Mary. We are told that

Mary stayed with him for the rest of her life, but who was he? It is most likely that he was Joseph of Arimathea, whom the Gospels describe as "a disciple of Jesus," because, as the closest male relative of Mary, he would have been responsible for her future care and well-being and in addition, by law, the closest male relative of Jesus would have had the task of organizing His burial. This was done by Joseph because presumably, Jesus's father was dead, or he would have been present at the crucifixion of his eldest son.

Jesus"s eldest brother should havde assumed responsibility for His burial, and we know from the Gospels that Jesus had siblings. We know, too, that Joseph and Mary lived together as a couple until Jesus was twelve years old and preached in the Temple, and the Gospels tell us that during that time they had other children. We know from various sources that Alpheus, the brother of Joseph, married and had children, and it is possible that Alpheus and the widowed Mary may have renewed their relationship, uniting their two families as step-brothers and sisters. Although there is no proof of this, if correct, James the less, the son of Alpheus (Clopas), who followed Jesus, was also the brother of Joses. If Levi was the son of the same Alpheus, Matthew and James would have been step-brothers. James is therefore the son of Alpheus and Mary the mother of James the less and Joses, which is a Latin rendering of Joseph, itself a Greek rendering of the Hebrew Yoseph. If Joseph of Arimathea was that particular brother, all becomes apparent:

> There were also women looking on afar off, among whom was Mary Magdalene, and Mary the mother of James the less and of Joses, and Salome; (Mark 15:40)

> And when the Sabbath was past, Mary Magdalene, and Mary the mother of James, and Salome, had bought sweet spices, that they might come and anoint him. (Mark 16:1)

The illusion of death could have been created easily with drugs freely available in the Middle East at that time. When Jesus was offered the sponge soaked in vinegar – "And straightway one of them ran, and took a sponge, and filled it with vinegar and put it on a reed, and gave him to drink" (Matthew 27:48) – which he had previously refused (possibly because the timing was not right for the illusion), he accepted it. The sponge had been soaked in a mixture of vinegar and gall, a derivative of *papaver somniferum*, or opium, a highly effective painkiller and narcotic.

In the Gospel of Matthew the sponge is offered on a reed, whereas in the Gospel of John it is on a hyssop, a soft-stemmed reed (John 19:29–30):

> Now there was set a vessel full of vinegar, and they filled a sponge with vinegar, and put it upon hyssop, and put it to his mouth.
> When Jesus therefore had received the vinegar, he said, It is finished, and he bowed his head, and gave up the ghost.

A hyssop would not have supported a dry sponge, let alone one soaked in liquid, but what if the spectators had witnessed from a distance a soldier offering Jesus the sponge on the tip of a spear? We know that Cana, or Kana, was at that time a source of reeds used in the shafts of spears. The Hebrew word for a spear was "hanith," and for a reed, "kaneth," so it is possible that colloquial Hebrew might use the word "kaneth" to refer to someone being speared (as, in the UK, one might say that someone had been "glassed" or "bottled" when hit with a glass or bottle). It is then possible that the writers of the original Gospel texts used colloquial Hebrew and referred to Jesus being "reeded." Translators of the Gospels might then have translated the word "kaneth" as "hyssop."

Having accepted the drugs presented on the sponge, Jesus would have given every appearance of being dead. A soldier then pierced His side (John 19:34): "But one of

the soldiers with a spear pierced his side, and forthwith
came there out blood and water." During the trauma of
crucifixion, body secretions build up in the pleural sac
causing pressure on the lungs resulting in suffocation. The
soldier would have pierced Jesus's side to prove that He
was dead. The fact that blood flowed from the wound
proves that at that point Jesus was still alive. The thrust
from the spear would also have enabled Jesus to breathe
by relieving the pressure on His lungs. The soldiers administered a coup de grâce to the other two men being crucified by breaking their legs, but they left Jesus's legs
unbroken; that in itself lends credence to the theory that
there was a plot to enable Jesus to survive His crucifixion.
The Romans would have known that blood flowing from
Jesus's side meant that He was still alive. Why, then, did
they not break His legs, too? The question remains a
mystery to this day.

According to the Gospel of John, with the Passover
approaching, Nicodemus and Joseph of Arimathea were
given the task of removing Jesus's body, whether dead or
alive, from the cross. If Jesus had still been alive, Joseph of
Arimathea would not have been breaking any Jewish law,
and if Jesus had been dead, he would have been absolved
from breaking his cleansing commitment for the Passover,
which allowed the eldest male relative to accept a body for
burial. When Jesus seemed to die on the cross, it was
Joseph of Arimathea who went to Pilate. The original
Greek text of the Gospel of Mark has Joseph use the word
soma, which means a living body. In responding to Joseph,
Pilate rephrases the request for the living body, using the
Greek word *ptoma*, which means a dead body. In front of
witnesses, Pilate then asked the centurion if Jesus was
dead. The request for the living body of Jesus appears only
in the Gospel of Mark.

The Gospels relate that with Jesus apparently dead, His

body was removed from the cross and Joseph of Arimathea removed the crown of thorns from His head and wrapped Him in a linen cloth. There is a legend that some close follower of Jesus planted the crown of thorns and from it grew a thorn bush, from which Joseph of Arimathea later cut a staff to take with him on his journeys. With the help of Nicodemus, Joseph of Arimathea put Jesus in the tomb, where, according to John 19:39: "Nicodemus brought a mixture of myrrh and aloes that was about a hundred pound in weight."

Why would the weight of a mixture of herbs and spices have survived two thousand years of translation, and why would it have weighed so much? Perhaps the package taken to the tomb included clothing, which Jesus would have required for warmth and to counteract the shock of trauma before he could leave the tomb.

For Jesus to stand any chance of being resuscitated following crucifixion, a skilled healer would have been required, and the Essenes possessed such skills. They would certainly have made available their finest healer to administer to Jesus, and, like any Essene, he would have been dressed in traditional white robes. Jesus, wrapped in a protective linen cloth, was in the tomb with a large bag containing medicinal herbs and spices, clean clothing, and two Essenes. We know there were two because when Mary Magdalene visited the tomb the following morning there were two men in the tomb, while Jesus was outside, preparing to make His escape. When Mary saw the two "angels" dressed in white she must have concluded that her Lord and husband was gone forever, but what if Jesus had wanted to see Mary for one last farewell? Was there a final farewell and possibly even a declaration of love between Jesus and Mary, one which would change the course of history? If Jesus did survive His crucifixion, He also disappeared from the historical record, though he certainly did not fade from Paul's theology – the meeting with Mary at the tomb created the myth of His resurrection, a central tenet of the Christian faith.

Joseph of Arimathea

Joseph of Arimathea was a rich man by the standards of his day, and through his association with Jesus, a financial backer of the Hasmonean cause. It is not possible, however, to establish definitively his relationship to Jesus, though there are sources to which we can turn for substatiation of what is written in the Gospels. References in the Talmud and in the Harlein Manuscripts in the British Museum support the claim that Joseph of Arimathea was a younger brother of the father of the Virgin Mary, and add that he had a daughter named Anna, who was Mary's cousin. Why would a rich man associate himself with Jesus when many of His teachings elevated the poor and suggested that the wealthy would have trouble entering the kingdom of heaven? And why would a rich man appear in the Gospels' accounts at such a late stage unless he was a member of Jesus's family, seeking to save his relative and king?

It would be reasonable to assume that Joseph came from Arimathea, as his name suggests, and there was a town in Biblical times with a similar name. Known today as Ramallah, it is to the north of Jerusalem and was the birthplace of Samuel. However, the Greek Septuagint version of the the Old Testament names the birthplace of Samuel as

Arimathaim. However Joseph was related to Jesus, he may
have come from Galilee, as did Jesus Himself. Capernaum
is a town in Galilee which was central to Jesus's activities.
Stone foundations of a village once known as Areimeh
have been excavated near the site of the ancient town of
Capernaum, but it is impossible to say whether Joseph
came from there or from Aimathaim. As a young
entrepreneur, however, he may have decided to venture
into the the great metropolis of Jerusalem. There he established himself as a prominent importer and exporter of
valuable commodities such as tin, which was brought to the
Middle East from Britain and was vital for the production
of bronze. Mary's husband, Joseph, disappears from
Christian scriptures when Jesus was about twelve years old,
suggesting that he died and left Mary a widow. Thus, when
Jesus began to visit Jerusalem from the age of twelve, it is
likely that a wealthy relative such as Joseph of Arimathea
would have kept a watchful eye on his young nephew of
royal descent.

Events in Jesus's life from the age of twelve to the beginning of his ministry at the age of around thirty are obscure.
During that time, Jesus and Joseph of Arimathea are likely
to have crossed paths many times. Perhaps Joseph gave
moral and financial support to Jesus, but, as a member of
the Sanhedrin, he would have had to keep quiet about his
relationship to the movement for the restoration of a
Hasmonean king, at least until the capture of Jesus left him
with no option but to blow his cover.

As Jesus hung on the cross he asked a disciple to take
care of his mother (John 19:26–27):

> When Jesus therefore saw his mother, and the disciple standing
> by, whom he loved, he saith unto his mother, Woman, behold
> thy son!
> Then saith he to the disciple, Behold thy mother! And from that
> hour that disciple took her unto his own home.

Although the disciple asked to take care of Mary is not named, Church tradition holds that it is John. However, Jewish traditions of that time required that the closest male relative should take care of and attend to the day-to-day requirements of a widow. According to the Gospels there were only two male relatives at the crucifixion; there is no record of Jesus bar Abbas being there, though that would not be surprising if Jesus had sacrificed Himself to save His son – Jesus bar Abbas would have been spirited away to protect the royal line. And neither were the twelve disciples there, so it would be reasonable to assume that one of Jesus's relatives, either Nicodemus or Joseph of Arimathea was named to take care of Mary. One, or both, of them must then have been close relatives. Certainly the Harlein Manuscripts maintain that Joseph of Arimathea was a close relative.

Long before Rome had become a superpower as the capital of the Roman Empire, the Phoenicians were using their naval expertise to establish trade routes throughout the Mediterranean and as far afield as the British Isles. Diodorus Siculus, a first-century BC Greek historian who was born in Agyrium, in Sicily, but who lived in Rome, travelled extensively throughout Asia and Europe. In his writings he names the Isle of Ictis as a Phoenician trading port for the export of tin from Cornwall. He states that this isle was joined to the mainland by a causeway at low tide, as is St Michael's Mount, which is widely believed to be the Phoenician's Isle of Ictis. The Phoenicians were traders who knew that the Celtic tribes of Cornwall and Wales were sitting on vast natural reserves of tin, an element used in the forging of bronze. The ancient Celts had discovered that when tin was smelted with copper, it formed a bronze alloy with much harder-wearing properties than copper, which could be used to manufacture weapons, household utensils, and jewellery. Originally the Celts had mined the tin for domestic consumption, but, when the Phoenicians arrived, a thriving export trade developed. The Phoenicians knew that the tin could be traded for Middle Eastern goods, but they also knew that they needed to keep the source of the tin a secret. For fifty years before the birth of Christ, the expanding Roman Empire had relied on the Phoenicians as the major suppliers of tin to Rome. In 55 BC Julius Caesar invaded Britain for the first time, but, due to strong resistance from the early Britons, the occupation didn't last long, and the Romans soon withdrew to France.

At the time of the crucifixion, Joseph of Arimathea is described in the Gospels as a wealthy businessman, and we know from other sources that he was an importer of tin from Cornwall. As an entrepreneur it is likely that he would have travelled to the outposts of the Phoenician trading empire to establish business links and to export Cornish tin to Rome. He would also have been a major figure in the Roman business world. Eventually, the Romans appointed Joseph of Arimathea as the official administrator for the mining and importing of tin, as recorded in the Vulgate, an early fifth-century version of the Bible in Latin (largely the work of Jerome, commissioned by Pope Damasus I to revise the old Latin translations). It gives Joseph's official Roman title as *Nobilis Decurio*, indicating that he had been appointed an administrator of mining for the Roman Empire. Thus Joseph of Arimathea switched his business from Phoenician to Roman control and, because of the Roman demand for tin, he was granted a monopoly as the sole exporter of tin from Britain to the Roman Empire.

It was at that time, during Jesus's formative years, that Mary's husband Joseph died, which left Joseph of Arimathea, Jesus's uncle and his next of kin, as His guardian. There are numerous legends that Joseph took Jesus with him on some of his voyages to England. There are clues regarding this in the Gospels, and in English folklore. From the age of twelve until He began His ministry at the age of thirty, Jesus was absent from Judea on numerous occasions. Matthew 17:24–27 (in the New American Standard Bible) offers one clue:

> And when they had come to Capernaum, those who collected the two-drachma tax came to Peter, and said, "Does your teacher not pay the two-drachma tax?"
>
> He said, "Yes." And when he came into the house, Jesus spoke to him first, saying,
>
> "What do you think, Simon? From whom do the kings of the earth collect customs or poll-tax, from their sons (nationals) or from strangers (foreigners)?"
>
> And upon his saying, "From strangers," Jesus said to him, "Consequently the sons are exempt."
>
> "But, lest we give them offence, go to the sea, and throw in a hook, and take the first fish that comes up; and when you open its mouth, you will find a stater. Take that and give it to them for you and Me."

This seems to suggest that Jesus and Peter were considered to be non-residents, or foreigners, due to their long absences from Judea. A further clue to their absence is given when John the Baptist, Jesus's cousin, fails to recognize him at the baptism. If Jesus and John had grown up in the same country, they would have met at the traditional feast days held three times each year. A further clue is provided in John 1:48, in which Nathanael, who lived in Cana, does not recognize Jesus.

There is also a wealth of English local traditions supported by old maps and even some church inscriptions, which add weight to the claim that Jesus visited England in his youth. Take, for example, the legend from the tin- and lead-mining communities of Somerset, England, that after Joseph of Arimathea and his young companion had visited the Scilly Isles to inspect Joseph's business interests, they sailed on to the Somerset port of Burnham which lies at the mouth of the River Brue which flows down from Glastonbury Tor. Joseph and Jesus are supposed to have visited the village of Priddy in the Mendips, a centre for the mining of copper and lead. Two thousand years after the ministry of Jesus, right up to the beginning of the Second World War, there was a common Somerset expression, "As sure as our Lord was at Priddy," used by locals wanting to emphasize the truth of a statement.

In Cornwall there are fourteen peculiar Christian relics depicting the boy Jesus. These relics, which resemble Celtic crosses, are known as the Tunic Crosses and are still to be seen at the roadside in the vicinity of churchyards – they are to be found nowhere else in Europe. One such cross is the Lanherne Cross at St Mawgan in Pydar. The Tunic Crosses depict, on their reverse side, carvings of a young boy dressed in a knee-length smock or tunic with his arms outstretched as if blessing the traveller.

Another indication that Jesus visited Cornwall is to be found on a stone arch over a south-facing church door of the private chapel in Manor Place near St Anthony in Roseland. The arch is over a thousand years old, pre-dating the Norman Conquest, and comprises a series of carved pictograms. Although weatherworn, the images can still be seen to depict an insignia of an anchor, a lamb, and a cross. E. Raymond Capt claims that an archaeologist familiar with Phoenician and Egyptian symbols had seen similar pictograms on a temple doorway at Denderah in Lower Egypt. Because the Phoenicians had been visiting Cornwall for hundreds of years, Phoenician symbols would not have been entirely foreign to the people of Cornwall. The archaeologist referred to by Capt interpreted the picto-graphs as follows: because the lamb and the cross are facing East toward the rising sun, the pictogram was intended to inform the viewer that Jesus had visited Manor

Place in his formative years before the the Passion. The pictograms above the lamb and cross show a boat in difficulty in rough seas, Jesus and Joseph being brought ashore by local fishermen, and a boat being repaired. Before Jesus left St Anthony in Roseland, legend has it that He erected a stone monument inscribed to tell the story of His and Joseph's visit. All of this seems to confirm that Joseph's mining interests in Cornwall were established long before the Passion of Christ.

After the crucifixion, the apostles lay low. Joseph settled Mary Magdalene in France before travelling to England. Somerset legends claim that Joseph came ashore on the Glastonbury Marshes – in those days Glastonbury was virtually surrounded by marshland and linked to the River Severn. Together with his party of twelve, Joseph ascended a nearby hill to survey the countryside. Once on the summit, Joseph apparently exclaimed that they were "weary all of them." He then plunged his thornwood staff, which he had cut from the bush grown from Jesus's crown of thorns, into the soft, fertile earth. The staff took root, and today, two thousand years later, a thornbush still grows on Weary-All Hill at Glastonbury.

Arviragus, a local tribal chief, is said to have given Joseph of Arimathea twelve hides, or approximately two thousand acres of land at Glastonbury on which to build the first English monastery. Thus the first and primary church in Christendom should be Glastonbury. In the fifth century, Gildas "The Wise" wrote that "Britain received the faith in AD 37 being the last year of the reign of Tiberius Caesar." Historians William of Malmesbury, Maelgwyn of Llandaff, and Polydore Vergil also claim that four church councils ratified the supremacy of the British Church. Each council stated that "the Churches of Spain and France shall both yield in points of precedence and antiquity to the Church of Britain because Joseph of Arimathea was the founder of the

British Church." The four church councils which made this proclamation were held in Pisa in 1409, Constance in 1417, Sienna in 1424, and Basle in 1434. It was because of this supremacy of the British Church that missionaries were sent out onto the European mainland. Lazarus, who had accompanied Joseph to England, was one of the first to return to France, where for seven years he served as the Bishop of Marseilles. French records also verify that during the early Christianization of France, the archbishops of Rheims and of Trèves were all appointed by the Mother Church of Glastonbury.

The Flight to France

Jesus was resuscitated at His tomb by two "angel" physicians dressed in the white robes of the Essenes. The two Essenes helped Jesus to dress and, with help on the outside of the tomb, the stone sealing the entrance to the tomb was rolled away. Jesus was about to leave to seek refuge either with the Nazorean Essenic community near Mount Carmel, or in the Essene community at Qumran. What happened next was unplanned: Mary Magdalene saw Jesus and ran to spread the news that He was alive. But for that unplanned meeting outside the tomb, Jesus might possibly have ended his days living the quiet monastic life in either the Qumran or Nazorean community; Christianity would not exist, and the course of history would have been entirely different, with no Holy Crusades – in all likelihood, Europe would have developed as part of the Muslim world. At this point in the story, Jesus, the man, fades from the story to re-emerge in the theological dogma of the Christian Church. But for the actions of Saul (later Saint Paul) and his Pauline doctrines, Jesus would be a forgotten minor Jewish king who lived two thousand years ago. Donovan Joyce theorizes in *The Jesus Scroll* that Jesus was involved in the revolt of AD 66. He claims that Jesus and a group of zealots made a last stand, dying, finally, during the fall of Masada.

With Jesus having been convicted and executed on a charge of sedition, his wife and any issue to the royal line would have been in danger. Pilate had allowed them some time, but soon after the "execution" of Jesus the full force of the Roman establishment would have been brought to bear on Mary Magdalene and the children of Jesus. The Romans were unlikely to tolerate claimants to the thrones of conquered kingdoms in their empire. Consequently Mary Magdalene, as the wife of the insurrectionist "King of the Jews," would have been forced to flee to escape the Roman authorities. It would have made sense for the escapees to split up and scatter to better protect the royal bloodline in countries which offered safe hiding places. During the early years of Jesus's ministry, He sent His twin brother, Judas Thomas Didymus, better known as Doubting Thomas, on a mission as an Essenic healing emissary to King Abgar of Edessa, who was chronically ill. The sick king, who had heard of the healing power of the Essenes, had written to Jesus with a request for Jesus to visit and cure him. Jesus declined and, in his place, sent his twin, Judas Thomas Didymus. It is worth noting that "Thomas" is Hebrew for twin, and "Didymus" is Greek for twin, suggesting that the Gospel editors were again at work to suppress the correct identification of "the twin twin." The correspondence between Jesus and King Abgar is referred to in Eusebius's *Ecclesiastical History*.

There is a legend that, after the crucifixion, Judas Thomas Didymus fled to Edessa and was given sanctuary by King Abgar. Mary Magdalene, too, fled from Judea, most probably with her mother-in-law, Mary the mother of Jesus. Some legends claim that Mary Magdalene was pregnant at the time of the crucifixion and that she escaped into Egypt with Joseph of Arimathea as her guardian. As a wealthy merchant, Joseph of Arimathea had the contacts and the money to effect an immediate escape. Once over the border in Egypt, both Marys and Joseph took refuge with the Essenes. There they would have been safe within the Essene cult which would have protected one of their own as they considered the future of their investment in the royal bloodline. We do not know how long Mary Magdalene stayed in Egypt, but, if pregnant, she would not have wanted to travel far during the final stages of her pregnancy. It is likely, therefore, that she would have stayed with the Essenes until the royal heir had been born, and the bloodline preserved.

Leaving Egypt for France, the refugees from Roman oppression settled close to present-day Saints-Maries-de-la-Mer. French legends claim that the Magdalene's descendants eventually became part of a French royal family through the Merovingian dynasty. After a period in France, the party of refugees again divided with the Magdalene staying in France, and Joseph of Arimathea moving on and finally settling at Glastonbury in England. It is possible that the Virgin Mary accompanied him on that last flight to safety, a theory which is explored by Graham Phillips in *The Marian Conspiracy*, in which he suggests that the Virgin Mary was finally buried on the island of Anglesey, in North Wales. Phillips's research draws on the Bible and on a letter from St Augustine to Pope Gregory written in AD 597, in which St Augustine claimed that he had found Mary's tomb in a church off the west coast of Britain. Phillips claims that when the island was under attack by the Vikings in the tenth century, Mary's remains were removed from the church and reburied beside a nearby well.

It was on the journey to France that Joseph of Arimathea is initially identified in legend as the guardian of the Holy Grail, but what is the Holy Grail? According to one French legend the "Sangraal," or Holy Grail, means "born in

Egypt." Another interpretation from medieval French is "Sang Rall," which equates to "Royal Blood." There is also a line of thought that maintains that the womb of Mary Magdalene was the symbolic chalice, the Holy Grail, that carried the royal bloodline of Jesus in the form of His son.

Jesus and Mary Magdalene's French Descendants

French legends relate how the Magdalene travelled to Aix-en-Provence in the company of Joseph of Arimathea, her sister Martha, and brother-in-law Lazarus, plus the remaining members of the group of refugees. On reaching France safely, the party dispersed through the regions of Provence and into Languedoc, where the Magdalene ended her days. The Priory of Sion claims that over the next three centuries, the descendants of Jesus and Mary Magdalene married into the Visigoths and were absorbed into the Merovingian dynasty. The Visigoths believed that they were descended from the House of Benjamin, and the Priory was a secret society with the goal of restoring the Merovingian line to the French throne. The Priory documents are first mentioned by Baigent, Leigh, and Lincoln in *The Holy Blood and the Holy Grail*, which investigated their claims that the Visigoth Arcadians were descended from the Benjaminites, who had been driven out of the Holy Lands by fellow Israelites for idolatry. These ancestors of the Visigoths had settled originally in the Greek area of Arcadia but around 1000 BC they had been forced to resettle in France, and, by the beginning of the fifth century, the Visigoths had formed a kingdom in the Languedoc, with Toulouse as its capital. Eventually, the kingdom of the Visigoths expanded from southern France into Spain.

Due to the influence of Mary Magdalene and her party, a form of Christianity evolved and flourished in the Languedoc over the next four centuries. In the fourth century, this French branch of Christianity absorbed another branch of Christianity known as Arianism, which was derived from a philosophy of Bishop Arius (AD 250–336), who rejected the dual divinity of Jesus Christ. Arianism thus also rejected the Holy Trinity, making the conversion of Europeans to Arianism a very real threat to the Catholic Church of Rome, particularly given that most French bishops were Arians. While this power struggle was being waged between the Roman Catholic and Arian faiths for the hearts and minds of the French Christians, the Roman Empire was crumbling and in AD 410 the Visigoths pillaged Rome. The treasure of Jerusalem that had been kept in Rome since Titus had sacked Jerusalem was taken to the Languedoc.

In AD 418, the Visigoths founded a town on a hilltop in the Languedoc named Rhedae that became a prominent city during the first millennium. The city then fell into decline, and remained neglected and partly abandoned for most of the next 900 years before regaining prominence in the twentieth century as a small village known as Rennes-le-Château.

In the fifth century, with the Christian world divided between Roman Catholicism and Arianism, the Visigoths opted to convert to the Arian faith. The Arian faith was eventually absorbed by the Cathars, and evolved into a non-violent, humanitarian religion, independent of the Roman Church. At around the same time, the Merovingian King Clovis I began his reign by murdering his three brothers so that he could rule an undivided Kingdom of the Franks. The practice of dividing a kingdom on the death of the father was a system that determined that the succession to the Frankish throne went in equal proportions to all of a king's sons. In reality it meant that each son inherited power over a particular territory within the kingdom, which resulted in the kingdom becoming fragmented and riven with fighting as the heirs attempted to recreate a single state. Clovis, in sole command, hedged his bets on which faith he should adopt, refusing, during the first part of his reign, to convert either to Arianism or to Catholicism despite constant pressure from his wife Princess Clotilde, who was a devout Roman Catholic. According to legend, during a battle which took place near Cologne, Clovis underwent a religious experience. The battle was going against Clovis and the Franks and, in a moment of desperation, Clovis cried out, "Jesus Christ!" At that moment an arrow fired from the ranks of the Frankish army hit and killed the opposing king, whereupon his army fled the battlefield, leaving Clovis victorious. Following Clovis's victory, his wife became even more insistent that Clovis should convert to Roman Catholicism, arguing that without the help of Jesus Christ, the Franks would have lost the battle. Eventually Clovis capitulated to his wife and, in AD 496, he and his subjects abandoned Arianism and were baptized into the Roman Catholic Church. The Church of Rome made an agreement with Clovis which pledged that all Roman Catholics in Gaul would acknowledge Clovis and his descendants as their lawful liege and king. A final tribute from the Church of Rome was to grant the Latin title *Novus Constantinus*, or "The New Constantine," to Clovis in acknowledgement of his conversion of the Frankish kingdom to Roman Catholicism. But the Church of Rome later reneged on this agreement.

The Priory of Sion maintained that the agreement of AD 496 established "the divine right of kings" by baptizing and receiving Clovis into the Roman Catholic Church. In AD 507, nine years after his baptism, Clovis defeated the Visigoths at Vouillé and subsequently sacked and burned Toulouse. The Visigoths withdrew to the fortified city of Carcassonne and made Toledo their new capital, but their kingdom went into decline; they lost most of their lands to the Merovingians and the city of Carcassonne soon became a Visigoth frontier town. To protect their treasures and records they were moved to the town of Rhedae, which had better natural defences and was more secure than Carcassonne. The Visigoth kingdom was in decline and eventually became so weak that it was reduced to an area that extended only from Carcassonne to Toledo, which eventually fell to the Moors. At his death in AD 511, Clovis was master of Gaul from the Loire to Cologne, and had extended the kingdom of the Franks as far as the Garonne River. Following his death, in accordance with the custom which had led Clovis to murder his three brothers, the Frankish kingdom was divided between his descendants into small principalities.

One hundred and seventy-five years after the death of Clovis another murder took place, instigated by the Church of Rome which had reneged on its agreement with Clovis. With the Visigoth kingdom in decline, Princess Giselle of the Visigoths married Dagobert II, a Merovingian from another branch of the French royal family. The issue from Dagobert and Giselle's union was a son and heir to the throne, whom they named Sigebert. Dagobert II is assumed to be the last French king in the Merovingian line, however, there are conflicting reports as to the fate of Dagobert II. Most records claim that both he and his son Sigebert were murdered while hunting, but records discovered in Rennes-le-Château claim that only Dagobert II was murdered, while Sigebert was rescued by two knights and therefore survived the assassination attempt. The records claim that Dagobert's wife hid with the young Sigebert at Rennes-le-Château. Thus the Merovingian line that was descended from Jesus and the Magdalene survived and continued underground through to future generations of French monarchy. Dagobert II, who was born in AD 651, was five when he inherited a realm that would become the foundation for the Hapsburg dynasty. Dagobert's kingdom lay in what is today north-eastern France, on the western frontiers of modern Germany. On gaining his inheritance in AD 656 he was kidnapped from the palace and taken to Poitiers where the Bishop of Poitiers spirited the young Dagobert II away to a monastery in Ireland. In Ireland he received a first-class education, which would not have been available to him had he not been abducted.

In AD 666, at the age of twenty-five, Dagobert II married a Celtic princess named Mathilde of York. The couple settled in York, and during the next three years they had two children. Dagobert also became acquainted with Saint Wilfred, the Bishop of York at that time. Saint Wilfred eventually became Dagobert's friend, mentor, and benefactor. During the fourth year of the marriage, Mathilde died during the birth of the couple's third daughter. Following her death, Dagobert II entered into a marriage uniting the Visigothic and Merovingian royal houses. This second marriage in AD 671 was to Giselle de Razes, who was part of a old Jewish Visigothic bloodline. The marriage agreement was arranged by Saint Wilfred and the wedding took place in the old Visigothic chapel of Mary Magdalene in Rhedae. A son and heir, Sigebert IV, was born two years later.

Within a couple of years, Dagobert II, who had territorial ambitions and strong authoritarian attitudes, was at odds with his old friend Saint Wilfred and became antagonistic towards the Church of Rome. The rift lasted the remainder of

Dagobert's short life, which ended five years later on 23 December, AD 679, when he was murdered while on a hunting trip with his family in the sacred Forest of Woëvres near the Royal Palace of Stenay. Legend has it that while Dagobert slept under a tree during a midday lunch break, his godson Jean took a lance and thrust it into Dagobert's eye. Queen Giselle and the infant Sigebert, protected by a small group of loyal knights, fled and took refuge in Rhedae.

The Merovingian dynasty, which had absorbed the Visigothic dynasty, had evolved from a tribe of Franks known as the Salian Franks. Dagobert II's murder marked the end of the Merovingian dynasty. His assassination was the result of a conspiracy between the Church of Rome and the Mayor of the Palace who had chosen Dagobert's godson Jean as their assassin. Although the young Prince Sigebert assumed his uncle's titles of Duke of Razes and Count of the Rhedae in AD 681, the Merovingian dynasty had become weak and was finally integrated into the Carolingian dynasty of the Franks.

The demise of the Merovingian kings occurred because of the treachery and murder that has always been associated with imperial politics; similar incidents took place in the eras of the Egyptian pharaohs, the Roman emperors, and the medieval English monarchy. Such treachery often occurs when associates or relatives of the royal household try to usurp the power of the throne, but in the case of the Merovingians, that power was usurped by a state-appointed civil servant known as the Mayor of the Palace. Palace mayors were supposed to administer the king's estate and kingdom, but after establishing government control of the land, this particular mayor seized the power of the throne for himself and established the Carolingian dynasty. The Priory of Sion claimed that the conspiracy was a betrayal of the Merovingians because the Church of Rome had proclaimed the Merovingian Clovis as *Novus Constantinus*.

The Merovingian dynasty experienced an upturn in its fortunes in October AD 732 when Charles Martel, the son of the Mayor who had conspired with the Catholic Church to assassinate Dagobert II, defeated the Moors, who had crossed the Pyrenees in great strength and raped and pillaged as far as the Loire, killing their leader Abd-er-Rahman, at Poitiers. This battle is regarded as one of the key events in Muslim and Christian history for it decided which faith, Christianity or Islam, would prevail throughout Europe. A further Frankish victory on the River Berre near Narbonne stopped the Moors from advancing further into the Languedoc, and, for the time being, Rhedae was saved from destruction.

With the absorbtion of the Merovingian dynasty, the Carolingian rise to power was gradual, but steady, until, aided by Charles Martel's victories, it became entrenched in AD 800 when the Pope crowned Charles Martel's son Charlemagne as Holy Roman Emperor. The Church had missed an opportunity to eliminate the bloodline of Jesus, which was being continued through Charlemagne. The Carolingian and Merovingian lines claimed descent from Jesus through the Visigoths, with a bloodline stretching all the way back to the Judaic kingdom of Saul and Solomon. It was at this time that legends of the Holy Grail began to surface in Europe.

Many researchers claim that the Holy Grail was not a sacred chalice used at the last supper, but is rather a corruption of the French term *sang real*, meaning "royal blood." This royal blood was betrayed by the Church with the murder of Dagobert II, but it survived through Charlemagne and into several royal houses in modern Europe. In consecrating Charlemagne, the Church again reneged on its agreement made at the baptism of Clovis, an agreement which was probably made without the Church understanding the true bloodline of the Merovingians. Louis XI of France, who reigned between 1461 and 1483, claimed that the French royal family were direct descendants of Jesus and Mary Magdalene. The Merovingians consolidated their hold on the Languedoc when they drove the Moors and Visigoths towards Spain. With their defeat, Charlemagne became ruler of an immense empire. As a reward he gave the city of Carcassonne to one of his commanders, thus creating the first Count of Carcassonne, who also had jurisdiction over the town of Rhedae.

When two royal households joined with the marriage of Almaric, the son of the Visigoth King, to Clothilde, a Merovingian Princess, the fortunes of Rhedae improved. Its status was further enhanced when a statute made Rhedae a Royal City. With its royal court and its troubadours it became the cultural centre of the region. Rhedae remained a centre of culture until the eleventh century when its fortunes and those of the Rhedezium region began to decline as a result of Ermengarde, the daughter of the Count of Carcassonne and the wife of the Vicomte of Bezier, having sold the whole region to a Spanish aristocratic family based in Barcelona. In 1170, the King of Aragon, Alphonse II, claimed his rights over Rhedezium when he attacked and destroyed Rhedae. The citadel survived that attack and remained in the hands of the Trencavel family, descendants of Ermengarde.

The Merovingian kings lived during the Dark Ages, consequently not a great deal is known about them. Old manuscripts and paintings show that they wore robes fringed with tassels, that they believed had magical curative powers, and, like the Nazoreans, they never cut their hair. The Merovingians were also adept in the occult. This was verified in 1653 in Tournai when archaeologists opened the tomb of the Merovingian King Childeric I, who had died in AD 481, and found various occult items, including a golden bull's head, a crystal ball, and three hundred golden bees.

The bee was the symbol of the Merovingian dynasty, perhaps intended to symbolize matriarchal descent of the line of David through the Merovingian "queen bee," or female, line. Legend also has it that all the Merovingian monarchs had a birthmark on their shoulder blades in the form of a red cross. The Carolingians may eventually have supplanted the Merovingians, but the Merovingian line was not totally extinguished by the usurpers. Claims have been made that the Merovingian lineage survived through the Carolingian Franks, through Charlemagne and into some European royal families. If the Priory documents are to be believed, when Dagobert's son Sigebert survived the assassination of his father, the Merovingian principality of Septimania continued to be ruled by Guillem de Gellon, an ancestor of Godfroi de Bouillon, one of the nine founding knights of the Templars.

The Priory documents claim that the Merovingian lineage survives to this day largely due to efforts to preserve it through intermarriage. The significance of such alliances is the key to the whole mystery of Rennes-le-Château, which came about because Dagobert married the daughter of the Visigothic Count of Razes and bestowed on his descendants the hereditary title to the lands surrounding Rennes-le-Château.

The Priory of Sion

So where did the Priory of Sion have its roots, and who promoted is foundation? In 1070 a group of monks from Calabria, in Italy, under the leadership of Prince Ursus migrated to Orval, in what is known today as the Ardennes. At Orval, Mathilde de Toscane, the Duchess of Lorraine, became a patron to the monks and gave them land on which they founded an abbey. Interestingly, the Duchess of Lorraine was also the foster mother and great aunt of Godfroi de Bouillon. Charlemagne, the founder of the Carolingian empire, ruled as king of the Franks and the Lombards over an empire that stretched from the River Elbe in modern Germany to the Pyrenees. Godfroi de Bouillon (1058–1100) was descended from the Merovingians and was to be one of the main advocates for the First Crusade to take Jerusalem for the Christians. Baigent, Leigh, and Lincoln suggest in *The Holy Blood and The Holy Grail* that Peter the Hermit, who was possibly the tutor of Godfroi de Bouillon, was also based at Orval. If that was so, then de Bouillon was about twelve years old when the monks arrived in 1070. Apart from being the tutor of de Bouillon, Peter the Hermit was one of the main advocates for the First Crusade. With de Bouillon as one of its leaders and with the Church sanctioning and even encouraging the crusade, was the Church about to reap the harvest sown by failing to eliminate the bloodline of Jesus?

In 1099, after taking Jerusalem during the first Crusade, de Bouillon founded an abbey on Mount Zion. It was from this abbey that a secretive group known as the Priory of Sion took its name. In Orval, the monks, who had remained there from 1070 until about 1108, suddenly disappeared, approximately eight years after the demise of their patron de Bouillon. Although there is no definitive evidence to link the monks of Orval with the Priory on Mount Zion the monks certainly moved to another monastery or priory, and both the monks based at Orval and those at Mount Zion in Jerusalem had the same mentor. It seems probable that the original headquarters of the Priory of Sion were based temporarily at the abbey at Orval only until they could move to their permanent accommodation on Mount Zion. If the establishment of a permanent home for the Priory of Sion was planned between 1070 and 1100, then perhaps when de Bouillon went on the First Crusade he took with him a group of advisers from Orval to let him know their political requirements for establishing a permanent home in the Holy Land. When the papal summonses came for the first Crusade, de Bouillon and his brother Baldwin mortgaged their entire property to finance their crusading expenses and joined the French knights leaving for the Crusade. This act alone suggests that the de Bouillon brothers weren't planning to come home, but intended to take up permanent residence in the Holy Land.

On 15 July, 1099, de Bouillon was at the head of a Frankish army which was the first to break through to Jerusalem. The crusaders then took part in the massacre of every man, woman, and child in the city, regardless of whether the victims were Jewish or Muslim. It is said that after the massacre the steps of the Temple ran with blood, while the crusaders took their spoils by claiming every building in the city for their own personal possession. On 22 July, 1099, a meeting was held in Jerusalem by a group which chose to remain anonymous, though it is likely that it was the elective body of the Priory of Sion, the advisers whom de Bouillon had brought with him from Orval. On the agenda for the meeting was the proposal to elect a King of Jerusalem. There were several proposals and claimants for the title, but the meeting eventually offered the title and the throne to de Bouillon. He accepted the responsibilities but declined the royal title on the grounds that it would be improper for him to wear a crown of gold in the city where Jesus had worn a crown of thorns. He eventually accepted the title of Defender of the Holy Sepulchre and, as such, became King of Jerusalem in all but name. De Bouillon ruled for little over a year before being laid to rest in the Church of the Holy Sepulchre. Almost immediately, and without hesitation, his brother Baldwin, or Baudouin, accepted the title of King of Jerusalem and succeeded his brother as Baldwin I of Jerusalem.

Following the First Crusade, a papal bull issued by Pope Paschal II in 1113 established permission for a monastic order of Hospitallers to be formed by the Blessed Gerard. Gerard began immediately to acquire territory and revenues for the order throughout the Christian world, in particular from within the Kingdom of Jerusalem. The order of Hospitallers played a large part in the Crusades and also, allegedly, in the eventual dissolution of the Templars, when hostility between the two orders surfacing in the English Peasants' Revolt of 1381. The Hospitallers were formed to offer care and sustenance to pilgrims who survived the journey to Jerusalem, but it was decided that it would be more effective to provide armed protection for the pilgrims as they travelled within the Holy Land. Towards the middle of the twelfth century, the Order of Hospitallers was divided into two arms, both of them under the authority of the Papacy. One arm was geared entirely towards caring for the sick and wounded, while the other arm was devoted to military matters. The Hospitallers grew into a substantial force, especially after their militia was reinforced by the formation of the Order of Templars. The Papacy granted the Hospitallers several privileges, the most notable being that they could erect religious buildings and defend them. They were also granted an exemption from paying tax. At the height of Christian supremacy in Jerusalem, the Hospitallers held seven large, strongly defended forts. When the two orders were on the field of battle – the Hospitallers in a black surcoat with a white cross, and the Templars in a white tunic with a red cross – they presented a daunting fighting force to protect Jerusalem.

After the fall of Jerusalem during the first Crusade, the European crusader knights were formed into an order of warrior monks which became known as the Knights Templar. These warrior monks strode onto the European stage and held the limelight for nearly three centuries until, in 1314, they were arrested, tortured, and executed by the King of France who was acting in collusion with the Pope.

Who were these warrior monks, and where did they come from? One early record, written at some point between 1175 and 1185 by the Frankish historian Guillaume de Tyre claims the Templar Order was founded in 1118 as the Poor Knights of Christ and of the Temple of Solomon. However, an even earlier letter written in 1114 by the Bishop of Chartres to Hugh, Count of Champagne, names the knights as the *Milice du Christi* or "Soldiers of Christ." At some point between 1109 and 1117, Hugues de Payens, a vassal of the Count of Champagne, presented himself and eight companions as a company of nine knights to Baldwin I, the King of Jerusalem. It is thought that they may have acted as diplomats to the Muslim leaders, but they also declared to the king that it was their intention, "as far as their strength permitted, to keep the roads and highways safe . . . with a special regard for the protection of pilgrims." Their declaration may have been intended merely to gain favour from the King, for there is no evidence that they protected a single pilgrim or even ventured out onto the roads leading to Jerusalem. In any case, protecting the pilgrim routes to Jerusalem would have been an impossible task for only nine Knights. Another theory suggests that the families of some of these original nine knights were part of the Rex Deus family tree. It is suspected that some time around AD 69, Rex Deus ancestors had secreted documents and artefacts in the vast caverns beneath the Temple in Jerusalem prior to its sacking by the Romans in AD 70. If those suspicions are correct, then the nine knights were perhaps attempting to claim their inheritance and restore their bloodline to the European monarchy. There is also evidence that three of the nine knights were Cathars (Bertrand de Blanchefort, the fourth Grand Master of the order, was certainly a Cathar).

Prior to 1118, the nine knights were provided with accommodation in Baldwin's palace, previously a Muslim mosque, which had been built on the site of the Temple of Solomon. There is substantial evidence that the nine knights spent most of the next nine years excavating and searching beneath the Temple Mount in Jerusalem, but what were they searching for? Was it the treasure of Solomon, or some records of births and marriages which would prove the bloodline of Jesus as the rightful king of Israel, or were they perhaps seeking the body of Jesus? The bloodline would have been important because if Jesus's heirs could unearth records to prove that he was the rightful king of Israel, a mortal prophet, a priest-king, and legitimate ruler of the line of David, his heir might well have proved acceptable to both Muslims and Jews, both of whom had held the same basic tenets since the time of Solomon. Thus the King of Jerusalem would have taken precedence over all the monarchs of Europe, and the Patriarch of Jerusalem would have supplanted even the Pope; the centre of Christianity would have moved from Rome to Jerusalem.

The Templars would then have implemented the main objective of their policy, which was the reconciliation of Christianity with Judaism and Islam throughout the world, but when Acre fell in 1291, the Templar's plan collapsed. The Merovingian (Frankish) kingdom of Jerusalem never materialized, and the Templars regrouped in Europe with long term plans to reclaim their right as the true defenders of the Royal House of David. Around the time of the first crusade, in AD 1105, Hugh of Champagne commissioned the Cistercian order to begin an in-depth study of ancient Hebrew texts, in which they were assisted by Hebrew scholars from the Kabbalah, a learning centre located at Troyes. Nine years later, in 1114, Hugh of Champagne made a second journey to the Holy Land and on his return to France, he again made contact with the Cistercians, possibly to make an interim report on his initial findings and those of his eight companion knights. At some point between 1120 and 1126 Hugh of Champagne and three other knights joined the original order of nine.

So what was the real brief that the nine knights had been given? Had they been ordered by some political masters to search for the ruined Temple of Solomon? The answer would seem to be yes, but who were their political masters? Could they have been the founder members of the Priory of Sion?

In 1117 King Baldwin I was dying, but before he died, the nine Templar knights made some preliminary searches of the stables, and then, under orders from their political masters, the Priory of Sion, they demanded a constitutional charter from the King. When that anonymous group – in fact, the Priory of Sion – met to elect a king of Jerusalem, whoever was chosen would be indebted to them. Thus when the nine knights presented themselves to the dying king, that obligation, according to Baigent, Leigh, and Lincoln, was about to be redeemed. King Baldwin was obliged to officially accommodate the Knights Templar in the stables under the ruins of the Temple of Solomon. Shortly after drawing up the new constitutional charter, the king died and was succeeded by King Baldwin II (1118–1131), who was called upon to ratify the charter drawn up by his predecessor. For the next nine years, the knights continued their searches and excavations under the Temple of Solomon and, towards the end of that time, they found something, though what exactly it was has never been disclosed, and remains to this day an object of speculation.

Following their find, Hugues de Payens and André de Montbard, two of the nine knights, travelled to Europe to visit the Cistercian monk Bernard of Clairvaux, the uncle of André de Montbard, who was later canonized. Bernard was so impressed with the knights' story of how they had been protecting pilgrims on the road to Jerusalem, that he promoted them in various noble houses in France in a bid to raise more funds. The future St Bernard also lobbied Pope Honorius II, who was so impressed with their motives that in January 1128 he provided them with their own constitution, or "rule," at a specially convened Council of Troyes. The council was presided over by the papal legate Cardinal Matthew of Albano together with two archbishops, ten bishops, and numerous other clergymen. The charter named six of the nine knights who attended the council: Hugues de Payens, Grand Master of the Templars and a relative by marriage to the St Clairs of Rosslyn and also a vassal of Hugh of Champagne; André de Montbard, the uncle of Bernard of

Clairvaux and another vassal of Hugh of Champagne; Geoffroi de St Omer, a son of Hugh de St Omer; Payen de Montdidier, a member of the ruling family of Flanders; Achambaud de St-Amand, also a member of the ruling house of Flanders; Geoffroi Bisol; and Godfroi. Hugues de Payens accepted the Holy Latin Rule on behalf of the other eight knights (the two ex-Cistercian monks are presumed to have remained in Jerusalem). Pope Honorius II had given the knights official recognition as warrior monks and established the Order of the Knights Templar. At the same time, the Knights were given their white vestments as a symbol of their purity. The charter makes no mention of the task of defending pilgrims or keeping the roads of the Holy Land safe. Another oddity is that while the original charter was in Latin, it was translated into French about ten years later, becoming known as the French Rule, with a number of changes to the original. In the original Latin Rule, the section on excommunicated knights has the following clause: ". . . moreover where you know non-excommunicated knights are gathered there we command you to go." But in the French Rule the equivalent clause reads as follows: "Where you know excommunicated knights to be gathered, there we command you to go; and if anyone there wishes to join the order of knighthood from regions overseas, you should not consider worldly gain so much as the eternal salvation of his soul." This about-turn on excommunication seems to imply that in the ten years since their inauguration the Templars had grown so arrogant and self-sufficient that they considered themselves above Vatican authority. However, eighteen years later, in 1146, Pope Eugenius granted them the right to use the red double-barred Cross of Lorraine as their standard. The Knights Templar were soon to become renowned for their combination of fanaticism and monastic discipline. They were sworn to chastity, poverty, and obedience. In 1139, Pope Innocent II issued a papal bull declaring that the

Templars were not permitted to hold allegiance to any secular or ecclesiastical power other than to the Pope himself. This gave the Templars the right to act independently and, if necessary, in total defiance of the rule of any local authorities, be they kings or princes. Although the Knights Templar were linked to the Church, they also maintained close and mutually respectful links with the Islamic and Judaic worlds. Consequently they were familiar with areas of scientific knowledge which were alien to the Church. By the middle of the twelfth century, the Knights Templar were in possession of both a constitutional charter and heraldic rights. They had papal approval and a nascent army recruited from the noble families of Europe whose sons flocked to join an order which demanded of recruits that they sign over all their property. Such a system enabled the order to accumulate virtually limitless wealth, which provided funds to train surgeons to work in the Templar hospitals. The Order was able to build and maintain its own fleet in its own shipyards at La Rochelle on the Atlantic coast of France. The Templars had other ports, too – northern ports for trade with England, and southern ports for access to the Holy Land – but the port at La Rochelle, situated in a natural bay which was easily defended against sea-borne invaders, was their principal port. There was also a good system of roads leading from Paris and the Mediterranean coast directly to La Rochelle, but there was another reason for La Rochelle's pre-eminence. In the days of sail, when it was vital to take advantage of prevailing winds, the most likely destination of ships sailing from La Rochelle would have been west, to the New World.

In the early twelfth century, with Jerusalem under Christian control, and with the Priory of Sion, the political arm of the Knights Templar, having been given a permanent home on Mount Zion, the Templars were acting as king-makers, with their chosen monarch on the throne of

Jerusalem. At that time the Templars and the Priory of Sion shared the same Grand Master who co-ordinated the Templar strategies. But which body was the power behind the throne, and could the liaison last? In fact, the relationship between the Knights Templar and Priory of Sion lasted for less than a century. In 1188 the knights quarrelled with their political masters, but the end of the relationship had been in sight in 1187 when several disasters caused the Templars to lose Jerusalem to the Moorish leader Saladin. The various disasters of 1187 were caused by psychological flaws in the character of their Grand Master, the Flemish-born Gérard de Ridefort.

Twenty-eight years previously, Gérard, a young adventurer and a member of the French crusading army, had nothing to draw him back to his native Flanders when the French contingent from the Second Crusade left the Holy Land and returned to France in 1149. So he stayed behind and settled in Jerusalem, becoming a vassal of Count Raymond III of Tripoli. Over the next few years, it is possible that the count recognized a flaw in the character of the young Gérard because he was overlooked when favours and contractual fiefs were granted. To understand the duties and obligations of a fief, it is necessary to appreciate that under the feudal system a vassal held land as a tenant and under the contract, or fief, he swore an oath of loyalty which required him to pay homage to his lord. In 1180 a vassal named William Dorel died in the service of Count Raymond, but Gérard was again overlooked and not given the rich heiress Lucia of Botrun in marriage. Instead, a wealthy merchant from Pisa, Plivain, purchased Lady Lucia and her inheritance from Count Raymond for her weight in gold, 140 pounds. This caused Gérard to bear a lifelong hatred of Count Raymond. In total disgust, he sought solace in the ranks of the Templars.

History condemns Gérard de Ridefort, who was Grand

Master of the Templars at the time of the loss of Jerusalem. His arrogance, deceitfulness, and incompetence in handling events is seen as inexcusable. The Battle of Hattin on 4 July 1187 culminated in the loss of Jerusalem, a decisive moment in history, the consequences of which are still felt today in the Middle East.

The Horns of Hattin

In 1180, when Gérard de Ridefort joined the Templars, he must have thought he was riding a whirlwind, because his rise through the Templar ranks was phenomenal. In 1183 he was appointed Seneschal of the Order, which made him second in command to Arnold de Torroga, the Grand Master. Within another two years, he had ascended to the office of Grand Master. During his first year in office, in March 1185, King Baldwin IV, known as the Leper King, passed away. This presented a problem because in his will King Baldwin IV had nominated his young nephew Baudoinet as his successor, to be known as King Baldwin V. The will also included a codicil which stated that until Baudoinet reached manhood, Raymond III of Tripoli was to rule as regent. King Baldwin IV had also covered other eventualities in the will, with a clause stating that should Baudoinet die without issue or before reaching manhood, the Kings of England and France and the Holy Roman Emperor should nominate a King of Jerusalem who must be sanctioned by the Pope. Due to Gérard de Ridefort's hatred of Raymond III, the Templars ignored the will of the dead king, which resulted in a power struggle orchestrated by the notoriously cruel Lord Raymond de Chatillon, Lord of Outrejordain and Kerak. Lord Raymond de Chatillon chose Kerak, the most impregnable and strongly defended crusader castle in the Middle East as his power base, from where, under the auspices of his Grand Master, he organized a coup d'état.

Lord Raymond was aided in his coup by Princess Sybilla and King Baldwin's sister Alice de Cortenay, who was also the Queen Mother. Once power had been seized, Princess Sybilla was immediately crowned Queen of Jerusalem, and one of her first actions was to transfer the crown onto the head of Guy de Lusignan, her husband. Gérard de Ridefort's immediate reaction to the inauguration of King Guy was to proclaim that the action repaid Raymond III of Tripoli for his mercenary behaviour in marrying the heiress Lucia of Botrun to the merchant from Pisa.

With an opinionated adventurer as Grand Master and a team of arrogant warlords, the ambitions of the Templars knew no bounds. With Lord Raymond de Chatillon holding the impregnable castle at Kerak, the megalomaniac Gérard de Ridefort launched a series of raids against Muslim caravans. The situation deteriorated until, in 1182, a caravan taking pilgrims to Mecca was attacked in violation of a guaranteed safe passage. The Muslim leader Saladin reacted by proclaiming a holy war, or jihad, against the crusaders which led to four years of skirmishes and guerrilla war with the Templars. In the winter of 1186–87, Raymond III of Tripoli, the regent designated in the will of King Baldwin IV, split the crusading forces in an act of treason when he openly rebelled against King Guy. To stoke the rebellion, Gérard de Ridefort used devious methods, including feeding King Guy lies about the loyalty of Count Raymond. As a result of the lies, King Guy harassed Count Raymond to the point where he felt forced to seek an alliance with Saladin, the Sultan of Egypt. At this point the Grand Master must have realized that he now had his adversary Count Raymond backed into a corner, and denounced Raymond as a traitor. The Templars were not fools, however, and had seen the course that their Grand Master had taken. As a result, most of the knights disagreed with the denunciation and King Guy was forced to seek a diplomatic solution to the crisis. On 29 April 1187, King Guy sent Lord Balian de Ibelin, a highly respected nobleman, and a team of negotiators, including the Archbishop of Tyre, to Saladin. On the way to the meeting de Ibelin left the party, claiming that he had forgotten an urgent appointment, but giving his word that he would rejoin the negotiators at Tiberius, Count Raymond's main stronghold. With the chief negotiator having left, it fell to Count Raymond to command the negotiators' Templar escort. Templar scouts soon reported that a marauding force of armed warriors led by Saladin's son, Al-Adfal, was in the area. Count Raymond, being a knight and bound by his alliance with Saladin, gave Al-Adfal's warriors safe passage through the area for a single day on condition that they did not raid or pillage. Gérard de Ridefort, who hated Count Raymond, was so incensed by this act of what he termed cowardice that he gave orders to Jacques de Mailly, Marshal of the Templars, to call for help from the ninety knights of the garrison at the Templar castle at Caco and from the forty secular knights of the Nazareth garrison. When they arrived, the 130 reinforcements joined the negotiators' escort to give them added protection. Thus reinforced, Gérard de Ridefort set out in search of Saladin's troops, whom they found camped near the Springs of Cresson. It was at this moment that the fate of the negotiators and the Templars was decided; their Grand Master ignored the advice of his subordinates and accused them of cowardice for not wanting to attack Saladin's superior force of five thousand men. Heavily outnumbered, Gérard de Ridefort, with his customary arrogance, led his 130 knights in a suicidal charge against Saladin's encamped forces. The battle did not last long, and by the time it was over, only three Templar knights, including De Ridefort, had managed to withdraw from the carnage, leaving the survivors to be beheaded. After this humiliating defeat at the Springs of Cresson, the crusading forces had to settle their differences and unite against Saladin.

Count Raymond of Tripoli was forced by the shame of the defeat into making his peace with King Guy de Lusignan, but there were still further disasters to come in 1187. As a reprisal for the crusaders' reneging on their offer of safe passage which had culminated in the attack and carnage at the Springs of Cresson, Saladin now attacked and took the coastal towns, including the city of Tiberius. The castle in which the wife of Count Raymond and her children were housed, managed to hold out.

On 3 July 1187, the crusaders mustered at the Springs of Saffuriya, a well-watered oasis which offered plenty of grazing for their horses, and was a key point in the kingdom's defence. Whoever held the oasis could hold off any further invasion by Saladin's army, but Gérard de Ridefort and Lord Raymond de Chatillon urged Count Raymond to attack the forces of Saladin and relieve Tiberius. Count Raymond pointed out that the road to Tiberius cut across harsh, rocky, arid scrubland, and that if the crusaders atttempted to cross this they could be drawn into a trap. If that were to happen, then both men and horses would suffer and quite possibly die during the heat of the day. Count Raymond declared that it would be better to lose his wife and children than to allow the crusaders to lose the kingdom to Saladin.

For a time Count Raymond's wise counsel prevailed, but in the cool of the evening, Gérard de Ridefort visited the king's tent, declaring that the Templars would willingly sell the clothes off their backs rather than give up a Christian city so easily. He called Count Raymond a coward and a traitor to the ideals of the crusading knights for not taking any action to save his own family. With that taunt aimed at Count Raymond, King Guy was persuaded to give the order to relieve Tiberius.

In the heat of the following day, the knights marched across the parched desert. During their forced march, they were harassed by Saladin's mounted troops who kept up constant skirmishing attacks, firing thousands of arrows into the crusader ranks. After an eight-hour march during which they had covered only fifteen miles, the harassed Christian forces had become almost deranged with heat and thirst when King Guy ordered an evening halt. Count Raymond, on hearing the order to halt for the night is reputed to have cried, "Alas, Lord God! The kingdom is finished, we are all dead men!"

That night, the crusading army camped on two hills known as the Horns of Hattin. Although the Christian army was on the cliffs and within sight of the Sea of Galilee and Tiberius, both were inaccessible due to a sheer, 200-foot cliff. The crusaders had little sleep that night due to the constant threat of attack from Saladin's forces, who fired arrows constantly into their camp. As dawn broke, the Christian army was completely demoralized and in desperate need of water, but there was worse to come. Just before sunrise, Saladin ordered the scrub-brush surrounding the crusader's camp to be set alight, causing choking smoke to irritate the already parched throats of the crusaders. With Saladin's army between them and relief, the crusaders could see and almost smell water, but could not get to it. Their already precarious position deteriorated further when the crusader's infantry mutinied, refusing to march any further. The cavalry could only watch in horror as Saladin's cavalry charged and massacred the Templar infantry. At that point, the Templars knew that they were trapped and doomed, that there could be no escape. With the infantry having been massacred and the main force routed, there were only 230 survivors of the original force of Templars and Hospitallers. Those who survived, the remaining nobility of the Kingdom of Outremer, were subsequently beheaded.

Only their Grand Master Gérard de Ridefort was kept alive, as a hostage to secure the surrender of any remaining Templar castles. Ultimately, Jerusalem fell, which left Tyre as the only city remaining under the control of the crusaders. De Ridefort remained a hostage for three months, before finally being released in September 1187 in exchange for the surrender of the Templar castle of Gaza. The Templars eventually lost their Grand Master de Ridefort when he was killed in battle at the defence of Acre on 4 October, 1189. So ended the life of a megalomaniac, beginning the process which led to the eventual split between the Templar's political arm, the Priory of Sion, and it's military arm, the Knights Templar.

Divorce and Settlement

To understand why the Priory of Sion and the Templars separated, ending their working relationship in a quarrel, it is necessary to examine events in Gisors, in northern France. French Masonic sources and research done by Baigent, Leigh, and Lincoln suggest that around AD 46 an Egyptian mystic named Ormus living in Alexandria and six followers were converted to Christianity by St Mark. Ormus then formed a holy order to which he gave the sign of a red cross, or *rose-croix*, which later became integral to the Priory of Sion. Ormus's Gnostic order had its roots in a combination of Christian and Pagan theology. A millennium later, in 1070, the Priory of Sion was founded when a group of monks from Calabria, in Italy, led by Prince Ursus, founded an abbey at Orval. In 1099, after the fall of Jerusalem, Godfroi de Bouillon formed the Priory of Sion. Not long afterwards, he is thought to have included the monks of the Abbey of Orval in his order – certainly they disappeared from Orval at that time. This relationship between the Knights Templar and the Priory of Sion lasted for approximately a hundred years until 1188, when Henry II of England and Philip II of France arranged to meet at Gisors on "a sacred field."

The English arrived early for the meeting and, to avoid the heat of the day, they sheltered under an ancient elm tree. After three days of negotiations in the heat, tempers frayed, and the French attacked the English, forcing them to take refuge in the town of Gisors. In frustration the French cut down the one-hundred-year-old elm. The "Cutting of the Elm" ended the relationship between the Priory of Sion and the Knights Templar, and from that moment, each group was free to choose its own Grand Master.

The Templars were left without their political arm and consequently without any astute guidance from political masters, other than the Church and the Pope. From this point onwards their fate was in the hands of others. The "Cutting of the Elm" took place exactly a year after the loss of Jerusalem, by which time the Templars had withdrawn to Acre, where they remained until their Grand Master, William de Beaujue, was killed in 1191 in the unsuccessful defence of that city. The Templars quickly regrouped, however, and elected a new Grand Master. In a heroic rearguard action, the surviving Templars, led by their new Grand Master, were, as usual, the last to leave the battlefield and the city of Acre. They made a strategic withdrawal to Cyprus so that they could maintain a Middle Eastern base at Limmasol. Although the Knights Templar fought with Richard the Lionheart against Saladin in the Third Crusade, the crusaders never retook Jerusalem. In Europe, the Templars established their administrative headquarters in the Temple Monastery in Paris and a military base in the Languedoc. After the "Cutting of the Elm," the Knights Templars went into decline, with their final demise coming in 1307 at the hands of King Phillipe le Bel, or King Philip the Fair, of France.

In their book *Messianic Legacy*, Baigent, Leigh, and Lincoln claim that after the "Cutting of the Elm," the Priory of Sion adopted the name Ormus, a title derived from early

Gnostic texts in which Ormus equates to the principle of light. In one of the French Masonic degrees, the ritual of Ormus is linked to the Alexandrian mystic of that name. In the ritual, Ormus is converted by St Mark and later becomes the founder of an order with the sign of a red cross, or *rose-croix*. The Priory of Sion also added the title of *Ordre de la Rose-Croix Veritas* to their mode of address. The origins of the Rosicrucians would seem to be considerably older than the traditional claims that they were founded in the seventeenth century.

The fact that the Priory of Sion elected Jean de Gisors as their first Grand Master raises a suspicion that the separation of the Templars and the Priory may have been premeditated and orchestrated by the Priory of Sion. The Priory would have had political contacts within the Royal Courts of Henry II of England and Philip II of France, who could have arranged the conference at Gisors. Under contrived circumstances in the heat of the day, it would have taken only a few insurrectionists within the French nobility to start the physical confrontation which led eventually to the split between the Templars and the Priory. Perhaps the Priory had realized that the Templars had outlived their usefulness, and that they could wield power behind the thrones of Europe without the strong-arm tactics of the knights.

Whatever the cause, the result was catastrophic for the Templars. Jean de Gisors was a member of the Gisors nobility. Did he orchestrate the split in order to advance himself? The second Grand Master was Marie de Saint-Claire, a descendant of Henry St Clair who had fought alongside Godfroi de Bouillon at the fall of Jerusalem in 1099. Marie de Saint-Claire's maiden name was Levis, which suggests that the Rosslyn branch of the Sinclair family had married into the Merovingian lineage with a connection through the line of David into Judaism.

Once the Templars had parted company with the Priory

of Sion, one of their objectives was to create a permanent home, or independent state, for their future advancement. The German contingent of crusading knights, who had already formed their own order similar to that of the Templars, aimed to secure a Teutonic state as their base. This German order was known initially as *Deutscher Orden zu Sankt Marien in Jerusalem* and had been formed to provide spiritual and medical care to German knights. Instead of the red cross of the Templars, the German knights had adopted a black cross as their symbol. After eight years of providing spiritual and medical care, the order expanded to include a military division. From that moment in 1198, when the Templars split with the Priory of Sion, the Teutonic Knights or *Der Deutsche Ritterorden*, began to have an impact on the future of European history with the foundation of the Prussian states.

Over the next fifty years, the Teutonic Knights converted the pagan populations along the Baltic Coast to Christianity, though there remains a mystery concerning the tiny Danish island of Bornholm in the Baltic Sea, where there are several round churches built in the Templar style. Were these built by the Templars, or by the Teutonic Knights? It is possible that both groups were co-operating with a common goal in mind, i.e., eventual domination of the known world. As the known world expanded with each successive discovery, the Templars finally decided that their homeland would be in North America, as planned by the Sinclair expedition to Nova Scotia.

In 1188, when the Templars split with the Priory of Sion, they managed their affairs fairly well and kept everything in their organization under control for the next 125 years. During that time they expanded their already established system of banking with a type of banker's draft that could be issued in one country and redeemed through a Templar organization in another country. This eliminated the risk of carrying large sums of gold or coins, but the system needed, of course, to have pre-arranged codes to identify the carrier of the draft. This need for secret identification procedures may have led to the secret handshakes followed by the use of specific words or phrases which are today part of Masonic identification procedures. By the end of the thirteenth century, the Templars had become the bankers to all the royal households of Europe and, at the height of their power, the Templars were also involved in establishing diplomatic liaison throughout Europe and the Middle East.

The Cathars and the Albigensian Crusade

In the mid-thirteenth century in what is now the south of France, there was an independent, wealthy principality known as the Land of Oc. The people of the Oc had their own language, hence the region became known as the principality with "the language of Oc," or *langue d'Oc* and subsequently as Languedoc. This principality was ruled by a few noble families, headed by the Count of Toulouse, and had one of the most advanced cultures in Europe, with a greater affinity to the Moorish cultures of Castile and Aragon than to the ill-educated nobility of northern France. It was in this tranquil country that the Cathars lived side by side in peaceful co-existence with other religious and cultural groups, such as Muslims, Christians, and Jews. In the Languedoc, the philosophies of the ancient world were studied, and because of the cosmopolitan background of the inhabitants, Hebrew and Arabic were also studied. Consequently the Languedoc was steeped in centuries of alchemical and esoteric learning. Several villages in the area today still bear witness to the secret and subversive preoccupations of some of their former residents who practised alchemy. One such village is Alet-les-Bains, near

Limoux, where the houses still have decorative esoteric symbols.

Nostradamus was born in Alet-les-Bains and presumably the local interest in alchemy and esoteric teachings influenced and guided him in his life's work. A twelfth-century church at Rieux Minervois displays many esoteric images in its windows which testify to the church architects' secret knowledge of alchemy, which, in the twenty-first century, seems to have been lost forever.

Among the many sects living in the Languedoc, there was a large "*primitive*" Christian group known as the Cathars, who contributed greatly to the knowledge and learning that was central to the area. These peace-loving people were so intellectually advanced that they had the Bible translated into their own language. They believed in God, but followed a very simple form of Christianity. They were one of the first European groups to practise birth control and, when considered necessary for the health or welfare of the mother, they even condoned abortion. These tenets obviously contradicted papal authority and eventually the Church branded the Cathars as heretics and launched a crusade to eliminate or cleanse the Languedoc of heresy.

To understand why the Church declared the Cathar practices heretical, it is necessary to examine their theological beliefs. The Cathars believed in dualism, or dual worlds of co-existent opposites. They held that there were two supreme beings, one being God, and the other, the Devil. This was substantiated by light and darkness, and good and evil. Both supreme beings were believed to be eternal, a belief derived from a passage in 2 Corinthians 4:4 which refers to Satan as the "earth god," or Rex Mundi. The Cathars saw the material world as corrupt and evil, and believed that Rex Mundi was the king of this world. They believed that Rex Mundi was their creator and that their physical bodies were enslaved by him, but that their souls belonged to God.

The Cathars also believed that if someone's earthly life had been lived in absolute purity, in total abstinence from the sins of the flesh, then his or her pure soul would be restored to God at death. To help them achieve this, there were three echelons in the Cathar hierarchy.

The *parfait* was the highest echelon, whose members achieved purity of soul through receiving *consolamentum*, which meant that from that moment of "ordination," the *parfait* were pure in spirit and absolved from any corruption of the flesh by becoming vegetarians and maintaining a state of celibacy.

The second echelon, comprising the majority of the Cathars, was the *credente*, who were not required to abide by the strict self-discipline of the *parfaits*. They did not have to be vegetarians, and could marry and raise families, but when one of the *credente* was on his or her deathbed, he or she would receive the *consolamentum*, and from that moment of "ordination" they were considered to have passed into a state of *endure* and were considered to be pure in spirit. Those in a state of *endure*, during their last few hours, could be comforted only with sips of water until they died and their souls joined God.

The third echelon comprised those who died without receiving the *consolamentum*. It was believed that those who had not been ordained before death, were subjected to successive re-incarnations until, eventually, they found an earthly life in a body that led them to perfection or a state of having a "pure spirit." These beliefs led the Cathars to see the Church as an earthly system that allowed corruption to flourish within its ranks.

In the eleventh century, around the time of the first crusade, there was a form of soul-searching by the people of Europe who wanted the clerics of the Church to live the type of lives that the Gospels had advocated for the early apostles. What the people actually witnessed was priests and other church functionaries living extravagant lifestyles. It was even rumoured that some priests had not said a mass for up to thirty years. All this led to dissent and a threat to the power of the Church. This threat was not readily apparent until the Church became aware, at the beginning of the thirteenth century, of an evolving bastion of pure Christian belief in love and equality as lived by the Cathars in the Languedoc, which was very different from what was advocated by the Church. This lifestyle of pure, Christian love gave rise to the legends of the Holy Grail, with their stories of true love for fellow men, celebrated in song by the troubadours. The origins of this lifestyle and subsequent legends were founded in Gnostic beliefs in tolerance and personal liberty.

In December 1945, two brothers, Mohammed and Khalifah Ali, while digging in an Egyptian cemetery near the town of Nag Hammadi, unearthed a large, sealed jar containing thirteen leather-bound books. The books, which were written in the Coptic script of ancient Egypt, were copies of even older texts. The Nag Hammadi texts, as they became known, offered a new understanding of the relationship between Jesus and Mary Magdalene which differs from that portrayed in the Gospels. The texts also contained tracts from hitherto unknown Gospels, such as the Gospels of Philip, Thomas, and Mary Magdalene, in which they offer insights into Judean customs at the time of Jesus. The Gospel of Philip actually gives a statement that is in direct conflict with the Christian faith: "Some say Mary was conceived by the Holy Spirit, they are wrong. They do not know what they say."

So what was Gnostic thought or teaching, and why did the Church feel so threatened by it? The Christian Gnostics believed in the living resurrection of Jesus, and, as such, they were in direct conflict with the Church which proclaimed that the only way to communicate with God was through the "Vicar of Rome" and his appointed clergy. The Cathars did not believe that the appointed clergy of the church were better suited to perform sacred services than their own non-ordained clergy, or even commoners. The Church took an opposing view that the personal behaviour of a priest was irrelevant because, if the church had ordained a priest, he was considered equally capable of dispensing grace and favour to the masses as a saintly priest.

The Church condemned the Cathars as heretics for their belief that clergy should be required to adopt a saintly lifestyle. From there it was a small step for the Cathars to advocate that an individual who led a good life was better suited to perform as a priest, than a corrupt ordained priest.

Due to the destruction by the Inquisition of Cathar records, the origins of the Cathar form of Christianity are obscure, though there is reason to believe that it evolved from Manichaeism. Manichaeism originated near Baghdad in what is today Iraq. Its founder, Mani, was born in the third century, and it is believed that while still a child, he had a religious vision which led him to proclaim himself a prophet in his twenties. As a prophet and spiritual leader, he gathered a following in a way which paralleled the life of Jesus. Mani's influence upset the Zoroastrian religious leaders in Iraq and they declared Mani a heretic. He was sentenced to be banished from the Persian Empire, and for the next twenty years, he preached as a self-appointed apostle of Jesus. His ministry, which took him from northern India, into Tibet, and back into central Asia, advocated the co-ordination of all beliefs, and his followers were what we might call today humanitarians. Mani acknowledged previous religious leaders and accepted that they were prophets, advocating the same beliefs as him. With this philosophy, Manichaeans could associate themselves with Christians in Christian lands, Buddhists in Buddhist lands, and, had Mani lived at a later date, with Muslims in Muslim lands. When Mani was well into old age, he returned from exile under the protection of the emperor, but once again the Zoroastrian clergy plotted against him until the weak emperor capitulated to their demands and had Mani executed as a heretic. Following Mani's martyrdom, his religion went underground, but it survived until the fifteenth century and during that period it had affiliations in Europe with the Cathars of northern Italy and the Languedoc, who advocated the pure Christian beliefs of the Manichaean faith. The Church even lost Saint Augustine to Manichaeism for a short time when he converted, but he quickly reverted back to Catholicism. In the thirteenth century, Cathar beliefs had spread to Switzerland, Germany, Italy, and parts of the Balkans, with particularly strong enclaves in Bosnia and Croatia. As well as respecting local cultures, the Cathars were affiliated with Muslim communities in the Middle East and Spain, and also had close links to Jewish Cabbalists. This is the real reason why the Church considered the Cathars to be heretics: they posed a threat to their dogma.

The Cathars believed that Jesus was a prophet, a priest-king, and Messiah, but not the son of God. Like the Templars, the Cathars respected the equality of the sexes and the tolerance of Muslim and Jewish cultures. They also believed that the soul or spirit was pure, but that all life on earth was defiled. Cathars accepted women priests, and the principle of praying directly to God without requiring the intercession of a priest. They did, however, have what might be called "holy men," known as *parfaits*, or perfect ones. As the Cathars in the Languedoc attracted more followers, they came more directly into conflict with the Church. It was this conflict that led to them being branded heretics.

The Cathars and the Church both followed the teachings

of Jesus Christ as set out in the Gospel of John, but the Church was more influenced by and rooted in the Pauline doctrines, a theology derived more from the Epistles of St Paul and the Acts of the Apostles than from the Gnostic beliefs of the early Christian church.

But what are Pauline doctrines? Acts 9:3–4 describe Saul (later Paul) on a road in or near Damascus where he has what the Gospels tells us was "a vision of blinding light." From that point onwards, he abandoned his persecution of Christians, and, after a period being taught by the Apostles in Damascus, Paul began to spread the Word. It was at that time that the Christian message began to be corrupted because, in his enthusiasm to adopt the teachings of Jesus, Paul deviated from the true message of the apostles, which was to bring salvation to the Gentiles by converting them by Hellenistic doctrines to Judaism. Paul embellished the Word with his own brand of salvation; he converted Jesus from the earthly Messiah of the Jews into Jesus the Son of God through whom one could be redeemed and attain eternal salvation. Paul made use of images of fire and damnation, and the wrath of the Lord from the Old Testament, and he began to draw crowds who would listen to him, spellbound. Paul's teachings, though, often had little to do with the apostolic message of Jesus, for example in Daniel 7:13–14:

> I saw in the night visions, and, behold, one like the Son of man came with the clouds of heaven, and came to the Ancient of days, and they brought him near before him.
> And there was given him dominion, and glory, and a kingdom, that all people, nations, and languages, should serve him, his dominion is an everlasting dominion, which shall not pass away, and his kingdom that which shall not be destroyed.

The crowds became ecstatic, so Paul began to elaborate on his misguided enthusiasm with increasingly outrageous claims of how the Lord would bring retribution to those who would not convert to Paul's theological standpoint. A typical message of Paul's new brand of Christianity is to be found in the first Epistle of Paul to the Thessalonians 4:16–17 where he writes:

> For the Lord himself shall descend from heaven with a shout, with the voice of the archangel, and with the trump of God: and the dead in Christ shall rise first: then we which are alive and remain shall be caught up together with them in the clouds, to meet the Lord in the air: and so shall we ever be with the Lord.

With Paul abandoning the milder messages and teachings of Peter and James, he set the wheels in motion for a modified brand of Christianity which the Roman Catholic Church, and subsequently the Anglican Church, adopted. The Pauline doctrines adopted by the Vatican were not what the Cathars were preaching; they had their own form of Christianity based on the messages of the early Church. This melting pot of disparate beliefs simmered throughout the twelfth century with various Vatican councils trying to convert the Cathars, but all peaceful methods of persuasion failed and things reached a point of no return in 1165, boiling over when an ecclesiastical council met in the Languedoc town of Albi and issued an edict which declared that all Cathars were heretics. The edict from Rome eventually spawned a Spanish fanatic, Dominic Guzman, who, in 1216, driven by a fervent hatred of heresy, established the Dominican monastic order, which, in 1233, initiated the infamous Holy Inquisition.

To understand why the Cathars had been condemned as heretics, it is necessary to go back to 1198 when Pope Innocent III had been elected to the papal throne. He had back-pedalled on the edict and once more tried the persuasive approach by dispatching two legates to Languedoc, but the legates, Peter of Castelnau and Raoul, had met with extraordinary opposition from the nobles who controlled the Languedoc. Then, in 1204, with the edict again an issue, the Pope suspended the authority of the Languedoc bishops because of their sympathetic attitude to the Cathars. In 1208, Peter of Castelnau was assassinated and Count Raymond of Toulouse, who had been excommunicated in 1207 by the legates, was suspected of having been involved. The situation was escalating and the Pope ordered all bishops who had a diocese in the Languedoc to place under interdict all those involved in the conspiracy and every town which offered the murderers shelter. Those who had been placed under interdict were denied all church sacraments and the right to burial and other facilities of the Church. This unrest and strife caused Pope Innocent III to initiate a crusade against the Cathars.

This crusade was authorized by the Church to eliminate a supposed heresy, but its ferocity was driven by the greed of the French nobility, who were envious of the wealth of the Languedoc. What was to become known as the Albigensian Crusade derived its name from the Albi Edict of 1165. Now, forty-four years later, Philippe Auguste, the King of France, dispatched Simon de Montfort and a crusading army of 30,000 fighting men to subjugate the Rhedezium, or the Languedoc, as the land of the Cathars was now being called. Simon de Montfort's brief was to claim the lands for the French Crown and to put Rhedae to the sword under the pretence of fighting against the Cathar heresy. Simon de Montfort led the crusade with the fervour of a bigot. He became notorious and much feared for his extreme cruelty in massacring the entire populations of towns during the crusade. To support the nobility in the Languedoc, Peter II, King of Aragon, personally led his troops in support of Raymond VI of Toulouse against the Albigensian Crusaders, but he died at the Battle of Muret in 1213 and, with immediate effect, the King of France dispossessed the fiefs of Toulouse and Béziers. This act brought to an end the independence of the area and the crusade now developed into an act of genocide against the peace-loving people of the Languedoc. Simon de Montfort did not survive to see the end of the crusade for he was killed in 1218, but the crusade, which lasted for forty years, was continued with equal fanaticism under new leadership. The Albigensian Crusade destroyed the civilization of the Languedoc, relegating the region to the Dark Ages.

The Crusade began with a brutal purge of the "heretics" at Béziers, where 20,000 men women and children were slaughtered. The town had a small enclave of 222 Cathar residents, but that was sufficient to warrant an attack. It is not certain if the Count of Béziers was a Cathar or just a sympa-thizer, but the crusaders besieged the town and demanded, on threat of excommunication of the mainly Catholic populace, that they hand over the Cathars or vacate the town so that the crusaders could do their work and deal with the Cathars. The Catholic inhabitants refused both options and, according to contemporary records, "they preferred to die as heretics rather than live as Christians." The Pope was informed that the townspeople had taken an oath to defend the Cathars. It is said that when a leader of the crusaders asked how they could determine which citizens of Béziers were Christians, the papal legate, Arnold Almaric, the Abbot of Citeau, offered this infamous response: "Show mercy neither to order, nor to age, nor to sex, Cathar or Catholic, kill them all. God will know his own." It is a strange fact that the massacre took place on 22 July, 1209, the feast day of Mary Magdalene. The Cistercian monk Pierre des Vaux-de-Cerny later wrote that "Béziers was taken on St Mary Magdalene's Day, a date which recurs frequently in this book. The heretics claimed that St Mary Magdalene was the concubine of Jesus Christ, so it was with just cause that these disgusting dogs were taken and massacred during the feast of the one they had insulted."

The Gnostic Gospels were supposedly unknown in the

thirteenth century, not surfacing for another six centuries, but it is apparent from translations of the Gnostic Gospels that early Christians had no difficulty in accepting the marital status of Jesus. It is uncertain why the Cathars and other inhabitants of the Languedoc had such a strong belief that Jesus had had a sexual relationship with Mary Magdalene, but it is certainly possible that the Cathars' belief was based on Gnostic texts.

As the Albigensian Crusade became more ferocious, whole villages and towns, including women, children, and even Catholics, were massacred, with the Church justifying its actions by declaring that the Cathar heresy must be eliminated whatever the cost in human life. In 1227, a Cathar bishop, Pierre Isarn, was burnt alive at the stake in front of the abbey gate at Caunes Minervois. The burning by the monks of Caunes, who were devout Roman Catholics, was done to frighten local Cathars into changing their faith. The genocide continued until, in 1233, the Inquisition was given almost unlimited power by Pope Gregory IX to suppress the heresy. Cathars were burned wherever they were found; the Inquisition sometimes even ordered the exhumation of Cathar corpses from church-yards for them to be burned in order "to save their souls." In its view, the Inquisition was burning heretics at the stake in order to save their souls.

One of the last atrocities of the Albigensian Crusade occurred at Montsegur, a castle stronghold perched on top of a rocky crag, 400 feet above a tranquil meadow. Today, an obelisk marks the grim event that took place in that meadow, known as "The Field of the Burned," on 16 March, 1244, when, rather than renounce their creed, 210 Cathars walked hand in hand, singing, into the flames.

The events leading up to that final atrocity of the Albigensian Crusade began in May 1243 when two Cathar sympathizers, the Lord of Montesegur and his son-in-law,

Pierre-Roger de Mirepoix, were besieged by an attacking force of 1,500 men. The besieged garrison numbered approximately 500, including 11 knights, 150 foot soldiers, and their families. The attacking force led by Hugues des Arcis expected a quick end to the siege by starving the defenders out of the fortress, but the siege dragged on all through the summer and autumn of 1243. In November, Hugues des Arcis changed his tactics and sent some lightly armed men to scale the precipitous eastern slope of Montesegur. In a dangerous night climb, the lightly armed attacking party acquired a foothold at the base of the fortress and began hoisting up siege engines. The siege lasted for ten months until 1 March, 1244, but with the defenders reduced to fewer than 400 through injuries and sickness, Montsegur was finally compelled to surrender. Most uncharacteristically the attacking army offered the defenders very lenient terms. The defenders requested a two-week truce with a complete cessation of hostilities so they could consider the terms of surrender. In return for the truce, the defenders volunteered hostages, accepting that the lives of the hostages would be forfeited if any defender attempted to escape from the fortress. On the night of 14 March, however, three *parfait* defenders were lowered by ropes from the fortress and managed to escape without being detected by the besieging army, consequently no hostages were killed. Why were these *parfaits* so important that they had to take such a risk to escape, or what were they taking out of the fortress? And why did they wait for the last night of the truce before making their escape? The night of 14 March coincided with the Spring Equinox so perhaps whatever it was that was smuggled out of Montsegur had to remain in the fortress for some ceremony on the night of the Spring Equinox. Normally someone making use of the cover of darkness will hope for as little light as possible from the moon or any other source. At Montsegur in 1244, there was no moon on the nights between

9 and 11 March, but by the night of 12 March there was a new moon, which enormously increased the risk that the escapers would be apprehended. So why did they wait until 14 March to make their escape? We shall probably never know, but on 15 March, the truce expired, and at dawn the following day, 210 Cathar *parfaits* walked out of the Montsegur fortress and walked calmly down the mountain and into a large stockade filled with brushwood. All 210 were burned en masse as the remainder of the defenders witnessing the burning.

With that final atrocity the Albigensian Crusade ended, but what role had the Templars played in the crusade? It seems that Bertrand de Blanchefort, the fourth Grand Master of the Templars, held Cathar beliefs and, as a result, the Templars remained neutral. While they kept a very low profile, they did offer some passive support to the Cathars. Evidence of that support can still be seen in the form of a Templar *commanderie* located at Montsuanés in the foothills of the Pyrenees. This *commanderie* was manned by the Templars throughout the crusade and kept open to protect and provide some sanctuary to pilgrims and those fleeing the massacres of Simon de Montfort and the other leaders of the crusade. The *commanderie*, which guarded the pilgrims' way from Toulouse to Campostella in Spain, was commanded by Bernard IV, Count of Comminges. Today, the lid of his damaged sarcophagus can still be seen in the chapel and there are other signs in the chapel testifying to the belief of the Templars that Mary Magdalene was the bearer of the bloodline of Christ, or Holy Grail. How different history might have been if the Templars had defended the Cathars, but through their silence and non-involvement, the Templars eventually exposed themselves to accusations of holding Gnostic beliefs, and they, too, paid the penalty for heresy. The youngest son of Simon de Montfort, who had been killed in 1218, also named Simon de Montfort, Earl of Leicester, founded the English

Parliament and played a major role in the Peasants' Revolt during the reign of Henry III.

There is an abundance of graffiti to be seen in the Languedoc today calling for independence from France for Occeania. It seems that the Cathar spirit of peace and independence still thrives in the ancient land of Oc. Interestingly, people in the Languedoc never talk simply of "God" – they always specify "the Good God," perhaps to differentiate Him from the evil God who condones wars in His name.

The Templars:
End of the Line

After the loss of Jerusalem in 1187, the Templars held on to Acre until 1291, but their position in the Holy Land was essentially untenable, so they looked for a new base. One possibility was the Languedoc, which, in the early twelfth century, was an independent principality ruled by a handful of noble families. When the Templars lost Acre, their last stronghold in the Holy Land, they withdrew and established their main headquarters in Cyprus; their treasury was in Paris, and they had a very strong military presence in the Languedoc. The Templars chose Cyprus for their headquarters because in 1191 Germany, France, and England decided to launch a Third Crusade against the forces of Saladin with the aim of recapturing Jerusalem. The crusaders needed to hold the port of Acre in order to be able to supply their armies. To achieve this, German crusaders marched their forces overland, while the forces of the French King Philip and King Richard the Lionheart of England travelled to Acre by sea. In the spring of 1191, the French and English fleets left Sicily, where they had spent the winter. The French fleet arrived safely in Acre and soon joined forces with the German contingent, but the English fleet encountered bad storms in the Mediterranean and had to seek sanctuary in Crete and Rhodes. During the storms, three English ships were blown off course and sought shelter in Cyprus; two of the ships ended up wrecked within sight of the Cypriot port of Limmasol, while the third English ship reached the harbour safely. On board that third ship was Johanna, the sister of King Richard and the Queen Dowager of Sicily. Also on board was Lady Berengaria of Navarre, King Richard's fiancée. The ruler of Cyprus, Isaac Commenus, eventually persuaded the royal women to leave the relative safety of the ship and disembark. Once they were ashore, Isaac Commenus imprisoned both women. The crews of the two shipwrecked boats who had escaped to land were also imprisoned and their property confiscated. Richard, concerned for the safety of his sister and his bride-to-be, left Rhodes and sailed with some of his fleet to Cyprus, where they landed at the port of Limmasol. Richard, having quickly assessed the situation, was so incensed at the outrages committed against his crusading army, and particularly those committed against his his sister and fiancée that he demanded an apology and compensation from Isaac. These demands were rejected and Isaac assembled his forces to repel the English. The astute Richard quickly realized that Cyprus offered a good base from which to supply the crusaders in Acre with timber and other commodities, and used the insults to his family as an excuse to declare war on the Cypriots. Richard's opening tactic was to lead fifty of his mounted knights in an attack against a group of Cypriot skirmishers located in an olive grove. Richard's cavalry pursued the Cypriots to within sight of Isaac's main defensive force which greatly outnumbered Richard's knights. The defenders were at a loss as to how to fight against mounted knights, as the Cypriot intelligence had not reported any cavalry on the island. Legend has it that an armed clerk, Hugh de la Mare, gave advice to Richard and begged him, "Retire, sire, their numbers are too great." Richard is alleged to have responded, "Sir clerk, return to your scrivening and leave the fighting to me!" and he led his fifty fully armoured knights in a charge that routed the Cypriots. Although Isaac was unseated by Richard himself, he managed to remount and escape to the mountains, leaving Richard to claim his battle standard with which to ride triumphantly back into Limmasol. Richard, the tactician, was determined to conquer Cyprus and subdue its population so he placed the Third Crusade on hold while he consolidated his base in Limmasol. The eventual fate of Cyprus was decided when Guy of Lusignan, the deposed Italian King of Jerusalem, arrived in Cyprus and offered his forces to Richard to help with subduing the Cypriots. Guy had come to Limassol to ask for Richard's support in reclaiming his throne when Jerusalem was retaken. He argued that he should be reinstated as the rightful King of Jerusalem because of his marriage to Queen Sybelle. His opponent, the Count of Montferrat, claimed to be the rightful King of Jerusalem by virtue of his defence of Tyre against Saladin. In exchange for King Richard's backing, Guy agreed to help Richard to conquer Cyprus.

In Acre, King Philip was growing concerned that the impetus for the Third Crusade was waning. He sent a deputation to Richard imploring him to join the crusade with haste. Richard responded, "Not for half the wealth of Russia, not until I have conquered Cyprus." Richard had decided that the only way to secure Cyprus was to capture Isaac, so he and Guy devised a two-pronged attack on Isaac's mountain retreat. Richard sailed around the coast to Famagusta, while Guy of Lusignan mounted a land attack which succeeded in capturing Isaac's wife and daughter. This two-pronged attack marked the end of the island's

resistance. Isaac surrendered the whole island, but begged
not to be put in irons. King Richard agreed, ensuring that
the imprisoned Isaac's chains were made of silver. Having
succeeded in conquering the island, Richard the Lionheart,
the Absent King, lost interest in Cyprus which resulted in
renewed Cypriot resistance. The island became a liability,
a thorn in Richard's side, and Robert de Sable, the Templar
Grand Master at that time, saw an opportunity. He made an
offer to Richard to buy Cyprus in order to give the
Templars a "homeland." Richard quickly agreed to the sale
for the sum of 100,000 bezants (bezants were gold coins
struck in Constantinople and used throughout the Middle
East as trading coinage). The financial arrangement was
that the Templars would pay 40,000 bezants as a deposit,
and the balance would be paid from future profits and
transactions made within the confines of the island itself. It
is an indication of the wealth of the Templars that having
recently suffered the monumental and disastrous defeat at
Hattin and their subsequent losses in the Holy Land, they
could still find 40,000 bezants with which to pay the
deposit for the purchase of Cyprus. The Templars used
Cyprus as a base in the Mediterranean from which to enter
the world of commerce. However, the Templar's commitment to the Third Crusade meant that Robert de Sable's
forces were overstretched and he could leave only a token
force of between fourteen and twenty armed knights to
police the island under the command of Armand Bouchart.
This small force soon asserted themselves, bullying the
islands's inhabitants and taking what they wanted. The
Cypriots revolted, confronting the Templars in their castle.
Bouchart led his knights in a charge, massacring the
Cypriots, but he realized that he could not hold the island
indefinitely with such a small force, and requested
reinforcements from Acre. Robert de Sable, realizing that
he had overstretched the Templar forces, offered to return

the island to Richard, but the English king was not interested in regaining the liability he had succeeded in
offloading onto the Templars. He did, however, offer to
mediate in the sale of Cyprus to Guy of Lusignan. The
purchase was funded by Italian merchants, and, although
the Templars were not reimbursed their 40,000 bezants,
they were allowed to retain a military presence at
Famagusta and Limmasol, as well as in the castles of
Gastria, Yermsoyia, and Khiokitia. A century later, in
1291, when the crusaders finally lost Acre, they and the
Hospitallers retreated to Cyprus, which then became their
main base in the Mediterranean.

Initially, things had boded well for the Hospitallers in
their working relationship with the Templars, but after the
loss of Acre, the French monarch, Philip the Fair, set in
motion his plans to destroy the Templars and seize their
treasures. In 1307 he took action against the Templars, but
not against the Hospitallers. At that time the Papacy had
suggested an amalgamation of the two orders, but the
Templars had resisted the merger. When, in 1312, the
Templar order was disbanded, much of their property was
given to the Hospitallers, inciting the surviving Templars to
perpetual hatred of the Hospitallers.

To prevent a takeover of the island, Henry of Lusignan,
a descendant of Guy of Lusignan, decreed that neither the
Templars nor the Hospitallers were permitted to gain any
further land or property, either by gift or by purchase. The
Templars were happy to remain in Cyprus as they still held
out hope of a new conquest of Jerusalem, but the
Hospitallers decided to move on and settled initially on the
island of Rhodes, later relocating to Malta, where they
became known as "The Knights of Malta." Cyprus
remained a Templar base and, in 1298, it became the home
of their final Grand Master, Jacques de Molay, who
remained on the island from 1291 until his imprisonment in

France on 13 October, 1307. In 1571, two centuries after the Templars had vanished as a formal institution, Ottoman Turks invaded Cyprus, destroying all remaining Templar archives, which would have been of inestimable value to modern historians in resolving some of the mystery surrounding the order and its sudden demise, which has baffled researchers for the last seven hundred years. At the height of their power, the Templars showed arrogance towards common people, they refused to bow down to any monarch, and, in the end, owed only nominal allegiance to the Pope. Undoubtedly, the Church played a leading role in the demise of the order, but did the Church switch allegiances when it discovered the true policies of the Templars, or was their demise the result of Pope Clement V appeasing the French monarch to whom he was indebted for his papal crown? If, in 1307, having finally woken up to the dangers inherent in Templar theology, the Church colluded with the French monarchy to eliminate the Templars, it failed, managing only to eliminate the front-line Templar troops. The Church failed to deal with the political arm of the Templars, the Priory of Sion, and, as a result, its ideology survived, into some eighteenth-century Masonic rituals. If so, that might explain why Pope Clement XII issued a papal bull in 1738 which excommunicated all Freemasons.

In October 1285, Philip IV, known as Philip the Fair, ascended the throne of France. Fifteen years later, at the beginning of the fourteenth century, Philip, having availed himself of the Templar banking system to borrow money, was heavily indebted to them. He hated the Templars because of several humiliations, the worst of these being the indignity of being rejected by them when he had tried to join the order as a postulant. His greatest objection to the Templars, though, was their allegiance to the Church, which revived the old conflict between Church and State.

Eventually, in 1307, Philip accused the Templars of heresy, though he may have begun to formulate a plan to get rid of them as early as 1303. But before Philip could carry out his plan to destroy the Templars, he had to have a Pope who was sympathetic to his cause. In 1303 the Templars were aligned with the Church and enjoyed the protection of the Pope. It took Philip two years, and two Popes had to be assassinated, before he could get his own man elected as Pope. The first assassination took place in September 1303, when, after a long, drawn-out quarrel between Boniface VIII and Philip over the relationship between the Church and the State, a French Minister for the State, Guillaume de Nogaret, recruited some men to kidnap the Pope. The plan was to kidnap the Pope from Anagni, in Italy, and take him back to France to face trial by a French-controlled Church council. With the aid of his ministers, Philip organized the kidnapping, but the plan went wrong. Before the Pope could be smuggled out of Italy, he was rescued by a party of loyal supporters, only for him to die a few days later on 12 October, 1303, of suspected poisoning. Under canon law, his attackers and Philip were automatically excommunicated, but the sanctions against King Philip were soon lifted, though the excommunication of Guillaume de Nogaret remained in force. The Church quickly elected Benedict XI as the new Pope, but being Pope in those days of intrigue was a risky business. Benedict XI reigned for just over eight months before the assasins struck once again; it is thought that Benedict was fed a dish of poisoned figs. Another Pope had fallen victim to Philip's assassins, so another conclave to elect a new Pope gathered in Perugia, where Benedict had died. It took nearly eleven months and much infighting before Philip could manipulate the Cardinals to elect Bertrand de Goth, Archbishop of Bordeaux, who was Philip's own candidate. When he was crowned in the presence of Philip at Lyons on

14 November 1305, the newly elected Pope took the name of Clement V. The new Pope did not take up the papal throne in Rome; instead he held his audiences first in Bordeaux, then in Toulouse, before settling on Avignon for his papal residence. Clement V's decision to establish his papal seat in France initiated seventy years of French domination of the Papacy. During those seventy years, there were seven French Popes, beginning with Clement V in 1305, and ending finally with the death of Gregory XI in 1378.

In 1305, however, with Philip IV still coveting the vast wealth and extensive land holdings of the Templars, and the new Pope owing his position to the French king, Philip conspired to execute a precisely timed plot to seize the Templars' assets. There is evidence that Philip met with Pope Clement V on several occasions between 1305 and 1307, though what they spoke about is less certain. Eventually Philip issued sealed orders to all his seneschals throughout France with instructions that they should be opened in the early hours of Friday 13 October. At dawn, the French seneschals moved swiftly to arrest the Templars, thus giving rise to the idea that Friday the Thirteenth is unlucky. On Saturday 14 October, Guillaume de Nogaret convened a meeting of clergy and university theologians in Paris where he presented them with a list of the charges against the Order of Templars. These charges included that they indulged in homosexual practices, worshipped a head they named Baphomet, and taught women how to abort their babies. The most bizarre charge levelled against them, considering that for two centuries Templars had been dying in the name of Christ, was that they denied Christ and spat on the cross. On that day, the king's men placed approximately 15,000 members of the Order of Templars, including knights, foot soldiers, clerics, and servants, under arrest. The secular authorities confiscated all Templar goods, which then became the property of the French Crown. However, the action against the Templars was only partially successful. Although the majority of the Templars were arrested, Philip's primary objective of seizing the Templar treasure was never accomplished. To this day its location remains a mystery.

During the following two weeks the proceedings against the Templars gathered momentum. On 19 October, the interrogations began in Paris, and five days later, Jacques de Molay made his first confession, which he confirmed by repeating it one day later at the University of Paris. The Church was not oblivious to what was happening in Paris and on 27 October Philip received a strongly worded letter from the Pope conveying his indignation at the arrests of the Templars. The indecisive and temperamental Clement V was probably hedging his bets by attempting to deny having colluded in the attack on the order. Clement continued to protest Philip's actions and to claim ignorance of the plot. Nine months later, on 5 July 1308, an official protest in the form of a papal bull *Subit Assidue* was made to Philip. Clement accused the French authorities of failing to warn the Church of Philip's intention to arrest all the Templars. One Templar command post, in Bézu in the Languedoc, was, however, left unmolested.

Towards the end of the thirteenth century a detachment of Templars from the Aragonese province of Rossillon were posted to the vicinity of Rennes-le-Château in the Languedoc, where they erected a command post and chapel on Mount Bézu. The commander of the Templars at Bézu was Seigneur de Goth, who was related to Bertrand de Goth, the Archbishop of Bordeaux before his elevation to Pope Clement V. Bertrand's mother was Ida de Blanche-fort, whose ancestor was Bertrand de Blanchefort, the fourth Grand Master of the Templars, who had been a Cathar. Part of the mystery surrounding the Templars and

Rennes-le-Château is the question of whether Clement V, as head of the Church, was privy to some secret entrusted to the Blanchefort family, or whether he was acting out of family loyalty to protect that particular group of Templars from arrest. The Templar arrests were, in fact, illegal because the French monarch had no jurisdiction over clerics, who were answerable only to the Church.

At the time of the arrests, Jacques de Molay was the twenty-third, and ultimately last, Grand Master of the Templars. His exact date of birth is unknown, but he was born at Rahon, Jura, in 1244, and joined the Knights Templar at Beaune in 1265, at the age of twenty-one. His rise through the ranks was rapid, and, before his appointment as Grand Master, he had served in the post of Grand Preceptor of England. On the death of Theobald Gaudin, the twenty-second Grand Master from 1291 to 1293, de Molay became the Templar Grand Master and moved his headquarters from England to Cyprus. Late in the year 1306, a year before Philip IV's plot to arrest the Templars was implemented, Jacques de Molay left his home in Cyprus to visit France. The purpose of his visit was to preside over the planning and the order of battle for a proposed Sixth Crusade to the Holy Land. After his arrival in France and before his arrest, de Molay had meetings with the Pope, who was in favour of a crusade and gave his blessing for de Molay to organize it. During one of these meetings with the Pope, de Molay presented a petition from the Templars that protested against any amalgamation of the Templars and the Hospitallers. Such a plan had been under review by the Church since the Council of Lyons, and had been accepted in principal by Pope Gregory X. On 21 March, 1313, exactly one year after the papal bull to sanction the dissolution of the Order of Templars, the Hospitallers made a large donation to Philip, in recompense for Philip's expenses incurred in disbanding the Templars, providing ample cause for the Templars to hate the Hospitallers.

A few days before the arrests in October 1307, Philip required de Molay to visit Paris so that he could be arrested along with the rest of his order. Jacques de Molay had no reason to suspect that he was about to be arrested. As a godfather to Philip's son, Jacques had complete faith in Philip, and believed that his presence was required for his godson's confirmation. Normally Templar rules forbade a Templar to be a godparent, but de Molay had made an exception in the case of Philip's son. At the ceremony, Philip deceitfully suppressed any bad feelings towards de Molay and the Grand Master was treated with respect as a friend of the King.

Two days after his arrest, de Molay made his first appearance before the Inquisition. Philip hoped that torture would enable the Inquisitors to get a confession of Templar guilt on the charges of heresy: that they denied Christ, worshipped idols, spat on the crucifix, and engaged in homosexuality. At his trial de Molay described himself as *miles illetteratus*, or an unlettered soldier; such knowledge as he possessed had been gained through his experiences as a Templar knight, without the benefit of any formal training in law or theology. As a result his defence was almost non-existent. The prosecutors asked him to record a plea of guilty or not guilty to the charges, the most serious of which was that as Grand Master, he was responsible for the indoctrination ceremony for new initiates, during which they were obliged to deny Christ and to spit on a crucifix. De Molay pleaded guilty to that charge, but refused to plead guilty to charges of homosexuality. At a later hearing on 25 October, de Molay made the same admissions and denials of guilt. Philip hoped that when the "evidence" obtained by torturing several Templars, was presented to Pope Clement, the Pope's objections would be silenced and he would ratify the imprisonment of the entire

Templar order. Philip was partially successful in that on 22 November, once Clement V had examined the confessions, he issued the papal bull *Pastoralis Praeminentiae*, which demanded that all Templars in Christian states be arrested and their property seized. The papal bull hinted at Philip's abuse of power and emphasized that all articles of property that were seized must come under ecclesiastic jurisdiction. This added fuel to the Church-versus-State conflict at the centre of Philip's witch-hunt against the Templars. The bull also stated that an ecclesiastical enquiry would determine the truth of the allegations of heresy, though that truth never surfaced because Philip suppressed certain witnesses and prevented the enquiry from interviewing key Templars. On 24 December, de Molay revoked his confession before the papal commission, then, in February 1308, Clement suspended the Inquisition in connection with the Templar case and appointed a commission of inquiry of eight cardinals with a mandate to interrogate the Templars without the use of torture. The establishment of a papal commission infuriated Philip, who retaliated on 24 March when he called a meeting of the States-General, which convened at Tours on 5 May, 1308.

King Philip IV had formed the French States-General in 1302 with a constitution that divided the populace into three estates: the clergy, the nobility, and commoners. The exact purpose of the States-General was unclear, as a succession of monarchs altered its brief to suit their own requirements, but basically it served as a forum for the monarch to gain approval for any anti-clerical policy that he wished to implement. The States-General which convened in 1302 performed their duty to the monarch and sanctioned actions against Pope Boniface VIII. In 1308, they sanctioned actions against the Knights Templar, following which the Church ordered a new enquiry under the auspices of a papal commission. The terms of reference for that commission were that the Church, not the monarchy, was to judge the guilt or innocence of the Templars. On the orders of Clement V, that judgment was to be reserved until Clement himself had been allowed to meet with the prisoners. Philip was once again embroiled in a conflict between the Church and the State, with the Templars at its centre. In June 1308, Clement V and Philip met. After lengthy discussions, the papal enquiry ended once the demands of the Pope had been rejected. Clement had asked for the prisoners to be placed in Church custody, but Philip had refused, so the Pope had suspended the power of the Inquisition to interrogate the Templars. On 27 June, 1308, Philip relented and decided to allow a select group of seventy-two Templars to be manacled and taken to Poitiers to meet and present their case in person to the Pope, but the senior members of the Templar Order, including its Grand Master, de Molay, were kept in isolation in dungeons at Chinon Castle. Philip used the excuse that they were too indisposed to suffer the hardships of a journey to Poitiers. Clement retaliated by appointing three cardinals as part of the commission to visit the prisoners in Chinon. This delegation of trusted and impartial cardinals included Cardinal Fredol, who, as Clement's nephew, had personally witnessed the abuse of power by the Inquisitors in their interrogation of the Templars.

The Church protested formally on 5 July, 1308, by means of another papal bull, *Subit Assidue*, in which Clement accused the French Inquisitor, Guillaume Imbert, of failing in his duty to warn the papal authority of the imminent arrests of October 1307. The Pope was obviously protecting himself against accusations that he had aided and abetted Philip in arresting the Templars. It was an embarrassment for the monarch to receive an official rebuke of this kind, but Philip had to substantiate the accusations against the Templars, so he sanctioned the use of torture to gather evidence. The Inquisition was expert at extracting confessions; its Dominican inquisitors first used lawyers to cross-examine the Templars, who were mostly uneducated soldiers. Once these cross-examinations were over, the Templars faced the torture chambers, where the thumbscrew, the boot, and the rack were used to crush and dislocate limbs. Other methods of torture used "in the name of God," included crushing victims with lead weights, or forcing a funnel down a victim's throat and pouring water down it until the victim drowned. One particularly hideous form of torture was called "the burning in the feet": the soles of a victim's feet would be smeared with fat, before being placed over a charcoal fire until they caught fire, burning the flesh off the bones. One Templar subjected to this torture was Bernard de Vaho; a few days after being tortured, the bones dropped off his feet. When de Vaho next appeared before the commission, he was helped into court, carrying the bones from his feet in a bag. The Inquisition forbade the spilling of blood during interrogation, but burning and racking were considered permissible forms of torture. However, when Clement suspended the authority of the Inquisition to investigate the Templars, Guillaume Imbert was acting outside the Inquisition's brief. That failed, however, to moderate his techniques because he continued to act under the jurisdiction of French secular justice, which allowed the spilling of blood in torture to obtain a confession. In August, de Molay was brought before the commission, and, according to the papal bull, *Faciens Misericordiam*, dated 12 August 1308, he repeated his admission of guilt. This brings into question the impartiality of the papal commission because when de Molay appeared before another commission a year later, on 26 November 1309, he appeared astounded. He twice crossed himself and proclaimed, "Would to God that such scoundrels might receive the treatment they deserve from the Saracens and Tartars." It seems probable that the papal commission of 1308 attributed to de Molay statements which were false. If that were indeed the case, the - commission's report probably had one of two objectives. De Molay may have had sympathizers among the cardinals who were trying to save him from the death sentence that would have been mandatory if they had reported to Philip that de Molay had relapsed and disavowed his confession of 1307. Another possibility is that Philip did not want to impose the death penalty at that stage because he still hoped to get his hands on the Templar treasure, so he instructed the cardinals to suppress de Molay's relapse to buy time in which to use torture to ascertain the location of the treasure. Philip had probably already decided that de Molay would go to the stake in the end. It is unlikely that the Commission for the Inquisition would have tried to save a heretic because heretics had to be "cleansed" by fire in order to redeem their souls. In the dungeons, de Molay secretly circulated a wax tablet of the sort used by scribes, asking the Templar prisoners to retract their confessions.

Retraction of a confession had severe consequences. Under medieval Inquisition law, there were three sentences for someone who confessed to heresy. If, following confession, someone repented his or her sins, he or she was set free, but if someone confessed yet refused to repent, he or she received a mandatory life sentence. The third and the most severe punishment was reserved for those who confessed, but then relapsed and retracted the confession, for they were said to be "in disavowal" of the confession, and disavowal was punishable by death at the stake. Between 1309 and 1311 most of the Templars were "in disavowal," and consequently Pope Clement suspended the order and left the fate of the Templars to French secular justice. As a result, fifty-four Templar martyrs were burnt at the stake on 10 May, 1310, for being "in disavowal" of their original confession.

Early that morning, fifty-four stakes were set up in a field at Paris's Porte Antoine gate, and piles of faggots were assembled, ready for the executions. As dawn broke, the fifty-four victims were led from their cells, together with witnesses drawn from Templar comrades who were in prison on similar, though lesser, charges. Members of the victims' families were also invited to the executions. As the faggots were piled up to waist height around each victim, family members beseeched their sons, or brothers, to save their lives by admitting their original confessions. When the pleas from their families failed, priests pleaded with the fifty-four knights, but not one of the fifty-four Templars relapsed and confirmed his original confession. The fires were lit and, gradually, as the flames took hold and their flesh began to blister, some Templars screamed in agony while others bade their comrades to be of stout heart. Gradually, the cries of the victims diminished until all that was left were fifty-four piles of greasy ashes. The Templar witnesses were then returned to their cells, most of them in a state of shock and trepidation, to await their fate. The shocked family members, too, went home. The Inquisition had used the psychological torment of witnessing the executions to break the spirit of those Templars still in prison. The execution of the initial fifty-four Templars was followed by the burning over a short period of another 120 Templars, of whom only two confessed to their sins to save their lives. The torture and subsequent commissions to hear confessions dragged on until, on 22 March, 1312, Clement issued the papal bull *Vox in Excelso*.

Philip had won, but it was only a partial victory because, although he had persuaded Pope Clement V to abolish the Order of Templars, he had not managed to lay his hands on the Templar's wealth, the treasure which had been spirited away five years before. The individual possessions of the Templars held by the Church of Rome were eventually handed over to the Hospitallers, and, in gratitude, the Hospitallers made a large donation to Philip's coffers in recompense for the expenses he had incurred in disbanding the Order of Templars.

During de Molay's interrogation between 1307 and his execution in 1314, the limits of Inquisition cruelty were boundless. Lomas and Knight, in their book *The Second Messiah: Templars, the Turin Shroud and the Great Secret of Freemasonry*, claim that during de Molay's imprisonment, the Grand Inquisitor, Guillaume Imbert, tortured him in a re-enactment of Jesus's crucifixion. They suggest that de Molay was scourged, before being crowned with a wreath of thorns. Then, with the wooden beams framing his cell door being used in lieu of a cross, de Molay was held against the door and nails were hammered into his wrists and feet, pinning him to the wooden structure, where he was left hanging in agony for several hours. Eventually, he was taken down, alive, and a two-edged knife thrust into his side to simulate the spear thrust into the side of Jesus. Then, unconscious or semi-conscious and in a state of shock, de Molay was laid face upwards on a burial shroud by the torturers. The upper section of the shroud was laid over his face and draped over his torso and legs; thus the still living body of de Molay was positioned to represent the living body of Jesus after his crucifixion. The term "living body" is used deliberately for both victims, as it is specifically relevant to the origin of the Turin Shroud. Whoever was wrapped in that shroud, whether it was de Molay or Jesus, the victim would have had to be alive to create the necessary bodily fluids to impregnate the shroud. According to Lomas and Knight, the scientific explanation for the Turin Shroud is that the mixture of flowing blood and lactic acid reacted with frankincense and calcium carbonate to form a whitening agent which etched the victim's features onto the shroud. De Molay's shroud was folded and kept at the home of Geoffrey de Charney, where it was stored as a symbol of loyalty between the two men. Fifty years later, in 1357, a three-and-a-half-metre shroud was taken from where it had been stored and put on public display. Today, we know it as the Turin Shroud. Whatever torture de Molay endured, on 18 March, 1314, together with his fellow Templar Geoffrey de Charney, he was burnt at the stake in Paris.

When de Molay and de Charney, the Preceptor of Normandy, were led out to publicly confess their sins and the sins of their order, in an act of extreme bravery and loyalty to each other and to their fellow Templars who had already been burnt at the stake, they recanted their previous confessions. De Molay claimed his only guilt lay in confessing to relieve his torture. Philip IV immediately had them both classed as relapsed and ordered them to be taken to the Ile de la Cité in the Seine to be publicly roasted to death over a slow fire made from green wood. As the smoke choked the life from the two victims, it is alleged that de Molay cursed Pope Clement and King Philip, his persecutors, and called on them to join him before God within the year to account for their sins. Pope Clement died, supposedly as a result of dysentery, within a month of de Molay, on 20 April, 1314, and, on 29 November, 1314, Philip IV, too, died in mysterious circumstances. It seemed that de Molay had indeed reached out from beyond the grave, but the deaths of the two men were most likely attributable to Templars taking revenge. The Templars had great expertise in using poisons and it is quite possible that Templars killed both King Philip and the Pope to see that justice was done. Members, or sympathizers, of the Order of Templars were still active during the French Revolution. It is claimed that when Louis XVI was guillotined in 1789, an unknown man jumped onto the scaffold, dipped his hand in the French king's blood and scattered some of it over the crowd of witnesses, crying, "Jacques de Molay, thou art avenged!"

The Templars could have anticipated that they would be attacked, but their arrogance led them to ignore most of the warning signs. They did, however, organize a group of Templars to smuggle the "treasure of the temple" by wagon to the Templar naval base at La Rochelle. In 1809, when Napoleon occupied Rome, some records were confiscated from the Vatican archives and brought back to Paris. Among those documents were a few relating to the Templar trials of the fourteenth century, one of which was a statement made by Jean de Chalons, from Nemours, in the diocese of Troyes. In the statement, de Chalons confirmed that on the evening of Thursday, 12 October, 1307, he witnessed three carts hauling three large chests that were concealed beneath straw. The carts left the Paris Temple shortly before nightfall, accompanied by Gèrard de Villiers and Hugo de Chalons at the head of fifty horsemen. As the Templar treasure was removed from Paris before the arrests, the chests hidden on the carts probably contained the entire Templar treasure from the Paris Temple. The wagons and escort took the road to the coast where they were to be transported abroad in eighteen Templar ships. There is no record of the Templar fleet being seen again, but it is possible that the ships made landfall in Nova Scotia, in North America, where some think that the treasure was concealed on Oak Island just off the coast. It is possible that the Templars knew about the New World two centuries before Columbus as a result of charts acquired in the East. Following the arrrest of the Templars in France, Philip tried to convince other European monarchs to eliminate the Templars in their kingdoms and in the whole of Christendom, but he received a very mixed response. King Edward II of England, Philip's son-in-law, received the demand without enthusiasm, and made only a few token arrests of Templars, before releasing them. In Scotland, no one even bothered to publish the papal bulls, and there are claims that the Templars were even given sanctuary. It is also claimed that the Templars led a cavalry charge to help the Scots defeat the English at the Battle of Bannockburn.

In medieval times the principality of Lorraine was allied to Germany, and the Templars were actively supported by the Duke of Lorraine, which led to some strange occurrences during the sixteenth century. Over a quarter of a century, the Houses of Lorraine and Guise made several determined attacks against the Valois dynasty with the aim of seizing the French crown by toppling the French monarchy. During that period, the House of Valois was systematically eliminated by the assassination of all their heirs to the French throne. The motive for the assassinations was that the House of Valois was descended from Philip IV, and it seems certain that the assassinations were all inspired by the Templars. It has also been claimed that Nostradamus, the court astrologer and visionary, was in the employ of the Houses of Guise and Lorraine. If Nostradamus was indeed a spy at the French Court, he would have been able to provide the Houses of Guise and Lorraine with confidential information on the movements of their enemies. Certainly some of the prophecies of Nostradamus concern the Templars, the Merovingian dynasty, and the House of Lorraine. Some even refer to the area of Razes that is associated with Rennes-le-Château.

Heretical Art and the
Black Madonna Cults

Artists such as Botticelli, Leonardo da Vinci, and Simone Martini all made heretical art, and in the galleries and museums of the world there are hundreds of examples. This chapter will explore the so-called Grail Heresy in particular.

Both Botticelli and Leonardo da Vinci were allegedly Grand Masters of the Priory of Sion, a society heavily steeped in the Grail legends, and believed to be the political arm of the Templars. The Grail Heresy can be seen in messages encoded in many medieval paintings. The heretical messages had two important purposes: the first was to display a message of hope that the royal line of David might be restored to a monarchy. The second purpose was to reiterate the Gnostic belief in the restoration of female equality within the Church, combined with the disavowal of Jesus as the Son of God, and acknowledgement of him as Jesus, the Son of Man. This belief held that Jesus was born of the flesh and had a family, together with Mary Magdalene. Because of the obvious danger to heretics from the Church and the Inquisition, the artists put these pictorial messages into their paintings to keep the "flame" alive and to convey the "heretic message" to initiates of future generations. One of the most common symbols integrated into paintings was the letter X. Margaret Starbird makes a very strong case for the use and origins of the X in Gnostic, alchemaic, and hermetic traditions. One possible, though obscure, origin of the symbol is given in the Book of Ezekiel, printed here first in Latin, and then in English (Ezekiel 9:4):

> *et dixit Dominus ad eum transi per mediam civitatem in medio Hierusalem et signa thau super frontes virorum gementium et dolentium super cunctis abominationibusquae fiunt in medio eius.*

> And the Lord said unto him, Go through the midst of the city, through the midst of Jerusalem, and set a mark upon the foreheads of the men that sigh and that cry for all the abominations that be done in the midst thereof.

So the mark of the X was placed on the foreheads of those who mourned the suppression of Sion within Jerusalem.

Another explanation of the origin of X as a symbol of truth and enlightenment is found in the hermetic use of the Latin word for light, which is *lux*. The Greek spelling of *lux* (ΛVX) was also used, soon elided to a single X. The use of X by alchemists also has Greek roots which can be traced back to the Greek God Hermes, who was the guardian of crossroads and the "one" who linked spiritual thinking with earthly matter. He was also the bearer of light to the un-enlightened, and is often portrayed with winged feet as a messenger from the Gods. Finally, the believers in the equality of female and male roles in the Church of the Grail combined the ancient symbolic sign for the female receptacle or chalice, V, with the ancient symbolic sign for the male blade which was Λ. The combination, or mating, of these two symbols creates a symbolic X as "the union." When the

Church of Rome became dominant in Christianity, it adopted the sign of the cross of St Peter, the Christian cross familiar to us today, but the Gnostic church saw the cross of St Peter as an instrument of torture. Therefore, the symbolic X, or mark of the truth, was retained by the Gnostic Church as the original cross, which subsequently became known as the cross of St Andrew. As a result, the cross of St Andrew became an heretical symbol to the Church of Rome and to the Inquisition, and the heretical sign, X, became associated with the wrong path – it is still used today by teachers to indicate that something is incorrect.

Another heretical symbol contained in many paintings is a pomegranate. To the ancients, the pomegranate with its many seeds was an obvious symbol of fertility. In the Middle East today, the fruit is still a symbol of fertility, abundance, and marriage. It has long been a mystery to art historians why paintings ascribed to Botticelli after 1483 are unorthodox and contain various symbolic messages, while prior to 1483 his paintings are very conformist in their content. Sandro Filipepi (better known as Botticelli) was allegedly Grand Master of the Priory of Sion from 1483 to 1510, and his first year as Grand Master marked the turning point in his style of art. Margaret Starbird has highlighted the use of symbols in Botticelli's paintings, asking, for example, why Botticelli included pomegranates in his paintings, placing one especially in the hands or lap of the infant Jesus? Was he sending a message that the King of the Jews was virile and produced offspring to continue the Line of David?

In Botticelli's *Madonna of the Pomegranate* an angel can be seen to the left of the Magdalene with a red cross across his breast, signifying the matriarch of the bloodline.

The works of medieval artists are filled with heretical signs, and the paintings of Carlo Crivelli are no exception. One of his paintings in particular, *The Virgin and Child*, portrays the Virgin Mary standing behind a low wall, while Jesus sits on a cushion on top of the wall in front of her. The wall has an obvious crack, thought to represent crumbling support for the orthodox doctrines of the Church of Rome, while the eyes of Jesus and the Madonna are fixed on a fly on the wall, which has been interpreted as an attempt by Crivelli to represent corruption within the church.

In *The Woman with the Alabaster Jar*, Margaret Starbird claims that a painting by Simone Martini, *Road to Calvary* (also known as *The Carrying of the Cross*) is another example of heretical art. Martini's painting depicts the Magdalene with a gash on her right cheek, while the cross which is carried by Jesus frames the face of the Magdalene, further drawing attention to the close relationship between them. In addition, both Jesus and Mary wear matching red cloaks. Many medieval paintings of the Madonna and of the Magdalene show them both wearing red cloaks. The Inquisition became so incensed at the portrayal of the Madonna wearing red that in 1649 it issued a decree ordering all portrayals of the Virgin Mary to be in blue and white, which left the Magdalene as the "lady in red," which came eventually to be associated with "the oldest profession."

But perhaps the best known piece of heretical art is *The Last Supper* by Leonardo da Vinci, painted on the rear wall of the dining hall at the Dominican convent of Sta Maria delle Grazie near Milan. In *The Da Vinci Code*, Dan Brown describes Leonardo's painting inaccurately as a fresco, which it is not. A fresco is painted on wet plaster, becoming an integral part of a wall in a way which gives a more permanent depth and colour to an artwork. *The Last Supper* has, in fact, been retouched many times, so it is possible that some of Leonardo's messages have already, inadvertently, been altered or obscured, but there are still a number of heretical signs and symbols to be seen in the painting.

(An extremely high definition image of *The Last Supper* by Leonardo da Vinci can be found on-line at http://www.haltadefinizione.com/en/cenacolo/look.asp)

Depicted, from left to right, are Bartholomew, James the less, Andrew, Judas (front), Peter, John (Mary), Jesus, Thomas, James, Philip, Matthew, Thaddeus, and Simon. A fellow researcher Gary Phillips claims to have found a symbolic message, a representation of the Holy Grail, hidden in the painting, above the head of Bartholomew. At first I was dubious of his claim, but after looking for some time, the Grail leapt out at me. Phillips comments that in a Gnostic Gospel attributed to Bartholomew, reference is made to Mary Magdalene; it is possible that da Vinci was implying that the faith in the historical continuity of the Holy Grail, or *sang real*, rests in the Gnostic Gospels. The Gospels of Bartholomew, Thomas, Mary, and The Book of John and Revelation are Gnostic and Essenic in origin.

There are other messages in Leonardo's painting. Andrew, depicted next but one to the right of Bartholomew, has his hands raised in alarm, possibly because of Jesus's announcement of his impending betrayal, or is it because of the knife held by a "phantom" hand which is pointed at his body? To the right of Andrew, Judas Iscariot is portrayed with a small bag in his right hand, presumably containing the thirty pieces of silver. In terms of the actual order of events of Holy Week, Judas would not yet have received his bribe, so presumably Leonardo used the small bag as a device to identify Judas.

One heretical symbol in the original painting was obliterated during an earlier restoration: a salt container on its side, with salt spilling onto the table. Symbolically, spilled salt was a sign of a broken trust. The figure to the right of Judas is generally thought to be John, but a closer look reveals a figure with breasts and a golden necklace. The figure has long, red hair and is thought by some to be a representation of Mary Magdalene. She is dressed in a red cloak and blue vestment, while Jesus, to her right, is dressed in a blue cloak and red vestment. Together, the figures of the couple seem to form two letters, the first being a V formed by the angle of inclination of their bodies to the horizontal. The V is understood as the feminine receptacle, or chalice. The second letter formed is an M, which can be interpreted as Mary or Magdalene. To emphasize that the two are a couple, they are depicted wearing complementary clothing. Peter, who is traditionally regarded as having been intolerant of the Magdalene, is shown making what appears to be a threatening gesture, with his hand across her throat, and to emphasize the hostility between the two, Leonardo has painted a pillar between Mary and Jesus. The pillar forms a wedge between Mary and Jesus which could be taken to mean that when Mary leaned towards Peter, a wedge would be driven between her and Jesus. With the figure of Thaddeus, it seems that Leonardo was declaring his own beliefs and also leaving a message for posterity, in that the figure resembles Leonardo himself and is turning his back on Jesus. That message was an heretical chain of thought known as the European Heresy, which existed in the minds of some of the most renowned artists in the world. The European Heresy venerates John the Baptist and Mary Magdalene, and is considered one of the great secrets of the Knights Templar, but why was this the case when there is nothing in the Gospels to justify this respect and reverence? This is one of Freemasonry's secrets today, but why is it guarded so closely? Leonardo's admiration for John the Baptist can be seen not only in his paintings and writings, but also in architecture associated with him, such as the Baptistery in Florence, which is octagonal in the style of Templar architecture, based on the Templar conception of the shape of Solomon's Temple. The Baptistery is the site of the only surviving example of a sculpture partly attributed to Leonardo. In the winter of 1507–08, Leonardo collaborated with the sculptor Giovanni Francesco Rustici to execute a bronze for the decoration of an outside wall of the octagonal building. It depicts John the Baptist with his right index finger raised in admonishment or warning, a gesture often associated with Leonardo's work.

In many European churches there are so-called Black Madonna icons, which are much revered. In the south of France, there is an annual gypsy festival for Saint Sarah, whom the European gypsies refer to as their patron saint, Sara-la-Kali. The festival requires a Black Madonna icon to be taken from the crypt of the local church and transported on horseback to the sea to commemorate the ancient knowledge that Sarah came from across the sea and landed in France. According to medieval legends, a party comprising Mary Magdalene, Mary Salome, Sarah the Egyptian, and others were led by Joseph of Arimathea in their flight from the Middle East. Legend has it that they came ashore in a boat without oars, landing near the Mediterranean village of Rha, which is now part of Saintes-Maries-de-la-Mer. Legend also has it that Sarah the Egyptian was a "dark-coloured child" who was possibly the daughter of Mary Magdalene. If that was the case, it is probable that the child was called "the Egyptian" because she was born in Egypt after the royal family of Jesus fled the Holy Land following the Crucifixion. The folklore of Provence claims that the Magdalene and her small entourage sought asylum in France thirteen years after the crucifixion of Christ, and the south of France generally abounds with legends from the life of Mary Magdalene, who reportedly lived out her last thirty years in a cave at Saint Baume in the Camargue, where a monastery was later established. Though literature in the monastery contains the story of the Magdalene's residence in the cave, this fact was suppressed by the Church, and prevented from filtering into mainstream Christian tradition until, in 1980, the Vatican sent an Apostolic Nuncio to celebrate a mass to commemorate the seven-hundredth jubilee of the discovery of the grave of Saint Sarah. The mass was celebrated with six bishops and numerous priests at the Basilica of Marie Madeleine in St Maximin. After 700 years, the Vatican had finally taken steps towards acknowledging St Sarah and her association with Mary Magdalene, lending credence to the legends. Statues of the mysterious Catholic Black Madonna adorn many of the cathedrals of Europe, in central and southeastern France particularly, where they are known as *Vierges Noires*, or Black Virgins. The most notable examples are to be found in Chartres, Marsat, La Chapelle-Geneste, Clermont-Ferrand, Lisseul, Vassivierre, Rocamadour, and Le Puy. The cult of the Black Madonna is often associated with the Merovingians and the Knights Templar, to whom the Black Madonna was Mary Magdalene. This is why, during the Middle Ages, the Black Madonna was associated with the Crusades and the Moorish occupation of Spain. Sarah, the black Egyptian, has travelled far and wide, and today Black Madonnas can be seen in the Americas, where she was introduced by the Spanish Conquistadors. Of all the Black Madonnas there is one which deserves a special mention due to the fact that the late Pope John Paul II held a special devotion to her image. That Madonna is Our Lady of Czestochowa, whom the Polish people credit with the protection of their nation during several conflicts. The Polish icon, however, has one unusual feature. On her right cheek is an ugly gash, the same symbol contained in the painting *The Road to Calvary*, which also depicts a wounded, dark-skinned Madonna. In the Book of Micah there is an intriguing reference to the "Leader or Judge" of the people of Israel, who has also been symbolically marked with a slashed cheek (Micah 5:1): "Now gather thyself in troops, O daughter of troops, he hath laid siege against us, they shall smite the judge of Israel with a rod upon the cheek."

But why have hundreds of icons been given black faces and hands, and what was the thinking behind the creation of the Black Madonnas? There is one school of thought which suggests that the Black Madonnas are iconic relics of pagan worship of the Earth Mother, which could link paganism with the Church. To pagans, darkness symbolized the earth, fertility, wisdom, life, and regeneration. Other schools of thought suggest that the Black Madonnas are linked to Egyptian, Greek, or Roman goddesses, such as Diana, Isis, Venus, or Cybele. This is substantiated by the fact that the first icons of a Black Madonna and child were not Christian, but pagan, symbolizing the Egyptian Goddess Isis with her child Horus in her arms. The Isis cult remained popular around the Mediterranean well into the first four centuries of Christianity, with Isis, a holy virgin, sharing her titles of "Queen of Heaven" and "Star of the Sea" with the Christian Virgin Mary. This adoption of a black icon by the Christian church occurred when the Roman Empire had extended into Egypt and Judea, and Horus and Isis were adopted as a god and goddess of ancient Rome. When the Roman legions spread throughout Europe, they erected shrines to the black Isis holding the black infant Horus. Later, with the arrival of Christianity, the early Church adopted the ancient shrines of the pagans. Subsequent development of one of these adopted shrines led to the construction of what is probably the most important French cathedral symbolizing the Black Madonna cult, the thirteenth-century Gothic cathedral at Chartres near Paris. This cathedral houses a Black Madonna, which is known locally as "the lady under the earth." It is possible that this local, colloquial expression for the Black Madonna springs from an ancient memory which links the Black Madonna to paganism. When those adopted pagan shrines were Christianized, they retained their black icons, which were made to represent the Christian Madonna, but which Madonna? The Catholic Church would have us believe that they are shrines to the Virgin Mary and the baby Jesus, but did the early Christians in France believe that they represented the Magdalene and her child, Sarah the Egyptian?

Rex Deus and the French Connection

While it is possible that a bloodline from the Jewish House of David, known as Rex Deus, survived through to modern times, it is a matter of fact that, in 1887, Johann of Hapsburg, the Archduke of Austro-Hungaria, allegedly a member of the Rex Deus family, travelled incognito to the Languedoc region of France. He travelled under the assumed name of Monsieur Guillaume, and presented himself to Saunière, the priest at Rennes-le-Château. Monsieur Guillaume was acting as an emissary from the Comtesse de Chambord, who was also of the House of Hapsburg and also, allegedly, a Rex Deus family member. She was the widow of Henri de Bourbon, the late, uncrowned King Henry V of France. Tim Wallace-Murphy, in his book *Rex Deus*, co-written with Marilyn Hopkins and Graham Simmans, claims that while giving a presentation at a meeting of The Saunière Society, he told his audience that, if he could obtain permission, he hoped to travel to Jerusalem where he intended to explore some of the excavations under the Temple Mount. After the presentation, a mysterious, middle-aged man, whom he knew only as Michael, spoke to him about some strange symbols that Tim might see under the Temple Mount. When asked for the source of his information, Michael said that it was part of an ancient family secret. Tim claims that he was intrigued, but was able to obtain only a brief synopsis of the tradition which led Michael to claim that he was a member of a clan of families known as Rex Deus, which claimed descent through both lines of Jesus's antecedents. One line was the Hasmoneans, who were of the House of David, and the other line was from the courses which had provided High Priests for the Temple in Jerusalem. The clan of Rex Deus families passed down their lineal heritage through the principle of uterine nobility, meaning that the succession went from father to a selected son or daughter. Michael alleged that the genealogies of these families for the pre-Christian era up to the Roman destruction of Jerusalem in AD 70 were inscribed on the walls of Solomon's stables under the Temple Mount. It is possible that these secret genealogies provided the Templars with the knowledge which made them so powerful and which contributed to Saunière's wealth, some of which came from the Hapsburgs, who were members of the Rex Deus family.

Michael went on to claim that other Rex Deus members include the Stuarts of Scotland and King Juan Carlos of Spain, one of whose many titles is Protector of the Holy Places of Jerusalem. So who were the founding members of the Rex Deus clan of families? In their book *The Second Messiah*, Christopher Knight and Robert Lomas, both of whom are Freemasons, claim that the Templars tunnelled under the Temple Mount and broke into a network of tunnels, where, it is alleged, the Hebrew priesthood had hidden their most valuable articles and sacred Temple artefacts from the Roman army when Jerusalem was conquered in AD 70. Among the treasures discovered by the Templars, was some of the silver and gold listed in the Copper Scroll found at Qumran, and records of the first

Christian Church of Jerusalem. It is also possible that they discovered the Ark of the Covenant.

The first Bishop of the Church of Jerusalem was James, the brother of Jesus, who led the small community of Judaic-Christians, more commonly known as Gnostic Christians, who were opposed to the Pauline form of Christianity, which was eventually to become the Church of Rome. Over the next thirty years, the Church of Jerusalem grew and, around AD 62, the Scribes and Pharisees of the Sanhedrin demanded that James moderate his preaching on the teachings of Jesus to the Gentiles and Jews, but James refused to deny the Gospel of his brother, and, as a result, was thrown off the city wall. When it was discovered that he had not been killed by the fall, James was stoned and then clubbed to death, becoming a Christian martyr. Following the death of James, Simon, another of Jesus's brothers, took over the leadership of the Church of Jerusalem. Four years later, in AD 66, the Roman Procurator Florus demanded a higher tax of seventeen talents from the Jewish Temple treasury. This was a final insult which provoked the Jews into open rebellion against Rome, but the Gentiles and the Gnostic Christians took no part in the rebellion. The rebellion was the beginning of the Jewish War which lasted until the fall of Masada in AD 73. According to Eusebius, when the Gentiles and Gnostic Christians in Jerusalem saw the might of the Roman army led by Titus Flavius Vespasianus, the majority fled to Pella, leaving the Romans to enslave or massacre the Jewish population. Vespasianus ordered the Temple to be levelled and its treasures removed to Rome. There is a triumphal arch in Rome on which some of the spoils of war are recorded, but it contains no record of the Ark, suggesting that the Ark remained in Jerusalem, perhaps hidden in the deepest secret caverns beneath the Temple. Eusebius goes on to write that after the destruction of Jerusalem and the

Temple, the Gentiles and Gnostic Christians returned to help rebuild the city. Eusebius also records that Simon remained as leader of the Gnostic Christians for forty years until, in AD 105, he was betrayed and tortured for several days before being crucified. For the next thirty years, the Gnostic Christians managed to maintain the Church of Jerusalem, but then the Second Jewish War broke out, in AD 135, as a result of an edict issued during Emperor Hadrian's visit to Jerusalem in AD 130. Hadrian had banned one of the cornerstones of the Jewish faith, namely circumcision. He had also commissioned a tomb for Pompey, who had desecrated the Temple in 63 BC. The final straw had come when Hadrian announced his intention to rebuild Jerusalem, including a new temple dedicated to Jupiter on the Temple Mount, and rename it Aeolia Capitolina. During the ensuing three-and-a-half years of war, the leaders of the Jewish revolt persecuted the Gnostic Christians in Jerusalem. When the Jewish army was finally defeated, Hadrian expelled all sectarian Jews from the city and left the Christian Church in Jerusalem to be controlled by the Gnostic Christians. The early Gnostics now controlled the Temple Mount and, although the Romans had destroyed the Temple, Solomon's stables were still intact, and more or less as they are today. They provided a perfect hiding place for the Gnostic Christians' secret documents. Thus, the documents of the Gnostic Church joined the treasure and artefacts already hidden, including the Hebrew Ark of the Covenant, and all remained hidden until their discovery by the Templars some time around 1118. Because the Jews and their priests had lost control of the Temple, they had no control over the safety of their treasure and, with the passage of time, the whereabouts of the artefacts became shrouded in the mists of time. The Gnostic Christians continued to control the Church of Jerusalem by paying lip service to their Roman masters and worshipping the pantheon of Roman gods. Two-and-a-half centuries later, when Constantine convened the Council of Nicaea in AD 325, and brought all the factions within the Christian Church together to form the Church of Rome, the foundation of the Catholic Church, the Gnostic Christians obeyed the emperor and subscribed to the form of Christianity advocated by papal authority. At the same time, however, the descendants of Jesus and James, the early priesthood, secretly practised Gnostic Christianity and thus kept alive the ancient knowledge relating to both lines of Jesus's antecedents. The descendants of Jesus, who, through James, formed the Gnostic priesthood in Jerusalem, and the other descendants of Jesus, who had escaped to France, eventually became known among themselves as the Rex Deus families.

Michael claimed that after AD 70 some survivors of the Rex Deus families fled and went into hiding in Europe. Each family member was required to maintain an accurate record of his or her own genealogy, and they were sworn to eternal secrecy regarding other Rex Deus families. The families intermarried to preserve the bloodlines through European Royal houses, ruling as the Hapsburgs, the Stuarts in Scotland, and as the present-day King Juan Carlos of Spain. The penalty for breaking the silence and disclosing secrets of Rex Deus is similar to the symbolic Masonic oath of having one's heart torn out and one's throat cut. Michael claimed that his disclosures to Tim Wallace-Murphy were a result of the publication of *The Holy Blood and the Holy Grail*, which had brought the subject of Rex Deus into the public arena, and also claimed that the original nine knights who worked on excavating Solomon's stables under the Temple Mount in Jerusalem discovered something that made them very wealthy and powerful in the twelfth and thirteenth centuries.

The tunnels under the Temple Mount, which the

Templars had excavated, were re-opened in 1867 by a team of British Royal Engineers led by Lieutenant Warren. Warren failed to find any artefacts or signs of treasure from the Temple of Jerusalem, but he did find the remains of a Templar lance, a small Templar cross, the major part of a Templar sword, and a spur. Knights Templar Chevalier Robert Brydon of Edinburgh, the Templar archivist for Scotland and Roslin, is responsible for preserving these Templar artefacts for posterity.

Robert Brydon also has a letter, written in 1912, to his grandfather from a Captain Parker, who was a member of Warren's excavation team in 1867. The letter recounts the discovery of a secret room carved into the rock beneath the Temple Mount. Captain Parker, breaking through the stone wall at the end of a passage, found himself inside the Mosque of Omar, and had to flee back into the tunnel to save himself from a crowd of angry Muslims, irate at having been disturbed at their devotions.

What were the Templars looking for that they spent nine years doing backbreaking work in one particular place? Who, or what, had driven them to undertake the project in the first place? Presumably they had inside knowledge, relayed to them, in all probability, through Rex Deus via Hugues de Payens, a Rex Deus family member and the leader of the nine knights. According to a chronicle written by Archbishop Guillaume de Tyre (William of Tyre) entitled *A History of Deeds Done Beyond the Sea*, Hugues de Payens, who had begun his adulthood as a Cistercian monk, was a vassal of Hugh of Champagne and a relative by marriage of the St Clairs of Roslin. The Archbishop goes on to write that among the original nine knights who founded the Templars were two Cistercian monks named Gondemar and Rosal. Hugues de Payens was chosen as the knights' leader possibly because of his links with the Cistercians, who were at that time deeply involved in deciphering Hebrew texts. The Cistercians and the Knights Templar were so closely linked by ties of blood, patronage, and shared objectives that they were practically two parts of the same organization. However, William of Tyre was wrong when he wrote that "no new knights were admitted to the Templars during their nine formative years." A letter from the Bishop of Chartres, dated 1114, was written to Hugh, Count of Champagne, congratulating him on his intention to join *La Milice du Christ*, or the Knights Templar, as they were more commonly known. The fact that Hugh of Champagne joined the Templars led to a bizarre chain of command within the Templar ranks because, under the feudal system, Hugues de Payens was a vassal to Hugh, Count of Champagne, but within the Knights Templar, Hugh, Count of Champagne, was subservient to de Payens, the first Grand Master of the Templars.

Bernard of Clairvaux, a Cistercian, nominated Hugues de Payens as the first Grand Master of the Poor Militia of Christ, the Templars. De Payens was consecrated in that post by Abbot Edouard in the northern Italian principality of Seborga. Ancient Templar documents, recently discovered there, in a secret Templar archive, claim that in 1113, Bernard of Clairvaux founded a monastery in Seborga, under the direction of an Abbot named Edouard. The documents claim that the monastery was formed to protect a "great secret." Gondemar and Rosal, the two Cistercian monks among the original nine Templars, were released from their Cistercian vows in November 1118 to rejoin the other seven founding members of the Templars. These Rex Deus members were sent to Jerusalem on a quest, possibly to locate the Ark of the Covenant and bring it to Europe, or perhaps to search for documents.

The Ark of the Covenant was built by Bezalel, who stored it in the Tabernacle, a portable Temple used by the Israelites under the leadership of Moses during their migration. As Moses approached death at the age of 125, he presented the children of Israel with their Law. According to Deuteronomy 31:26, Moses instructed them to, "Take this book of the law and put it in the side of the Ark of the Covenant of the LORD your GOD that it may be there for a witness against thee." Over the years, the Israelites carried the Ark into battle and on most occasions won, but, during the Priesthood of Eli, the Jews suffered a crushing defeat at the hands of the Philistines, who captured the Ark. After almost a year of various misfortunes, including plague, the Philistines decided to send the Ark back to the Israelites, along with expensive gifts. The Ark was taken back to Beit Shemesh and then transported to Kiryat Yearim, where it remained for twenty years. King David had the Ark transported to Jerusalem, where it remained until Solomon's construction of the First Temple, where the Ark was kept until the Babylonians, under Nebuchadnezzar, captured Jerusalem. The defeat of the Jews led to the destruction of the First Temple and their enslavement. After the Jews' period in Babylonian captivity, most references to the Ark of the Covenant cease in conventional biblical texts, except for one verse in Chronicles. There is a reference to the Ark in the non-canonical Apocrypha, where it states that when the Israelites rebuilt the Temple at the time of Ezra and Zechariah, the Ark could not be found.

The Apocrypha is one of a number of texts omitted from the official, or canonical, version of the Bible, which appears in other versions. These anomalies began in AD 450 when Jerome translated the Bible into Latin, creating the so-called Vulgate. He rejected the Apocrypha because no Hebrew version of the texts could be found, although they do appear in the Greek Septuagint, or Old Testament. Eventually, some of the texts were accepted by the Church of Rome, and became part of the Catholic Bible, but, during the Reformation, Protestants rejected the Apocrypha, and either edited them out or inserted them in a third section of the Bible. In 1546, the Council of Trent accepted the Apocrypha or Deuterocanonical Books as being of divine origin and ruled that they should be included in the Catholic Bible as a second canon. Today the Apocrypha is included in only some Protestant Bibles, between the Old and New Testaments. It comprises the Books of Baruch, Judith, Maccabees, Tobias, and the Wisdom of Solomon, but excludes the Epistle of Jeremiah and Laodiceans, Susanna, the First and Second Books of Esdras, the Book of Bel and the Dragon, and the Prayer of Manasseh and Azariah. The only reference in the Apocrypha to the loss of the Ark concerns a character who lived before the Babylonian invasion, Jeremiah, who, it is written, hid the Ark of the Covenant in a cave on Mount Nebo, which is why it was not incorporated into the Second Temple when it was rebuilt around 535 BC. The Ark is mentioned only once more in the Old Testament in 2 Chronicles 35:3 in which King Josiah orders that the Ark should be returned to the temple: "Put the Holy Ark in the house which Solomon the son of David king of Israel did build; it shall not be a burden upon your shoulders."

That biblical reference dates King Josiah's command to around 623 BC so the Ark must have remained in the Second Temple as the Bible does not mention it being moved, which surely it would have done if the Ark had been moved again for reasons of safety. If we assume that the Ark remained in the Second Temple, if well hidden, up to 63 BC, when the Roman general Pompey conquered Jerusalem, it would have been there when he demanded to be allowed to enter the Holy of Holies. On his exit, it is alleged that he commented that he could not understand why there was so much secrecy about the sanctuary when it was just an empty room.

The Ark is mentioned only twice in the New Testament. One mention comes in Hebrews 9:2–5:

> For there was a tabernacle made; the first, wherein was the candlestick, and the table, and the shewbread; which is called the sanctuary.
> And after the second veil, the tabernacle which is called the Holiest of all;
> Which had the golden censer, and the Ark of the Covenant overlaid round about with gold, wherein was the golden pot that had manna, and Aaron's rod that budded, and the tables of the Covenant;
> And over it the cherubims of glory shadowing the mercy seat; of which we cannot now speak particularly.

The second mention is in Revelations 11:19: "And the temple of God was opened in heaven, and there was seen in his temple the Ark of his testament, and there were lightning, and voices, and thundering, and an earthquake, and great hail."

From these references it can be assumed that the Ark was so well hidden that it avoided being added to the plunder during the destruction of the Temple by Titus in AD 70 and, although it remains hidden today, its hiding place may have changed several times in the last two millennia. There is, of course, a legend that the Ark of the Covenant disappeared from Jerusalem more than 3,000 years ago, during the reign of King Solomon. According to the *Kebre Negast*, the Ethiopian version of the Bible, the Ark was taken to Ethiopia by Menelik I, the love-child and son of Solomon, born as a result of his union with Queen Makeda of Ethiopia, popularly known as the Queen of Sheba. According to Ethiopian records, the Ark has remained in Ethiopia since then. There is also a more widely accepted and credible version of the legend which claims that when Menelik reached manhood, he went to Jerusalem to meet Solomon, his father. While in Jerusalem, Solomon had a copy of the Ark made for his son and it was this copy that went to Ethiopia with Menelik. Today, some Ethiopians claim that the Ark of the Covenant is still located in a shrine in the Ethiopian town of Axum. Presumably this is the copy that Menelik took to Ethiopia because the Hebrew priest-hood would surely have done everything in its power to prevent the true Ark from leaving the Temple. In the tunnels under the Temple Mount, the Ark remained undis-covered by Roman, and later Muslim, occupiers until the Templar quest which began in 1108.

Two hundred years after the dissolution of the Templars and the flight of a few survivors to Scotland, Templar tradi-tions were incorporated in Masonic rituals. Early texts of these rituals state categorically that the Ark of the Covenant was hidden in a cave under the site of King Solomon's temple:

> In pursuance of your orders, we repaired to the secret vault, and let down one of the companions as before. The sun at this time was at its meridian height, the rays of which enabled him to discover a small box, or chest, standing on a pedestal, curiously wrought, and overlaid with gold, he gave the signal of ascending, and was immediately drawn out. We have brought the Ark up, for the examination of the grand council.

The Templar artefacts discovered by Warren and the letter written in 1912 by Captain Parker confirm the existence of a secret room carved into the rock beneath the Temple Mount, and there is circumstantial evidence that the Templars found the Ark of the Covenant. By the north door of Chartres Cathedral, there is a pillar with a carving which depicts the excavation of the Ark of the Covenant. Some have suggested that the carving depicts Menelik, the first emperor of Ethiopia, taking the Ark back to Jerusalem, but that is unlikely because Menelik I was unknown to Europeans before the fifteenth century and the great fire of

1194 which led to the rebuilding of Chartres Cathedral in 1209 had taken place two centuries earlier, so the masons would not have depicted Menelik unless the following legend was true. White-skinned Europeans were supposedly unknown on the African continent before the fifteenth century, but there is an Ethiopian legend which claims that a one-hundred-foot obelisk, made from the largest single piece of stone ever to be quarried, was erected at Axum by blond, fair-skinned men who did so by making use of some power from the Ark of the Covenant. It is possible that these mysterious blond men were Templars, and that they retrieved the Ark and bought it back to Europe because the carving on the pillar at Chartres Cathedral shows the Ark on a wheeled vehicle, and local legends claim that the Ark was hidden for decades in the crypt of the cathedral. Other legends have it that the Templars also discovered an archive of documents beneath the Temple Mount. Another piece of evidence, uncovered by Patrick Byrne, concerns the way in which most accounts of Templar history refer repeatedly to their "treasure." In 1291, when the Templars lost their foothold in the Holy Land, Tibald Gaudin, the Templar treasurer, was revered for having saved this "treasure" from the Muslim enemy, which suggests that the Templars considered that saving their "treasure" was more important than saving the people that they were supposed to be protecting. Tibald Gaudin's very act of saving the "treasure" warranted his immediate promotion and he became the penultimate Grand Master of the Templars. It would have been a disproportionate honour if Gaudin had been promoted simply for having brought a quantity of gold with him when escaping from the Muslim forces, but if he had saved the Ark of the Covenant, it would have been small recompense for his achievement. A third piece of circumstantial evidence relates to the disbandment and arrest of the French Templars in 1307, when they removed their "treasure" from their Temple in Paris, another occasion on which protecting their "treasure" seemed paramount when danger threatened.

No one knows the final resting place of the Ark, but, on the evidence available, and given that Hugues de Payens returned to France along with most of the rest of the original nine Knights Templar once the excavations beneath the Temple Mount had been completed, it would be reasonable to assume that the Ark returned with them to France. Of the original nine knights, Hugues de Payens, a Rex Deus family member, became the first Grand Master of the Knights Templar, under the political leadership of the Priory of Sion. Together, these two organizations aimed to unify Europe and the Middle East under a single monarchy. An extension of that aim was to see one God worshipped through the mediation of three prophets, namely Elijah, Jesus, and Mohammed. The Templars and the Priory of Sion wished for a utopia, in which humanity co-existed peacefully, with no religion held to be better, or more "true," than any other.

During the thirteenth century, the Priory of Sion and Rex Deus took charge, clandestinely, of what they claimed to be documented proof of Jesus's bloodline. At the same time, the Templars, too, secretly possessed documents proving Christ's bloodline, as well as possibly possessing the Ark of the Covenant, which they had retrieved from the Temple Mount in Jerusalem.

By 1120, the Templars had at least some of these powerful artefacts, and it was time for them to consolidate and expand. On one tour of recruitment in 1128, Grand Master Hugues de Payens and his lieutenant, André de Montbard, travelled to England to obtain from the Norman King Henry I safe conduct in England and across the border into Scotland. Once in Scotland, the two knights visited the St Clairs at Roslin, who were related by marriage to

Hugues de Payens. On hearing of the Templars' charter and their official backing by the Church of Rome, the Lord of Roslin granted immediate ownership of land to the new order. The land at Ballontrodoch is today named "Temple" after the Templar headquarters of Scotland.

It seems clear that the artefacts discovered by the Templars were kept hidden, available only to those with "eyes to see," within their political arms, the Priory of Sion, for example. It also seems clear that there is something hidden in the crypt at Rosslyn Chapel, but what it is, we cannot know until the keepers of the secret decide that the time is right for it to be revealed.

The Mystery of
Rennes-le-Château

In 1059, a church in the medieval city of Rhedae was
dedicated to the Magdalene. Once a large, prosperous, fortified town, Rhedae is now little more than a hamlet named
Rennes-le-Château, but it is at the very centre of one of the
greatest mysteries of our age. Of the countless books which
have been written about the village and its mysterious past,
one of the best is probably *The Holy Blood and the Holy Grail*
for those wanting a more detailed examination of the
mystery.

At the end of the second millennium, Rennes-le-Château
was a small, tranquil, mountain-top village set in the
beautiful countryside of the Languedoc. A few years later,
Dan Brown's book *The Da Vinci Code* had disrupted the
tranquility of the village, but the countryside remains as
beautiful and peaceful as before. The region was not always
as peaceful, though, as witnessed by the hundreds of
ossuaries dotted all over the region, which serve as a
reminder of the many bloody battles which took place in the
area. In 1908, when a road was being built up to the village,
the workmen discovered one such ossuary. It was several
hundred yards long, with skeletons stacked six to eight layers
deep, all of them oriented east to west. More recently, while

digging the foundations for a new water tower in the car park in Rennes, workers uncovered a ravine full of skeletons of bodies which had been unceremoniously dumped. The workers immediately filled in the ravine and relocated the foundations of the new water tower.

During the late nineteenth and early twentieth century, Bérenger Saunière, the priest at Rennes-le-Château, obtained large sums of money from a source which has never been established, and it is this wealth which lies at the root of the mystery. Saunière became a local benefactor, using some of his acquired wealth to fund the construction of the afore-mentioned road. (It should be stressed that Bérenger Saunière is in no way connected with the fictitious character who appears in *The Da Vinci Code*, although the history of Rennes-le-Château does form part of the plot of Dan Brown's novel.)

In the thirteenth century, the city of Rhedae was system-atically pillaged over a number of years and became almost a forgotten town. Then, in 1231, during the Albigensian Crusade, Pierre de Voisins, a military man founded a family dynasty, beginning work on the present château. De Voisins also assisted in the rebuilding of parts of Rhedae, but it was left to his grandson to build a church, which was dedicated to St Peter. Rhedae became the most important city of the region once again, but then misfortune befell its citizens in the form of hordes of armed bandits, who attacked the city. This was the beginning of a campaign of systematic rape and pillage, in which harvests were burned and Rhedae's citizens mercilessly slaughtered. A final act of terrorism occurred when a Spanish bandit, Count Henri de Trastamarre, besieged Rhedae. Despite strong resistance by de Voisins and the inhabitants of the city, the attackers razed the fortifications, destroyed the Church of St Peter, and slaughtered most of the survivors. Rhedae's final demise as a city came when plague struck the handful of survivors who had escaped slaughter. From that time, the city of Rhedae ceased to exist, and only nearby Carcassonne remained to provide testimony to two millennia of turbulent history. Today, only the small village of Rennes-le-Château, with its few houses located around the château of the de Voisins family and the Church of St Magdalene, remain. The de Voisins family name seems to have died out in the late fourteenth century with the birth of a daughter named Jeanne de Voisins, who married a Spaniard, Sicard de Marquefave. They had a daughter, Blanche de Marquefave, who, in 1422, married Henri d'Hautpoul. Her dowry to her husband included the title of Baron of Rennes. Henri, Baron d'Hautpoul, immediately took the title of Seigneur de Blanchefort. In 1732, the last Marquis de Blanchefort married Marie de Nègre Dables, who became Lady d'Hautpoul de Blanchefort. Thirty years later, Lady Marie d'Hautpoul de Blanchefort was left a widow, with no male heir. In January 1781, Lady d'Hautpoul de Blanchefort, who was the trustee of a great secret which had been passed down in her family from generation to generation, felt that her death was imminent and prepared herself to join her husband in the family vault. Without a male heir and not wanting to take her secret to the grave with her, Marie de Blanchefort confided in, and gave some important documents to, her confessor, Father Antoine Bigou, who had been the parish priest at Rennes-le-Château for seven years. Although many church records were destroyed during the French Revolution, surviving records show that Father Bigou was also the personal chaplain to the de Blanchefort family, the prominent local landowners. On her deathbed, Marie requested that Father Bigou pass on the mysterious secret to someone worthy of receiving it. Whatever that secret was, it terrified Father Bigou.

A page in the parish records from the late eighteenth

century contains the words, "... *us de galillée n'est point ici*," which translates as, ". . . us from Galilee is not here." Was Father Bigou recording his thoughts that Jesus from Galilee was not represented here in the church at Rennes-le-Château? On 17 January, 1781, the Marquise Marie d'Hautpoul de Blanchefort died peacefully at the age of sixty-seven at her château in Rennes, and so began the mystery.

In 1781, France was in a state of pre-revolutionary unrest which led eventually to the revolution of 1789. From 1781 until the revolution began, Father Bigou lived in terror of the secret which he had been told. He decided to hide the documents which he had been given in a Visigothic pillar which supported the altar in his church, and he left clues for future generations as to the nature of the terrible secret which had been confided to him. In 1791, fearing for his life, Father Bigou made plans to escape to Spain, but before he fled, he took steps to prevent his dreadful secret from falling into revolutionary, or atheist, hands. He concealed the entrance to an ancient crypt inside the church with a sculptured stone slab, placed face down. The slab's hidden face portrayed a knight and a child on the same horse. In the churchyard, he had a large gravestone laid flat on the tomb of Marie de Blanchefort, and a headstone placed on the grave of the marquis. The inscription on the headstone had numerous irregularities in the form of Latin cryptograms, one of which, when translated from Greek, read "*ET IN ARCADIA EGO.*"

In 1792, with the guillotine in daily action to rid France of right-wing church authorities and the nobility, the revolutionary Committee for Public Safety declared that Father Antoine Bigou was a rebellious priest. Fearing for his life, Bigou fled to Sabadell, in Spain, where he died eighteen months later. During those eighteen months, he became acquainted with Father Cauneille, another exiled French priest, to whom he passed on his secret. Before he, too, died, Father Cauneille passed the secret on to two other priests, who, once the Terror was over, returned to Republican France. One of the two priests was Father Jean Vié, who, from 1840 to 1870, was the parish priest of Rennes-les-Bains. The other priest was Father Emile Francois Cayron, the parish priest of Saint-Laurent-de-la-Cabrerisse, in the Aude. Supposedly, the two priests claimed that a vast, price-less treasure was buried in the district between Rennes-le-Château and Rennes-les-Bains, in twelve hiding places which Marie de Blanchefort had confided to Father Antoine Bigou. The two priests knew that Father Bigou had left a coded message, the key to which had been inserted in the epitaph on the headstone of the marquis's grave. As to the documents hidden in the church, both priests were aware of their existence and of their extraordinary historical impor-tance. In 1872, Father Henri Boudet succeeded Father Jean Vié as the parish priest of Rennes-les-Bains. The second priest, Abbé Cayron, who had been Boudet's tutor and had been entrusted with the secret, informed Boudet of the Mystery of Rennes-le-Château.

Jean Jacques Henri Boudet was born in Quillan in 1837. He came from a poor family, but showed great intelligence at an early age, which persuaded Father Cayron to become Boudet's tutor and to help form his character. Boudet became a highly educated and cultured man, who was well versed in Latin and Greek. For some unknown reason, he also learnt Saxon, but his main interest was archaeology. Eventually, he entered the Carcassonne seminary and gained a degree in English. He was always a thin, sickly man with a taciturn nature, and so took up walking in order to improve his poor health. In December 1861, Boudet was ordained a priest, and appointed to Durban the following month. Six months later, in June 1862, he transferred to Caunes, in the Minervois, where he stayed for four years until November 1866, at which time he was sent to Frestes. Father Boudet remained at Frestes until his transfer to Rennes-les-Bains in 1872, where he took over from the deceased Abbé Vié. In 1887, at the age of fifty, while he was the priest at Rennes-les-Bains, Father Boudet published a book, *The True Celtic Language and the Stone Circle of Rennes-les-Bains*. The book made Father Boudet a significant figure in the unravelling of the secrets of Rennes-le-Château, but it was also much criticized. It was suggested that the author of the book lived in a fantasy world, and had falsified gravestones in the cemetery. Some critics also alleged that the author had falsified some of the evidence presented in the book by changing the locations of some stone crosses, and actually erecting new ones. The book received only one good review from a critic named Reverend Father Vannier, who came close to under-standing the contents of the book when he wrote, "Father Boudet is the keeper of a secret which could be the cause of major upheavals." Father Boudet concealed in the text of his book the secret which Marie de Blanchefort had confided to Father Bigou over one hundred years previously, of a treasure hidden in twelve chests in twelve different locations. The author specifically stated that the text in the book was written in such a manner as to allow the reader to locate the treasure by interpreting a word in the book composed in a foreign language and then by deciphering the text. Father Boudet also claimed that the contents of the book would be incomprehensible to anyone who did not possess the keys to the ciphers. Any reader who knew the secret code or number, which was also hidden in the text of the book, would therefore be able to locate the chests. Father Boudet also wrote of a sculpted head, which became known as the *Tête du Sauveur*, which had originally adorned a small shrine near the village, and had a code engraved on its back. Boudet claimed that he had been given the head by local residents because of his interest in archaeology, but there were claims that Father Boudet had actually removed the head from the shrine and fixed it to the garden wall of his presbytery. Today, the head is on display in a local museum. Henry Lincoln claims that the head was removed from its original site and located close to the garden wall so that the engraving on the rear of the head would be hidden from the public. As a result of the criticism of his book, Father Boudet conspired with Father Bérenger Saunière, who had become the parish priest of Rennes-le-Château in June, 1885, to make a permanent record of the d'Hautpoul secret. The permanent record was to be contained in the décor and artefacts of the Church of St Magdalene, where Bérenger Saunière was the priest. Thus Father Saunière became the accomplice of Father Boudet in the renovation of the dilapidated Church of St Magdalene in Rennes-le-Château.

François Bérenger Saunière was born on 11 April, 1852, in the small village of Montazels, across the valley from Rennes-le-Château. He went to school at St Louis, in Limoux, but soon earned a reputation as an insolent, independent fundamentalist, who rebelled against authority. In June 1879, at the age of twenty-two, he entered the seminary in Carcassonne and was later ordained as a priest. He served at Alet, and was appointed, in 1882, as priest in the deanery of Clat, until 1885. During his period of service at Clat he became a teacher in the seminary in Narbonne. It was during those early years that the first of several mysterious deaths of Saunière's associates occurred. Apparently, the young Saunière had found some documents written in an old form of Latin dating from Virgil's time. Saunière's Latin was not adequate to the task of translating these documents, so he sought the help of a notary in the village of Quillan. The contents of the document are unknown, but it is possible that they contained something that Saunière wished to be kept secret because, after the notary had translated the document for Saunière, something strange happened. That summer, the notary and Saunière took a party of children from the village for a ramble on a local, rocky hillside. As they led the group of children up the steep path, disaster struck: Saunière slipped and fell, injuring himself, and, in doing so, caused the notary to fall to his death. The police enquiry and subsequent inquest absolved Saunière of any blame, but this was not the only mysterious death that cast a shadow over Saunière during his lifetime.

Saunière's superiors found him undisciplined and, in June 1885, after the death of the notary, he was appointed to the sleepy village Rennes-le-Château where it was hoped that he would fade into obscurity and no longer trouble the Church authorities. But it was not to be, for when Saunière first came to Rennes-le-Château, he lodged at the presbytery with the Denarnaud family, who had a daughter named Marie. Saunière was not on the best of terms with Marie's mother so he eventually moved, into a building next to the churchyard and appointed Marie Denarnaud as his "housekeeper." The relationship between Saunière and his "housekeeper" continued until his death in 1917. Saunière, never one to hide his light under a bushel, caused more trouble for the Church authorities when, during the elections of 1885, he preached two inflammatory sermons, encouraging his parishioners to vote against the Republicans, who were anti-Catholic. The sermons confirmed Saunière's anti-Republican or, to be more precise, royalist tendencies, which must have made him quite a few enemies within the establishment. The prefect punished him by forcing him to leave the diocese from December 1885 to July 1886 and to teach once more in the seminary of Narbonne. But the villagers of Rennes-le-Château protested to the prefect and petitioned for Saunière's return. It is also possible that Father Boudet intervened with the authorities to have Saunière reinstated at Rennes-le-Château. The authorities finally relented, and the royalist Saunière returned to the fold of his local monarchist friends. Early in 1887, Johann of Hapsburg, who, as a member of a Rex Deus family, and also the Archduke of Austro-Hungaria, travelled incognito to visit Saunière. The Archduke travelled under the name of Monsieur Guillaume, and presented himself as an emissary from the Comtesse de Chambord, who was also of the House of Hapsburg, and also a Rex Deus family member.

The Comtesse de Chambord was the widow of Henri de Bourbon, the uncrowned Henri V of France. Henri, the Pretender to the throne of France, had died in 1885, and with his death had gone any hope of an imminent Bourbon restoration. This left the Comtesse de Chambord with only one option, which was to attempt to establish her children's position as claimants to the throne. To do this, she sought the help of the staunchly royalist Saunière. It is alleged that the emissary made an offer to Saunière, and, as a royalist, it can be assumed that Saunière would have agreed to help the Comtesse, even without an offer of a financial reward. The emissary offered Saunière 3,000 francs towards the restoration of the church if the priest would search for something that was supposed to have been hidden by Father Bigou, one of Saunière's predecessors. Whether Saunière knew what he was looking for or to what use it would be put is a moot point, but he may have received a hint that there were genealogical records hidden in the church that related to the bloodline of the French royal family. Saunière accepted the emissary's offer, and began to search for the documents. The search proved difficult, but in 1891, when Saunière removed the altar in the course of the restoration, two sixth-century, Visigothic supporting columns were revealed, one of which had the Visigothic "cross of silence" sculpted into it. It was originally claimed that hidden inside one of the columns, preserved in wooden tubes, were four parchment scrolls, however, it is now known that the pillars were not hollow, so the parchments could not have been found in this way. What is certain is that the parchments had been hidden inside the church, but where exactly Saunière found them remains a mystery. Another report claimed that while the heavy altar stone was being handled, it cracked a flagstone and a *capsa* was revealed beneath the flagstone. *Capsa* is the Latin word for a box or chest, and a capsa would often be buried in a secure place near the altar and used to store holy relics, such as the bones of saints. It is claimed that in the *capsa* in the church in Rennes-le-Château were a few gold coins and pieces of jewellery, which had belonged to a local aristocrat, who had entrusted them to Father Bigou following the execution of Louis XVI, and before the aristocrat escaped from France. It is alleged that when Saunière found the treasure hoard, he suspended all work on the church, though not, it is claimed, before a workman had seen Saunière remove a wooden tube with wax seals from inside the *capsa*.

It is possible that documents were found in the *capsa*, or elsewhere inside the church, though there is no conclusive proof that Saunière found any parchments at all. According to Alan Scott, the only verifiable evidence of any parchments was a small scrap discovered by a bell ringer as he entered the belfry. At the time, the stairs to the belfry were being replaced, and the baluster had been thrown out for disposal. The bell ringer saw something glinting in a crack in the wood and, when he looked more closely, he saw a small glass vial with a scrap of parchment inside. He handed this to the priest and, the next day, Saunière ordered a hole to be excavated, just in front of the altar. It does not really matter where in the church the parchments were found; what is important is the allegation that Father Bigou, one of Saunière's predecessors, had written and hidden the scrolls in the pre-revolutionary late 1780s. It is claimed that two of the scrolls contained genealogies covering the period from 1244 to 1644. Among these parchments were Latin texts of extracts from the New Testament, one of which was illogically spaced, suggesting a coded message. As a student of Latin, Saunière must have been intrigued by the poor Latin grammar. He sought help with the coded parchments from Father Boudet, who now had Saunière as his inside man firmly entrenched in Rennes-le-Château. Boudet recommended that Saunière take the parchments to Monsignor Félix Billard, the Bishop of Carcassonne. When Monsignor Billard saw the manuscripts, he paid for Saunière to travel to the seminary of Saint Sulpice, in Paris, were Saunière was ordered to have the parchments examined by religious scholars schooled in ancient Latin. Saunière stayed in Paris for five days, during which time he was introduced to an esoteric circle of acquaintances, including the famous occultist, Emile Hoffet, an acknowledged author on Freemasonry. Another of those to whom he was introduced was the singer Emma Calvé, who, it is alleged, became for many years Saunière's lover. Another member of this esoteric circle was Joseph Péladan, who, in 1891, founded the cabbalistic order of the Rose Cross of the Temple and the Grail. Over the next few years, these people would be frequent guests of Saunière at Rennes-le-Château. When Saunière returned from Paris, he reported back to Boudet, and the pair went to work to unravel the secret of Rennes-le-Château. It is possible that Father Henri Boudet used his knowledge of the secret to prompt the emissary to visit Saunière in the first place, but what is certain is that after the emissary's visit, Saunière and Father Boudet became close friends, and both of them threw themselves into attempting to unravel the secret of Rennes-le-Château for the rest of their lives. Father Boudet remained as priest of Rennes-les-Bains until ill health forced him to retire in 1914. He died of stomach cancer the following year.

In the Dagobert Parchment, it is clear that certain letters are raised above the line of the text. When these letters are abstracted from the Latin text, they form a message in French, which reads:

"*A DAGOBERT II ROI ET A SION EST CE TRESOR ET IL EST LÀ MORT*," which translates as, "THIS TREASURE BELONGS TO DAGOBERT II KING AND TO SION AND HE IS THERE DEAD." In the Dagobert Parchment, a simple code can be found, which was originally decoded by Henry Lincoln. While on holiday, Lincoln was reading a French paperback, *Le Tresor Maudit*, in which the parchment was reproduced. The simple code contained in the parchment was not mentioned in the book and Lincoln could not understand the omission given that it was a very basic code. Thus began his lifelong quest to solve the mystery. The code was a reference to the assassination of King Dagobert II, allegedly orchestrated by the Church when it reneged on a contract between itself and the Merovingian dynasty, made when King Clovis was baptized into the Catholic Church in AD 496. King Dagobert II, the last Merovingian monarch, was murdered in AD 679. It is possible that the Church betrayed Dagobert because his dynasty claimed descent from Jesus, and the Church wanted the alleged bloodline eliminated, for obvious reasons. The parchment also contained other codes, written deliberately ungrammatically. In the second parchment, which Lincoln calls the Geometrical Parchment, he draws attention to what he calls "the geometric substructure of the parchment." This pentagonal geometry can be found on large-scale survey maps of the area of Languedoc surrounding Rennes-le-Château. It can also be seen in man-made and natural features in the landscape. The Geometric Parchment was deciphered using the moves of a "knight's tour" on a chessboard. The "knight's tour" is a logic puzzle in which a player uses a knight's moves to "jump" once, and once only, to every square on a chess board. There is only one solution to the puzzle. When the "knight's tour" is applied, it reveals a strange, coded message, which reads, "SHEPHERDESS NO TEMPTATION THAT POUSSIN TENIERS HOLD THE KEY PEACE 681 BY THE CROSS AND THIS HORSE OF GOD I COMPLETE THIS DAEMON GUARDIAN AT MIDDAY BLUE APPLES." It is uncertain to which of the *Temptation* paintings by the artist Teniers the Younger it refers, but the encoded message certainly adds to the mystery of Rennes-le-Château. Two of the *Temptation* paintings have as their subject St Anthony the Hermit, which could offer a clue. St Anthony's feast day is celebrated on 17 January, a date which recurs continually in the Rennes-le-Château mystery. It is also to be found on the vertical tombstone, part of the inscription on which reads, "Here lies the noble Marie de Nègre d'Arles, La Dame d'Hautpoul de Blanchefort, aged sixty-seven, died 17 January 1781. May she rest in peace." Interestingly, the date inscribed on the tombstone is incorrect; it should be MDCCLXXXI, rather than MDCOLXXXI.

Father Bigou had hidden the parchments in 1781, during his time at Rennes-le-Château when he was the confessor to Marie d'Hautpoul Blanchefort. Saunière's investigations led him to discover that the same coded message on the parchment was on the tombstone of Marie d'Hautpoul in the churchyard. In 1906, the Scientific Research Society of the Aude made a field trip to Rennes-le-Château and made a copy of that particular tombstone. The following is an extract from the *Bulletin de la Société d'études scientifiques de l'Aude* (Bulletin of the Scientific Research Society of the Aude), Volume XVII, 1906: "A visit to the cemetery enabled us to discover, in a corner, a wide tombstone, broken in the middle, on which one could read a very crudely engraved inscription. This tombstone measured 1.3 metres by 0.65 metres." The horizontal tombstone, or flagstone, laid on the marchioness's tomb by Father Bigou in 1791, ten years after her death, has carved into it the words, "ET IN ARCADIA EGO," which translates as, "I who am also in Arcadia."

Saunière later obliterated the inscriptions on the tombstones, but he was too late; a copy had already been made. The secret that the priest tried to suppress by vandalizing his own churchyard was out, but what was he trying to hide? Perhaps we will never know, but the church holds enough other mysteries, along with some answers, to keep the most energetic sleuth occupied for years to come.

To add to the mystery, until the late 1980s, there was a tomb in the village of Arques, approximately three miles from the Château de Blanchefort and six miles from Rennes-le-Château, which featured in Poussin's famous painting *Les Bergers d'Arcadie*, or *The Arcadian Shepherds*. The Poussin painting shows shepherds around a tomb containing the mysterious inscription, "Et in Arcadia Ego." The tomb at Argues was destroyed in April 1988 by Monsieur Roussett, the owner of the land, with the full agreement of the local authorities because trespassing on his property by treasure hunters had reached an unacceptable level. The destroyed tomb dated back to the beginning of the twentieth century, but local traditions claimed that it had replaced a much older tomb on the same spot.

The initial gift of 3,000 francs from the Comtesse de Chambord to induce Saunière to begin a search of the church property was not Saunière's only source of money. During the late nineteenth and early twentieth century, Bérenger Saunière received large sums of money from sources which have never been established. For most of his time at Rennes-le-Château, Saunière used the money to lead the life of a very rich man. He ate only the best food, and his cellar was stocked with the finest wines, though he also spent vast sums on the refurbishment of the local church and the development of the church property, and on improvements to the village to benefit the inhabitants. One of the additions to the church property was the *Tour Magdala*, the Tower of the Magdalene, built to overhang a precipitous chasm. The location of this structure could be considered a rich man's folly, but, in times of danger – and Saunière certainly had enemies – he could shut and bar an iron door, which gave access to a flat castellated roof, which would provide sanctuary until the danger had passed. The basic purpose of the *Tour Magdala* was to house Saunière's library, but it also had a more important use. From the tower's roof, Saunière was able to view all the compass points that can be aligned on a map to form the sacred geometric pentagon, the points of which are the crux of the mystery of Rennes-le-Château. *Magdala*, in Hebrew, means "tower," and Tour Magdala can be translated as "the tower of the flock," which was a title given to the Egyptian goddess Isis. There is also a reference in the Book of Micah to "the tower of the flock," who became the *magdala*, or shepherd of the people (flock) of Israel (Micah 4:8): "And thou, O tower of the flock, the strong hold of the daughter of Zion, unto thee shall it come, even the first dominion; the kingdom shall come to the daughter of Jerusalem."

Margaret Starbird also makes the point that the epithet *Magdala*, which means, literally, "tower," or "elevated, great, magnificent," when applied to Mary, Jesus's companion, would have been the Hebrew equivalent of calling her "Mary the Great." The Magdala was also symbolic to the custodians of the secret of Rennes-le-Château, and to the Priory of Sion which adopted the mantle of the shepherd of Zionism, the object of which was to restore the line of David to a European royal house.

On 17 January, 1917, Saunière suffered a fatal stroke and died five days later. The day after his death, a chair was positioned on the doorstep of his library on the terrace of the Tour Magdala, and Saunière's body, robed in a tasselled cloak, was placed in the chair. A cortege of mourners passed by the robed body and each mourner plucked a tassel from the robe. This may have been a symbolic gesture when one considers that the robes of both the Merovingian monarchs and the Nazoreans were similarly fringed with tassels. Folklore claims that the tassels held curative powers. The bizarre act of plucking off the tassels has never been explained and can surely only be understood in terms of Saunière having been a champion for the restoration of a Merovingian dynasty, in which case supporters were giving him a symbolic farewell. Equally bizarrely, and mysteriously, Saunière's housekeeper, Marie Dernaud, allegedly ordered a coffin for Saunière just five days before he had his stroke. With Saunière's death, the secret of the source of his wealth passed to Marie Dernaud, who promised to reveal it before she died.

After Saunière's death in 1917, Marie Dernaud continued to enjoy the benefits of his wealth, but, in 1945, at the end of the Second World War, the French government issued new French francs and any money that Marie Dernaud had accumulated became valueless. Local residents in the village recall her burning vast quantities of the old paper francs in her garden in 1945. Marie Dernaud had lived in the Villa Bethania with Saunière, as his "housekeeper" for half a century, but the revaluation of the French currency had impoverished her, and she was forced to sell the Villa Bethania to raise funds. The house was bought by Monsieur Noel Corbu, who let Marie Dernaud live on in the house on the understanding that she would one day tell him the secret that he hoped would make him a rich and powerful man. Unfortunately, in 1953, Marie Dernaud, too, suffered a stroke, which left her paralysed and unable to speak. In her last few days, Noel Corbu nursed her and, if he learned anything from her before she died, he, too, took the secret to his grave when he was killed in a suspicious car crash in 1953, which had all the hallmarks of having been an "arranged accident." Was the source of Saunière's wealth the lost Templar treasure, the gold which had disappeared along with the Templar fleet in 1307? Perhaps it was the lost treasure of the Cathars who had lived in the area, or alchemists' gold, the source of which lies hidden in the mysteries of alchemy? At least one Grand Master of the Priory of Sion, Nicolas Flamel (1398–1418), was an alchemist. Could Saunière have been making gold? The wealth could also have come from gold buried by the Visigoths. Or it is also conceivable that Saunière was blackmailing the Vatican with a secret that had the potential to seriously harm the Vatican. There is some circumstantial evidence which points to the last possibility, for example, the priest who attended Saunière to grant absolution was so shocked by his confession that he denied him final absolution and the last rites.

The source of Saunière's wealth, however, is only one aspect of the mystery of Rennes-le-Château. There have also been a number of unexplained deaths and unsolved murders. Jean-Antoine-Maurice Gelis was a priest, who, towards the end of his long life, became a hermit with paranoid tendencies. He would allow only his niece to visit him, to bring him food and other necessities. Eventually, she became his only contact with the outside world and the only person he would admit to his presbytery. However, despite his precautions, he was murdered, on All Saints' Eve in 1897. He was assaulted with fire tongs, and then killed with four well-aimed blows from an axe. Bizarrely, the killer then re-positioned the Gelis's body with his hands crossed over his chest, seemingly in an act of respect, before he or she ransacked the room, as if searching for something. It is not known if the murderer, or murderers, found what they were looking for. No money or valuables were taken and the killer, or killers, were never apprehended.

Another mysterious death occurred in December, 1901, when Monsignor Billard, Bishop of Carcassonne and a staunch supporter and friend of Saunière, died while under investigation by the Vatican for the mismanagement of money left to the Church in the wills of rich parishioners. A statue in Saunière's garden commemorates a visit in June, 1897, from Monsignor Billard, who was replaced as Bishop of Carcassonne by the Abbé de Beausejour, who became an opponent of both Saunière and Boudet.

In 1956, three sets of human remains were found buried in Saunière's garden. They were all male, aged between thirty and forty at the time of their death, and all three had died of gunshot wounds. There is no record of any investigation relating to the remains. The men may have been killed during the Second World War, or perhaps they were the murderers who had killed Father Gelis, before making an unsuccessful attack on the occupants of Saunière's house. It is likely that no one will ever know.

The Church at Rennes-le-Château

To understand more fully the mystery of Rennes-le-Château, it is necessary to know the history and artefacts of the Church of St Madeleine in some detail (pictures of the artworks at Rennes-le-Château can be seen on-line at www.cleveleyswriters.co.uk). The church was consecrated in 1059 and lies in the Languedoc in the heart of what was once Cathar country. The exterior of the church is typical of many village churches in the area, except for the small entrance porch with a pitched roof which was added by Saunière. The small roof helps to protect some ornate carvings above the door, above which there is a cross with a ribbon-like motif draped over it which reads, "*In Hoc Signo Vinces*" (In This Sign You Will Conquer), the vision supposed to have appeared in the sky before the Emperor Constantine's victory at the Battle of Milvian Bridge. Beneath the cross is a carved figure of Mary Magdalene (her identity is indicated on a circular plaque below her feet) carrying a cross which points south-east. Below the plaque is a lengthy Latin inscription which contains deliberate errors, such as the words *soeculi*, *anorem*, *quen*, and *cremini*, all misspelled. The original, complete with spelling errors, reads, "*Regnum mundi et omnem ornatum soeculi contempsi propter anorem domini mei Jesu Christi quem vidi quen amavi in quem cremini quem dilexi*," which translates as, "I have had contempt for the kingdom of this world, and all temporal adornments, because of the love of my Lord Jesus Christ, whom I saw, whom I loved, in whom I believed, and whom I worshipped."

Together, the words can be formed into two Latin anagrams. The misspelled words (*soeculi*, *anorem*, *quen*, and *cremini*) form the first anagram, "*norma sic inire lucem nequeo*" which translates as, "normally I cannot enter the light this way." This may be a message from Saunière that the way to the truth cannot be found through the Church.

The second anagram of the four words is "*e lumine es norma circinoque*" which translates as, "You are conformable to the light by means of the square and the compass," which seems to hint at a connection with Freemasonry, which has the square and the compass as its emblem.

The final inscription in the porch is taken from the Vulgate Book of Genesis 28:17: "*pavensque quam terribilis inquit est locus iste non est hic aliud nisi domus Dei et porta caeli*." Saunière paraphrased the original Latin text and divided it into three sections. The prominent central section above the door reads, "*TERRIBILIS EST LOCUS ISTE.*" The Latin inscription on either side of this paraphrase is an oblique reference to a quotation from the Gospel: "my house will be a house of prayer; you have made it a den of thieves." Was Saunière hinting, subversively, at misdeeds of the Church?

At the entrance to the church, there is the usual water stoup, but a very unusual one. It is supported by a statue of Rex Mundi, also known as the devil Amadeus, who is mentioned in the Book of Tobias. Amadeus was supposedly the bad god of this earthly kingdom, while a good god ruled over the afterlife. This concept of two gods is known as dualism, and was the central concept of Cathar belief. The figure of Rex Mundi appears to be staring, wide-eyed, at the sixty-four black and white squares paving the floor of the church, as if drawing attention to it. The right hand of the devil forms a circle. Some suggestions have been made as to the significance of this gesture, but, in fact, there is nothing mysterious in the encircling fingers. The hand in question originally held a trident, traditionally believed to be the devil's weapon, which has long since been removed, either by souvenir hunters or by the wardens of the church. The statue of Amadeus has a belt, or ring, of gold around his waist. Some claim that this is a clue directing the initiated towards the coat of arms of a descendant of King Sigebert I, who was named King Jean XI, and bore the Latin motto "*Et in Arcadia Ego*" on his coat or arms.

The coat of arms comprises the upper part of a suit of armour placed on a vertically striped heraldic field, with a fleur-de-lys in its centre, encircled by a ring of gold. Above Rex Mundi and below the water stoup is a pair of salamanders, which mythology claimed were born from flames, surrounded by a carving of rising flames. Above the salamanders is a small oval plaque with the letters BS, which may be simply the initials of Bernard Saunière. The original lettering was considerably more ornate, as can be seen in older photographs, but the plaque has been crudely painted over.

Crowning the water stoup are four angels, each one making one of the hand movements required in making the sign of the cross. The uppermost angel appears to be gazing into the distance, and the angel at the bottom is pointing down with her left hand.

So the stoup depicts Rex Mundi, the devil or lord of the earth, accompanied by two salamanders, which mythically represent fire; and it is filled with water and adorned by four angels, who represent the free spirits of air. In other words, it depicts earth, fire, water, and air: the four basic elements of alchemy. Did Saunière dabble in alchemy? Is it conceivable that alchemy might offer some explanation of the source of his wealth?

The chequered floor of the church is laid out to represent a chessboard with sixty-four black and white squares, aligned with the four points of the compass. During the restoration and redesign of the church by Saunière and Father Boudet, they used two chess boards in Boudet's studio to give a field of 128 squares, instead of the usual sixty-four squares of a single chessboard, to help decode the parchment created by Abbé Bigou, the resident priest before the French Revolution. After many nights spent contemplating the manuscript and trying to decode it, Father Boudet finally used the "knight's tour" of the chessboard to reconstruct the text of the message. The deciphered text, which is given in full in a previous chapter, ends with the "signature" blue apples, which, coincidentally, are to be found in an anagram on the gravestone of the Marquise d'Hautpoul de Blanchefort.

Beyond the stoup is the confessional. Set into the domed ceiling above the confessional is an extremely elaborate, and most peculiar, three-dimensional fresco, which depicts the Sermon on the Mount, though it contains some strange elements. With the exception of Jesus, the fresco depicts only three other males; the remaining figures are six females, a baby, and young child. One woman, to the right in the foreground, is asleep, reclining against a man. At the base of the mount is a moneybag with a hole torn in it, through which can be seen what appear to be gold coins. The mount itself is adorned with scattered pink roses, possibly a clue to Masonic Rosicrucians. To the left of the landscape in the background, perched on a hill, is a castle or monastery, while to the right of Jesus is what appears to be a walled city. One very peculiar feature of the fresco is a small, stooped figure to the right of the mount, who is peering into a bush. Henry Lincoln has deciphered part of the inscription below the fresco, which, in French, reads, "*VENEZ A MOI VOUS TOUS QUI SOUFFREZ ET QUI ETES ACCABLES ET JE VOUS SOULAGERAI*" (Come unto me all you who labour and are heavy laden and I will give you rest). In the original French text, Saunière changed one word from the standard French biblical quotation, but retained the meaning of the whole. Lincoln discovered that there is a thin white line in the fresco to draw the reader's attention to the two words, and the letters are written in different sizes: "*ETES ACCALBLES*." When the words are divided into *SAC A BLES*, we are left with the message to look at the "sack of corn", which is French slang for "sack of money."

To the right of the confessional is a strange statue depicting John the Baptist dressed as a Roman soldier and carrying a cross in his left hand, which has a ribbon draped over its crosspiece. Why would Saunière have chosen to depict John as a Roman soldier? The ribbon bears the Greek letters for Alpha and Omega, and John is standing over a figure of Jesus, who appears submissive to Roman authority in a posture which is almost a mirror image of the posture of Rex Mundi. What did Saunière mean by these strange images?

At the top of each Station of the Cross is the usual crucifix, but in Saunière's church, the base of each crucifix is adorned with five pink roses, which seem to imply some link to the Rosicrucians. Many of the stations have other strange features. Station I shows Jesus being interrogated by a red-haired Pilate. Alongside Pilate, is a black child holding a white dish which contains the water in which Pilate washes his hands. Lincoln suggests a link between the white dish and the black child, pointing out that on a nearby road to Rennes-les-Bains there is a Templar *commanderie* named Blanchefort (white castle). The commanderie is located on top of a black rock, known as *le Roco Negro*, above a *plateau blanc*, which can be translated as "white dish." In the Station painting, Pilate wears a long, purple headpiece which reaches down his back and has a piece of purple cloth draped over his knees and falling onto the pedestal steps, purple being the colour that denotes royalty. In the background, behind Pilate, a man is depicted with his right arm raised above his head, clutching a golden egg; he has his back to the proceedings. Below the black child's feet, there is a golden griffin, a mythical animal with the head of a lion and the wings of an eagle, which was held to be the protector of golden treasure. What does the golden egg symbolize? Does it represent some actual treasure, or does it symbolize "hush money" that the Church had been paying to Saunière to suppress the truth about the Magdalene and the Holy Grail (*Sang Raal* or Holy Blood)?

Station II seems to have only one unexplained mystery: why is there a man stooping to retrieve a stick at Jesus's feet? Station VI depicts Veronica wiping Jesus's face. It has been suggested by some that the cloth depicted in the painting has been painted in the form of a pelican, a bird which stores food in its pouch to feed its young. To the ancients, this seemed to be an act of regurgitation, which gave rise to the myth that the pelican pecked at itself to draw blood to feed its young. This, in turn, led to the pelican being adopted as a symbolic icon in alchemy, to represent the touchstone or Philosopher's Stone, which was supposedly used to transmute base metals into silver or gold – another message, perhaps, from Saunière.

Station VI contains another pictorial message, again recognized by Henry Lincoln, who chanced upon it when he was writing descriptions in French for some of the actions in the painting. In the top, left-hand corner is a

Roman soldier grasping a "high shield" (in French, *haut bouclier*); behind the tower can be seen the right-hand half of a tower (*demi tour*), which can also mean "half a turn"; Station VI is often referred to as "Veronica with the Cloth" (*Veronica au Lin*); and, finally, the man helping Jesus with the cross is Simon of Cyrene, whose gaze seems to be up and away from the scene (in French, *Simon regarde*). Lincoln combined all these phrases in a sentence: *Haut bouclier demi tour Veronica au lin Simon regarde.* Pronounced phonetically, this would resemble: *Au bout clier demi tour, vers haut nid kaolin, Simon regarde*, which, in English, is, "At the enclosure, make a half turn towards the high China-clay peak Simon looks at." If the "enclosure" is taken to be the church cemetery, a "half turn" would leave one facing towards Cardou, a mountain of kaolin, or China clay; in the middle distance is the Temple *commanderie* of Blanchefort.

Station VIII seems to hint at a Masonic connection. The customary daughters of Jerusalem are shown meeting Jesus, but one woman with a black veil could be a widow, who is holding the hand of a child dressed in tartan. Freemasons often describe themselves as the "Children of the Widow," and in cryptic Masonic language, "Will no one help this poor son of the Widow?" is a request for help from another mason. Or perhaps the tartan is intended to draw attention to the House of Stuart, which had strong Masonic connections in France.

In the painting of Station IX, as in all the other paintings, Jesus is wearing a red cloak, perhaps signifying the House of Austria and the Hapsburgs. As Jesus stumbles and falls for the first time, a bare-chested soldier wearing a Frankish helmet grasps his cape. Could the red cape be intended to indicate that the Hapsburg dynasty of Austria was descended from Jesus? There is evidence that Archduke Johann von Hapsburg, cousin to Franz Josef, Emperor of

Austria, made several visits to Saunière; bank statements prove that Saunière and Archduke Johann opened consecutively numbered bank accounts on the same day, and that a substantial amount of money was transferred from the archduke to Saunière that same day.

Station X shows Jesus divested of his clothes, but there is an anomaly in the artwork: a soldier dicing for Jesus's robes has thrown two dice, but the soldier's hand appears to be detached from his body, and the cast dice show impossible combinations: the die on the left shows a three and a four, which could not be adjacent to one another, while the die on the right shows a five.

Station XIV depicts the scene at the tomb. Jesus should be shown being interred in daylight, but Saunière has had a full moon placed in the sky. Perhaps this is not, in fact, Jesus being interred, but Jesus being removed from the tomb, either alive or dead, under cover of darkness.

There is much else in the church that is strange. For example, just beneath the altar is a large and ornate bas-relief depicting Mary Magdalene sitting on her haunches before a rustic cross with a skull at her knees. The background seems to be a mirror image of the background of the fresco above the confessional. The position of the Magdalene's hands are extraordinary, as it is almost impossible to interlock one's fingers in the criss-cross pattern of a net, or grid, as Mary is shown to have done, which suggests that the positioning of the fingers must have been deliberate. Alongside Mary's left arm is an open book. The text on the open pages is illegible except for the number "64" on the middle line,which, taken with the grid formed by Mary's fingers, could suggest a chessboard, used by Saunière and Boudet in their "knight's tour" solution of the code in the second parchment. There was originally an inscription below the bas-relief, but it was vandalized, and has never been replaced. The inscription, in ungrammatical

192 *The Church at Rennes-le-Château*

Latin, read: *JESU MEDELA VULNERUM SPES JOINS POENITENTIUM PER MAGDALENAE LACRYMAS PECCATA NOSTRA DILUAS*. It should have read: *JESU VULNERUM MEDELA PAENITENTIUM JOINS SPES MAGDALENAE LACRYMAS PECCATA NOSTRA DILUAS*. Saunière was well versed in Latin, so it seems likely that he intended to convey some coded message by means of his "mistakes," but again the message is open to interpretation.

Alchemy

Could there possibly be some scientific basis to the ancient alchemist's hope that they might transmute base metals into gold? In 1897, a British scientist living in New York, Dr Stephen Emmens, claimed to have discovered how to transmute silver into gold. For his experiments, Emmens used Mexican silver dollars, certified by the US Mint to contain less than one part in ten thousand of gold. Records show that between April 1897 and August 1898, Dr Emmens sold more than $10,000 worth of gold to the Wall Street Assayer's Office. Following an article in the *New York Herald* regarding Dr Emmens and his selling of gold, the Assayer's Office admitted to buying the gold. Records from the Assayer's Office in 1897 show that the gold purchased from Dr Emmens ranged in fineness from 305 to 751 (the gold content per 1,000 parts of an ingot – a normal ingot has approximately 995 parts pure gold per five parts other metals or impurities). In 1898, when Dr Emmens sold more ingots, the fineness of his gold had increased, though it was still variable; the Assayer's Office records indicate that the final quantity of gold purchased from Dr Emmens varied in fineness between 313 and 997, the latter being almost entirely pure. The Assayer's reports indicate that the ingots contained an alloy of silver and gold, with occasional traces of other metals. To give some indication of the quality of Emmens's gold, the following are carat equivalents to parts-per-thousand measurements: 24 carat (999); 22 carat (916); 18 carat (750); 9 carat (375).

When Dr Emmens died, the eminent English physicist Sir William Crookes duplicated Emmens's experiment and succeeded in increasing the gold content in an assayed silver dollar by twenty-seven per cent. Dr Emmens was not a charlatan, but a scientist, and an inventor of remarkable ability. One of his inventions was an explosive named Emmensite which was accepted by the US government for use by its ordnance depots. Dr Emmens became a member of the American Ordnance Board, and was also a member of the American Chemical Society. As a result of his technical ability, he was selected to be a member of the US Military Service Institute, a member of the American Institute of Mining Engineers, and of the US Naval Institute. Because of his impeccable track record as a chemist he was internationally renowned in the scientific world.

Ancient alchemy was not restricted to the manufacture of gold; alchemists claimed that they could also manufacture precious gems. If their claims are to be believed, they had invented synthetic gemstones. In 1969, a Nobel Prize winner, Dr Willard Libby, in a very expensive experiment, sandwiched a block of graphite between two nuclear devices to create synthetic diamonds. Is it possible that ancient alchemists possessed a more cost-effective method? Although there were doubtless hundreds of charlatans, the transmutation of mercury and lead into gold was considered possible. To understand what may be considered transmutation, we can look at the nuclear industry. The element plutonium does not occur naturally on earth, but is created by means of a nuclear reaction.

Theoretically, then, it is possible to alter the atomic structure of elements. Until 1919, modern science had considered transmutation an impossibility, but in that year, an English physicist, Ernest Rutherford, transmuted nitrogen into oxygen and hydrogen by bombarding the basic elements of nitrogen with a stream of alpha particles (which have a similar structure to helium nuclei) thereby vindicating transmutation, in theory at least. Even Dr Frederick Soddy, the Nobel Prize winner, who coined the word "isotope" and pioneered nuclear physics, did not deride alchemy in his book *Interpretation of Radium*. In 1879, Mendeleyeff formulated a periodic table of the elements in a cascading scale of increasing weight according to their atomic structure. On the periodic table, it can be seen that gold (atomic number 79), mercury (atomic number 80), and lead (atomic number 82), are closely associated. An element is defined by the quantity and arrangement of its electrons, protons, and neutrons. By rearranging those components, it is at least theoretically possible to transmute one element into another. Did the medieval alchemists have some knowledge of this?

The alchemist, by the very nature of his craft, placed himself in a very dangerous position in society. His ability to "manufacture" gold left him open to envy that might result in robbery, violence, or even murder. To protect their secrets, alchemists resorted to using coded text when writing their notes. But the danger to the alchemist came not only from his peers and the state, but also from the Church, in the form of Inquisitors. During the Middle Ages, the interest in alchemy was so pervasive that, although many clerics were alchemists, Pope John XXII issued a papal bull in 1317 entitled *Spondent Pariter* which condemned alchemists to exile and subjected them to heavy fines if they were caught profiteering from transmutation. Pope John XXIII, on the other hand, having read some documents confiscated by the

Inquisition, wrote a paper, *Ars Transmutatoria*, on alchemy, in which he described how, while living in Avignon following the disbanding of the Templars, he had practised alchemy and manufactured two hundred bars of gold. In *Ars Transmutatoria*, he stated that each gold bar weighed one quintal, or approximately 107.7 pounds. Because revenue from Rome was limited, the bulk of that treasure seems to have been used to pay for the Pope's expenses while the Papal See was based in Avignon. After Pope John XXII's death in 1334, 800,000 gold florins were found in his treasury. Pope John XXII claimed to have implemented his right of *jus spolii*, or right of spoils, which permitted him to divert the estate of a deceased bishop into the papal treasury, which was perhaps a smokescreen to hide the true source of his wealth which had been gained by means of alchemy. The Church acknowledges that several treatises on alchemy are attributed to St Thomas Aquinas, who performed an in-depth theological investigation into whether gold produced by alchemy, as opposed to gold found in the natural world, could be sold as real gold. Aquinas concluded that it could, if it truly possessed the properties of gold.

Over the centuries there have been several church leaders and heads of state who have issued edicts banning the transmutation of base metals into gold. Those leaders presumably foresaw a time when the economy of a country could be undermined if alchemists were allowed to produce vast quantities of gold. If transmutation were impossible, why would church leaders and statesmen have gone to such lengths to ban the practice? Around AD 197, at the beginning of the reign of the Roman Emperor Septimus, an incident occurred which was still causing shock waves to reverberate through the Roman establishment one hundred years later. This incident was probably the catalyst which caused the Roman Emperor Diocletian to issue an edict in Egypt around the year AD 300 proclaiming that "all manuscripts and books that divulge or promote the art of gold-making should be burned." This occurred when Didius Marcus, a wealthy senator, became a Roman Emperor and bought control of the empire for what would today be the equivalent of about thirty-five million dollars. He was the highest bidder in an auction for the support of the Praetorian Guard, which had assassinated his predecessor, Emperor Pertinax. Where did Didius Marcus get the gold to pay for this transaction? Whatever he was up to, Didius Marcus suffered the extreme penalty under Roman law when he was beheaded in AD 197 on the orders of Emperor Septimus.

The ban on alchemy in the ancient world was not restricted to the Middle East and Europe. There are references to alchemy and its banning in both China and India. In China, a law was passed around 175 BC which prohibited the manufacture or counterfeiting of gold by alchemy. During the Hundred Years' War and in the middle of all the associated civil unrest which gave rise to the Peasants' Revolt, the English monarch Henry IV found time to issue a declaration in 1404 stating that it was a "crime against the crown to multiply metals." A subsequent monarch, Henry VI, took an entirely different stance and granted work permits to two alchemists, John Mistelden and John Cobbe, granting them permission to "practise the philosophic art of the conversion of metals." Parliament, considering these licences to make gold one method to supplement the depleted royal coffers, approved them. The original Act of 1404 that forbade the making of gold was still on the statute book when William and Mary came to the throne in 1688, and it was only in 1689 that they finally repealed the Act of Suppression of 1404. The writer, philosopher, artist, mystic, and occultist Manly Palmer-Hall, who had his collection of manuscripts indexed and catalogued, had a copy of the act of 1689 in his archives. The manuscript of that 1689 act is entitled "An act to repeal the statute made in the 5th year of King Henry IV against the multiplying of gold and silver or use of the craft of multiplication, and if any the same do they shall incur the pain of felony." A new act passed by William and Mary goes on to decree that "all the gold and silver that shall be extracted by the aforesaid art" shall be turned over to Their Majesties' Mint in the Tower of London where the precious metals would be bought at the full market value.

William had initiated experiments while Prince of Orange and a member of the Dutch royal family and destined to become William III the future British monarch. He had became involved in alchemy when he employed Johann Friedrich Schweitzer, better known as Helvetius, as his personal physician. In 1666, the physician allegedly managed to transmute lead into gold. The Inspector-General of the Royal Dutch Mint, Porelius, personally supervised a test when he visited the laboratory of Helvetius. Porelius had the grains of a test piece checked before it was subjected to "treatment" by the alchemist, then, after observing the alchemist at work, Porelius took the gold test piece to the Royal Minter, Brechtel, for analysis. Brechtel, who was also the royal jeweller to the Prince of Orange, performed a supervised test on Helvetius's gold sample and declared it to be the finest and purest gold he had ever tested.

Nicolas Flamel, allegedly the Grand Master of the Priory of Sion between 1398 and 1418, was also an alchemist. As a young man he had trained as a professional notary and a bookseller in Saint-Jacques la Boucherie, in Paris. Once established, he had purchased a house in the old rue de Marivaux and converted the ground floor into his business premises. As his business expanded, he employed copyists and illuminators and occasionally gave writing lessons to the nobility, some of whom could only sign their names with a cross. Flamel also illuminated manuscripts and books and in his youth a very old manuscript written in an unknown language and titled *Abraham the Jew* came into his possession. For many years, Flamel and his wife Pernelle worked to translate the manuscript, eventually coming to the conclusion that it was a book on alchemy. On 17 January, 1382, sixteen years before he was elected Grand Master, at the age of fifty-two, Nicolas Flamel allegedly conducted his first transmutation of a base metal. Flamel produced eight ounces of pure silver from mercury, but surpassed that four months later, on 25 April, 1382, when he is alleged to have made his first alchemical gold. For the next thirty-six years, until his death in 1418, Nicolas Flamel funded fourteen hospitals and three churches in Paris. Five years before his own death, Pernelle died and, in acknowledgement of her contribution to the translation of the original manuscript, Flamel made inscriptions and signs from the translated text in the Cemetery of the Innocents at the Paris churches of St Jacques de la Boucheries and St Nicolas des Champs. Those inscriptions could still be seen in the late eighteenth century, but were later vandalized, probably during the French Revolution. It is not known what happened to Flamel's original manuscript, but there are reports that it was last seen by Cardinal Richelieu in the seventeenth century, who claimed that it contained marginal notes made by Flamel. In 1654, Dr Pierre Borelli recorded the existence of the manuscript in his *Catalogus librorum philoso Phicorum hermeticorum*, and there are rumours that copies of the manuscript of *Abraham the Jew* circulated in the world of alchemy for the next two hundred years.

Examples of alchemist's gold exist in some of the world's top museums. One example is held in the Department of Coins and Medals at the British Museum, indexed with the registration number M2036. The exhibit, described as an "Alchemical Bullet" was acquired by the museum together with a note written in an early-nineteenth century hand. The note reads, "Gold made by an alchemist from a leaden bullet in the presence of Colonel MacDonald and Doctor Colquhoun at Bapara in the month of October 1814."

Over the years, the bullet has been put on show in a number of temporary exhibitions. In 1971, a specific gravity test was done which demonstrated that the bullet is an object of the purest gold. There is no information regarding the act of transmutation, but the fact that the object is recorded as an example of alchemical gold by the British Museum suggests that the science of alchemy should be treated with some degree of seriousness.

The British Museum is not alone in having this type of exhibit. The Medal and Coin Room (*Münzkabinett*) of the Viennese Kunsthistorisches Museum contains an extraordinary exhibit that provides supporting evidence of the authenticity of alchemical transmutation in the Middle Ages. The exhibit, held under catalogue number 27ß, is described as an alchemist's oval medallion, made in 1677 by Johann Permann. The medallion is 8.14 in (37 cm) by 8.8 in (40 cm) and weighs 15.87 lb (7.2 kg). It is composed of 47 per cent gold, 43 per cent silver, and 7 per cent copper.

In 1833, at the request of Professor Bauer of Vienna, four sample notches were made on the medallion's edge in order to analyse the metallic content of the plate. This analysis confirmed that two-thirds of the medallion was solid gold, with no evidence of a joint or weld between the silver/copper portion and the gold portion. The medallion's history began in the sixteenth century with the birth of an Austrian named Wenzel Seiler. Although his mother was aristocratic, his father was a commoner, so young Wenzel lived the life of a poor young man who grew up within the confines of an Augustine monastery and eventually took holy orders. The young monk soon became bored with the quiet and solitude and wanted to leave the order, but because of his poverty, he was unable to do so. Then something happened which was to change Wenzel's life forever. An old friar, who was Wenzel's patron, mentioned that there was supposedly hidden treasure buried within the monastery. After a long search, the old friar and the young monk found an old chest which contained four jars of reddish powder and a parchment with strange signs and letters. The old friar eventually managed to decipher enough of the manuscript to conclude that the red powder was a product of alchemy, used in the transmutation of metals. Wenzel, a free spirit at heart, stole an old, tin plate from the refractory, and, after applying the red powder to the plate, the two men heated the plate in a fire. Allegedly, the plate turned to gold. It is not known who sold the plate, but it was sold in the nearby city for twenty ducats. Shortly after the discovery of the powder and the parchment and the sale of the plate, the old friar died, leaving Wenzel Seiler in sole possession of the money and the secret. Some time later, Wenzel and another young monk, Francis Preyhausen, escaped from the monastery. Wenzel took with him his only possessions, the remainder of the money and the jars of red powder. Free of the religious order, both young men made their way to Vienna, where they are said to have parted company, and nothing more is known of the young Preyhausen.

Wenzel, now a young man about town with a little money and a secret, met and secured the patronage of Count Peter von Paar, to whom Wenzel confided the secret of the red powder. The count was a confidant of the German Emperor Leopold I, who was interested in alchemy. Wenzel was summoned to the court, where he demonstrated transmutation in the presence of two witnesses, Father Spies and Dr Joachim Becher. During the course of the experiment, which lasted a quarter of an hour, Wenzel transmuted an ounce of tin into pure gold. After the demonstration, the witnesses to the experiment signed a written declaration as to its authenticity. Wenzel was taken under the personal protection of Emperor Leopold I and, in 1675, the emperor, with the aid of a Count von Waldstein, the captain of his bodyguard, made alchemical gold using the red powder that Wenzel had brought to court. The Imperial Mint struck a special ducat from the alchemical gold; on one side of the ducat was an image of Leopold I, and on its reverse side an inscription proclaimed "With Wenzel Seiler's powder was I transformed from tin into gold." At the Viennese Palace of the Knights of St John, Wenzel performed more successful transmutations of base metals into gold, some of which was made into a gold chain, on the orders of Count von Waldstein. On 16 September, 1676, the emperor appointed Wenzel Seiler as Court Chemist; he also knighted him, granting him the title of Wenzelaus von Rheinburg, the maiden name of Wenzel's aristocratic mother. In 1677, with his supply of red powder almost exhausted, Wenzel and Leopold I coated a large silver medallion with the remaining powder and the subsequent and last transmutation took place when the medallion was dipped into the transmuting compound and its lower part turned to gold. It is that medallion that can be seen today in the Imperial Treasury room of the Viennese Kunsthistorisches Museum.

There is one final aspect of alchemy which is worth examining. Did the medieval stained glass-makers use alchemy to produce the beautiful translucent stained glass windows in Chartres Cathedral? The process for the manufacture of the super-translucent glass in those windows has never been surpassed, and it has been suggested that the glass was made by alchemists. The story of the stained glass in the gothic cathedrals begins at the

Abbey of St Denis, to the north of Paris, built in memory of the patron saint of Paris, and, by association, the patron saint of the medieval French monarchs of the House of Capet. The abbey is built on the site of a ninth-century Carolingian church, which, over the years, had become the family chapel of the Capet dynasty because of its ancestral links to Charlemagne. Towards the end of the eleventh century, a male child named Suger was born into abject poverty in the village of St Denis. As the child grew, he developed a superior intelligence. The local priesthood recognized his genius at an early age and accepted him into the Prieuré de l'Estrée school in the local monastery. During his schooldays, Suger formed what was to become a lifelong friendship with another student who was destined to become King Louis VI of France. Between 1118 and 1121, Suger was given several diplomatic missions to the Holy See, where he so impressed Pope Callistus II that, in 1123, he was elected Abbot Suger of St Denis. As Abbot of St Denis, Suger was to be responsible for the creation of one of the most beautiful Gothic cathedrals in Europe, due almost entirely to the contents of a book that Suger found in the abbey library. The book had been written in the second century by the Gnostic philosopher Dionysius the Areopagite, and had been given to a son of Charlemagne by the Byzantine emperor known as Michael the Stammerer. The rediscovery of the book by Abbot Suger led to his development of a Gnostic theory of continuous light, or *lux continua*. The theory held that light was a "gift from God" and had spiritual roots in the Gnostic illuminism of alchemy. Inspired by that theory, Suger became involved in the development of a new style of architecture, seen today in Gothic cathedrals throughout Europe. The roofs of the new cathedrals were supported by flying buttresses, opening their interiors up to light cascading through brilliant stained glass windows. The beauty of the glass in these Gothic cathedrals was the wonder of the age, allowing the windows to be translucent even when the light outside was dim, as in the middle of winter. To develop the translucent effect that he required, Suger employed the best scientific minds of the day, including experts from Persia, to manufacture stained glass. It has been suggested that the glassmakers applied secret techniques to a type of sand found only in the Middle East. If so, it is a secret technique which has been lost to modern science. What is certain is that the particular quality of translucence of the stained glass created in the mid-thirteenth century for Chartres Cathedral has never been replicated. It has been suggested that the Persian experts used mathematical formulae to transmute mineral elements in the silicon sand to create the translucent effect.

It is interesting to note that the original stained glass windows in Europe's Gothic cathedrals did not include a single portrayal of the crucifixion. Any windows depicting the crucifixion were added following the demise and dissolution of the Templars in 1312. The reason for this omission is that the Templars and the Gnostic Christian church had always denied the crucifixion, perhaps the reason why Templar rituals included spitting on the cross.

In 1125, Suger was elevated from Abbot of St Denis to cardinal, but before his appointment could be ratified, the Pope died. In fact, it was a timely death because, for the remainder of his life, Suger was able to devote himself to building the great Gothic cathedrals of France, while he remained an adviser to his old school friend Louis VI, and later to Louis VII. During the Second Crusade, Suger was nominated Regent of France, governing France for two years during Louis VII's absence.

Rosslyn Chapel and
the New World

To the south of Edinburgh, on the edge of a gorge in the beautiful Esk valley, is a small, fifteenth-century Gothic chapel in a small town named Roslin. The chapel, since achieving fame through Dan Brown's *The Da Vinci Code*, is no longer peaceful due to the number of visitors, but it is still worth a visit.

The town is actually called Roslin, but, due to some quirk, the chapel is known as Rosslyn Chapel, or the Collegiate Chapel of St Matthew. When William Sinclair commissioned Rosslyn Chapel in 1446, it was during an age when books were often destroyed or edited by an establishment which wished to suppress ideas or facts. It was for this reason that the idea of building a chapel which would serve as a "book" in stone, appealed to William Sinclair. The "book" would have every carving or statue deliberately positioned to tell future generations of "readers" a story, but such readers would be required to "read" with an open mind. Sinclair envisaged that his "book" in stone would survive the ravages of time and decay, and be a permanent record for future generations. Rosslyn has been described as a miniature cathedral, which, in many respects, resembles Chartres Cathedral, transplanted onto a Scottish hillside. From the outside, the chapel appears unfinished, or partly in ruins, because its west wall has what appear to be the ruins of a larger structure. This is not the case; the original builders deliberately built the west wall as a symbolic monument to the ruin of Herod's Temple, which the Knights Templar first entered in their exploration of Jerusalem in the early eleventh century.

The story of the construction of Rosslyn Chapel has its roots in France, on Friday 13 October, 1307, when King Philip IV had most of the Knights Templar arrested. It is very likely that the Templars had some forewarning of their impending arrest because they had secretly removed their treasure from their Temple headquarters in Paris during the night of Thursday 12 October, when a witness claimed to have seen laden wagons winding slowly through the dark suburbs. From there, they made their way on to the open road leading to their fleet of eighteen galleys, waiting at La Rochelle. With the treasure safely stowed aboard, the Templar fleet sailed out into the Atlantic carrying some Templars who had escaped being arrested. The fleet having sailed, the treasure disappeared from history, its destination remaining a mystery to this day. Some of the Templars escaping from France reached the west coast of Scotland, but it is not known if only a few Templars disembarked before the fleet sailed on, or if the entire fleet concealed itself somewhere in the remote Western Isles of Scotland. There, the fleet would have been safe from prying eyes until a more suitable permanent home could be found for the treasure. Those Templars who disembarked established a Scottish branch of the St Clair family, the Sinclairs. Seven years later, in 1314, they resurfaced at the Battle of Bannockburn, where the Scottish army led by King Robert the Bruce was outnumbered three to one, and in danger of suffering a heavy defeat at the hands of the English forces of Edward II. Scottish folklore relates that Henry St Clair, a Templar knight, together with his two sons, William and Henry, led a charge by mounted knights in full armour, turning the tide of battle, and routing the English. Legend has it that the knights rode off without disclosing their identity. Perhaps the Templars were paying off a debt to the Scottish king, who had given them sanctuary seven years previously; there is a Scottish Masonic degree based on the re-enactment of this legend. Forty-four years later, in 1385, long after the French Templars had fought at Bannockburn, Sir William St Clair died, and his son Henry St Clair became the Baron of Rosslyn at the age of thirteen. In 1365, at the age of twenty, Henry married for the second time, his first wife having died very young, and fathered ten children, three sons and seven daughters. Twenty years later, King Hakkon of Norway, realizing that he could no longer control the rebellious inhabitants of the Orkneys, offered the thirty-three-year-old Henry St Clair the earldom of those islands, handing over power in an official ceremony on 2 August 1379.

In order to maintain law and order over his new lands, Henry St Clair built Kirkwall Castle, and commissioned a fleet of thirteen ships with which, in 1390, he invaded and subdued the Shetland Isles. According to legend, two events then occurred which could have been the catalyst which changed the course of Henry's life. The first event was the dramatic return to the Orkneys of a fisherman who had been missing at sea for twenty years. He claimed that he and another crew member had been swept west in his boat by severe storm-force winds, eventually making landfall somewhere on the North American mainland. For the next twenty years, the natives had held the two of them in friendly "captivity." After some time, his crewmate had died, and he had been freed to return home and tell his story in the Orkneys. The second event happened while Henry and his men were subduing the rebellious Shetlanders. One day, after a brief storm, Henry's men came upon a marooned and storm-damaged Venetian vessel. Henry and his small force had saved the damaged boat from the marauding islanders, who had claimed that they had salvage rights to any vessel washed up on their shores. As well as salvaging the boat, Henry also protected the crew and captain from the fierce Shetland islanders. The Venetian Captain, Nicolo Zeno, said he was leading a voyage of exploration with his brother Antonio Zeno. The brothers were from a long-established trading family with such influence in Venice that it was the only family ever to have had a private chapel in the Basilica San Marco. Today it contains the tomb of Cardinal Giovanni Battista Zeno, a nephew of Pope Paul II, who died in 1501. The Zeno brothers had been shipwrecked on the Shetland Islands while searching for new trading routes, possibly to the New World. The exploration had become an economic necessity if the Venetian family were to survive and compete with the Hanseatic League of Baltic traders whose North Sea ports virtually excluded the Venetians from trading with the Low Countries and England. How did they know, one hundred years before the voyages of Columbus, that there was a New World to the west? Their knowledge came from ancestral maps of the North Atlantic which showed Greenland as a landmass discovered by the Vikings. When Columbus's three ships crossed the Atlantic to the New World, they sailed under the flag of the red cross of the Templars, possibly because the wife of Christopher Columbus was the daughter of a former Templar. Columbus would have had access to the charts and diaries of his father-in-law, which were from the same source as the maps used by the Zeno brothers on their voyage of exploration.

While the Venetian ship was undergoing repairs, Henry

told the Venetians the story of the shipwrecked fisherman. This was just the spur that Henry and the Zeno brothers needed to attempt to find for themselves the distant lands that were to become known as the New World. Legend does not say if the repaired Venetian vessel formed part of their fleet, but there is some circumstantial evidence that it did, or at least that some of the ordnance from the Venetian ship did, because in 1849 a cannon was retrieved from Louisbourg Harbour, Cape Breton Island, in North America. The cannon was identified as a late-fourteenth-century Venetian gun of the type that would have been fitted to the Zeno brothers' ship.

Further circumstantial evidence of Henry St Clair's visit to Nova Scotia is found in the legends of the Mimac people of North America. A Mimac legend tells of "a king with three sons, who visited from an island far across the sea. The king landed with many soldiers, stayed for a year, and then departed." The fact that Henry had three sons fits the Mimac legend, and it is known that Henry's stay in the New World lasted for about a year. South-west of Nova Scotia lies New England, and, while Henry was waiting for favourable winds to take him home, he decided to explore that part of the coastline. While the exploration party was ashore, one of Henry's knights died, and a record of his demise was left, which is still to be seen on Prospect Hill, in Westford, Massachusetts. The shore party carved a motif into the face of a stone ledge on the hill in the form of a series of punched holes, which vary in size and depth, carved using a sharp tool of some kind and a mallet. The motif shows an armoured medieval knight in a bassinet helmet and mail surcoat. He is shown with his mailed fist resting on a fourteenth-century sword and pommel of the type used between 1350 and 1400. The heraldic emblems on the shield have been positively identified as those of the Clan Gunn, and Sir James Gunn of Clyth was indeed a member of Henry's party of explorers. Adjacent to the motif of the so-called Westford Knight is a plaque with the following inscription: "Prince Henry First Sinclair of Orkney born in Scotland made a voyage of discovery to North America in 1398. After wintering in Nova Scotia, he sailed to Massachusetts and on an inland expedition in 1399 to Prospect Hill to view the surrounding countryside, one of the party died. The punch-hole armorial effigy which adorns this ledge is a memorial to this knight."

There is further evidence that the Templars visited the New World. For example, at Newport, on Rhode Island, there is a round tower which has been preserved as an historic monument. The tower is constructed from local materials, such as laminated slate, sea-worn stones, and mortar. Much thought must have been given to the positioning of the Newport Tower because it is strategically located about half a mile from the eastern and western shoreline of Newport, and gives a commanding view of all the tributaries of the Narragansett Delta. This would have been one of the builders' prime considerations in determining where to locate such an observation tower. Mr James P. Whittall, Jr, a director of the Early Sites Research Centre in Massachusetts, who investigated the architectural style and the construction methods of the Newport Tower, reached the following conclusions: "The tower is constructed in the style of Norman Romanesque architecture inspired by the Holy Sepulchre in Jerusalem. The unique style of the Newport Tower was further influenced by the round Templar churches of Scandinavia. Local building traditions from whence the builders came also influenced its style. Determination of the date of original construction is usually based upon the study of features, such as arches, windows, niches, beam holes, key stones, mortar, and the orientation of openings. Those found within the Newport Tower have been dated in the broad range of

1150–1400. However, some specific features narrow the range to the late 1300s."

Even without the benefit of that report, it is apparent that the Newport Tower is architecturally similar in style to Scandinavian and other European Templar churches of the Middle Ages. The round churches in Europe and also those built by the crusaders in the Holy Land used a design philosophy to simulate the Church of the Holy Sepulchre in Jerusalem (built around AD 330) which had round altars at which the Templars worshipped. When the Templars returned from the Crusades in the twelfth century, they introduced round and octagonal churches into most of Europe. The Newport Tower has eight pillared arches. On the inside of the tower, above the arches, there is evidence that at some time there was a wooden floor supported by beams set into the circular wall of the tower at the level of the first floor, on which there is also an integral fireplace with two chimneys built into the wall of the tower (two chimneys allowed smoke to be drawn from the room irrespective of the direction of the prevailing wind). Located opposite the fireplace is a window, which would have acted as a beacon to ships in the estuary whenever a fire was lit. A few feet above the floor, there are small alcoves built into the wall, and a channel is cut into the wall below and between the alcoves. The channel appears to have been designed to support an altar stone. When an altar stone was in place, the alcoves would have been used to hold religious icons or relics, as found in pre-Reformation churches. In the more recent past, the New England states were Protestant, so the placing of the alcoves adjacent to the altar stone in the style of Catholic churches, provides more circumstantial evidence that the Newport tower predates the seventeenth-century colonization by protestant immigrants. A final piece of circumstantial evidence regarding the builders of the tower is found in the unit of measurement used during its design and construction. The men who built the tower used an old Scottish measurement known as an "ell," which was in use in England until the middle of the sixteenth century.

In 1399, Henry and the surviving members of his party returned to the Orkneys, with every intention of returning to the New World, but it was not to be. An English army led by Henry IV was making incursions into Scotland and, when a band of English raiders attacked Kirkwall Castle in 1400, the brave, but foolhardy, Henry St Clair left the relative safety of his castle to fight the marauders. Henry died in battle and the Mimacs were left waiting in vain for his return. It has been suggested that it was at the instigation of the Hanseatic League of shipping merchants, who had a vested interest in silencing rumours of new trade routes, that the band of English marauders left the main English army to silence Henry St Clair. A final piece of evidence of Henry St Clair's epic voyage to Nova Scotia was recently discovered by the historian Andrew Sinclair, who visited the Zeno library in Venice, where he uncovered a map of Nova Scotia, dated 1398. The map is embellished with an effigy of a Templar Knight with his arm resting on a shield, which bears the St Clair family crest.

When William St Clair, the grandson of the explorer Henry St Clair, commissioned Rosslyn Chapel, he employed the best stonemasons in Europe to create a chapel that has been described as one of the greatest examples of medieval stonemasonry and architecture in Britain. The interior of the chapel incorporates so much Christian, Pagan, and Arabic symbolism that every inch of the interior is adorned with carvings, many of which are redolent of North America, in particular, the carvings of maize on the Apprentice Pillar. The mystery is that William St Clair knew something of the North American flora and fauna almost fifty years before Columbus landed there. In 1442, only 132 years after the dissolution of the Templars, Sir William St Clair, the Earl of

Orkney, began planning a church for Rosslyn. He intended to build a chapel in the Templar tradition to the "Glory of God." The chapel he built stands 40 ft 8 in tall, 34 ft 8 in wide, and 68 ft long. It was designed in the shape of a cross with a Lady Chapel, and with a high tower at its centre. To house and support the many stonemasons and ancillary workers, William St Clair provided accommodation, which became the nucleus of the small village of Roslin. After four years of planning, the foundation stone for the chapel was finally laid on St Matthew's Day, 21 September, 1446. The chapel is described as a perfect example of the "sacred geometry" of the Masonic brotherhood, with literally hundreds of examples of Templar and Masonic symbolism incorporated into the intricate carvings and hieroglyphics in the stonework. The chapel's magnificent ceiling features hundreds of carved stone cubes intricately inscribed with symbols. One theory is that the ceiling is a coded puzzle, and a prize of £5,000 has been offered to anyone who can crack the code, but the most intriguing symbolism is reserved for the two pillars at the south end of each of the main aisles. The pillar on the right-hand aisle is known as the Apprentice Pillar, while the pillar on the left-hand aisle is the Master's Pillar. According to legend, while the Master Mason was away visiting Venice to gain inspiration for the design of the pillar, an apprentice mason, on his own inititive, designed and constructed such a beautiful work of art that on the return of the Master Mason, the latter was so consumed with jealousy at the quality of the work that he killed the apprentice in a fit of rage and jealousy. Since then, the pillar has become known as the Apprentice Pillar. The base of the Apprentice Pillar is composed of carvings of what appear to be eight dragons or serpents, which support the intricately carved pillar with coiling spirals that form a perfect double helix, coincidentally the form taken by DNA, the fundamental building block of life. Consider that the pillar was

carved five hundred years before modern science discovered
the meaning of the double helix in basic structure of life.

To the right of the Apprentice Pillar are steps leading
down to a small crypt with a sealed stone arch, which is
allegedly the entrance to a larger, sealed subterranean
crypt, thought to contain the remains of ten knights in full
armour. Others believe that the crypt contains the Ark of
the Covenant, or other artefacts removed by the crusaders
from the cellars of the ruined Temple of Solomon in
Jerusalem. The Sinclair family has repeatedly refused
permission for this crypt to be opened, thus fueling
speculation as to what is hidden behind the sealed entrance.

During the Middle Ages, Rosslyn Chapel proved to be
a haven for Gypsies, who are today probably the only
European members of a cult of goddess worship which can
still be witnessed at the annual Gypsy Festival held at
Saintes-Maries-de-la-Mer, on the Mediterranean coast of
France. The festival requires the veneration of a black
Madonna and commemorates St Sarah, whom the
European Gypsies refer to as their patron saint, Sara-la-
Kali. Sarah arrived with Mary Magdalene in an open boat
after they had fled from the Holy Land. Today, the Gypsies
are long gone from Rosslyn, but why were they attracted to
Rosslyn in the past, particularly when poor roads made the
chapel almost inaccessible?

Down through the centuries, Rosslyn has survived
several invading armies, the brutality of the Reformation,
and the English Civil War in the mid-seventeenth century,
which spilled over into Scotland. The Civil War provides
another mystery relating to Rosslyn Chapel, and connected
to the violence of those times. The Sinclair family were
royalists, opposed to Oliver Cromwell. When the
Roundheads, under the leadership of Oliver Cromwell, a
Master Mason, captured and destroyed Rosslyn Castle, he
gave orders that the chapel was to be left alone (he did

allow the chapel to be used for stabling his horses, but his soldiers were prevented from desecrating the building). Perhaps because he was a Master Mason, Cromwell was showing respect for the Chapel and its Masonic symbolism. He may even have been privy to some of its many secrets.

In 1312, the Knights Templar were disbanded in France, and, in 1314, their Grand Master, Jacques de Molay was burned at the stake; many years later, in 1736, the first Grand Lodge of Scotland was formed as a governing body of the Scottish Masons. Their first Grand Master was Sir William St Clair of Roslin, a Templar, who, prior to the formation of the Grand Lodge, was the hereditary Grand Master Mason of Scotland. The St Clairs, or Sinclairs, are one of the oldest Scottish families, and have allegedly been the keepers of the Templar treasure and holy relics that are supposed to have been sent to Scotland after the dissolution of the order in 1312. When Michael Baigent and Richard Leigh were researching *The Temple and the Lodge*, they discovered a hidden churchyard, at Kilmartin, near Loch Awe, containing old Templar graves, which they took as proof that a considerable number of Templars had indeed settled in Scotland.

Oak Island

There is no report of the Templar fleet of eighteen galleys
which sailed out into the Atlantic from La Rochelle after
the mass arrests of the Knights Templar in October 1307
ever having been seen again. The fleet's intended destination has remained a mystery for 700 years, but most
probably it was Scotland, and then Nova Scotia. It is
possible that the Templar fleet used the same Venetian
charts as Henry St Clair and travelled to the New World to
hide their treasure. There is a group of small islands off the
coast of Nova Scotia, one of which is Oak Island, the site
of one of the world's greatest archaeological enigmas for it
is believed to conceal a mysterious treasure which has
defied detection and extraction since 1795. The secret has
already claimed six lives, and consumed large parts of the
wealth of some very well known people, including Franklin
D. Roosevelt, John Wayne, and even Errol Flynn, all of
whom have funded schemes to try to recover the treasure.
But whose treasure is it? Some suggest that it is pirate
treasure, buried by Captain William Kidd, rather than the
mysterious wealth of the Templars. Following Kidd's
execution in London, several treasure maps surfaced, all
allegedly showing the hiding places of his treasure. For

several years following the pirate's death, there were stories of deathbed confessions by dying seamen who, claiming to have been members of Kidd's crew, claimed knowledge of the hidden treasure. Some of those stories hint at a North Atlantic island, possibly Oak Island, as a location.

The mystery of the buried treasure began in 1795 when Daniel McGinnis, a sixteen-year-old boy, took his father's boat and rowed out to the island to explore. Back then, the island was covered with a thick stand of trees, very similar to red oaks in appearance. As Daniel wandered into a small wooded area, he noticed a depression beneath an old oak tree. It gave the appearance of someone having dug a trench or hole, before filling it in again. Daniel observed that there was some damage to one of the main branches of the tree, as if a pulley or ropes had scuffed the bark. An excited Daniel rowed back to the mainland and, with tales of hidden pirate treasure in his mind, he enlisted the help of his two best friends, John Smith, nineteen, and Anthony Vaughan, sixteen. The boys were to remain treasure seekers for the rest of their lives. The following day, the three boys sailed back to Oak Island, armed with picks and shovels. The sandy soil was not hard to shift, and soon they had dug down to a depth of about four feet, where they uncovered a flagstone floor. The boys removed some flagstones and dug down a further six feet, where they uncovered another floor, comprising oak logs embedded in the hard clay walls of the shaft. The next day, the three boys rigged up a block and tackle on the scuffed branch of the old oak tree to hoist out the oak logs and soil. Over the next few weeks, the boys returned as often as possible to Oak Island to continue excavating. At a depth of twenty feet, they discovered another log platform, and, at thirty feet, another. The shaft was now too deep for the three boys, and with the onset of the long, cold Nova Scotia winter, deep snow covered the site. Nothing more could be done until the ground thawed in spring.

Seasons came and went, and Smith and McInnis got married and built homes on the island. Then, one day, Smith made another find, this time on the beach. It was a hand-forged iron ring-bolt, visible only at low tide. It was embedded in a boulder at Smith's Cove which suggested that the natural harbour of the cove had in the past been a frequent mooring place for ships. Modern sea charts show that it is possible to sail due north-west into Mahone Bay at Oak Island, without making landfall on any of the hundreds of other islands in the area, which points to the route that would have been taken by the Templar fleet, sailing from La Rochelle via the Western Isles of Scotland to Oak Island.

In 1803, eight years after the initial discovery, Smith's wife was about to have her first baby. She was taken to Truro, Nova Scotia, to the home of a young doctor named John Lynds, who, after safely delivering the baby, listened to their story of the buried treasure. He was hooked, and visited the island, agreeing that there was something to their story of buried treasure. Dr Lynds formed a business syndicate, the Onslow Company, which raised enough capital to conduct a thorough excavation of the pit. Digging commenced and the workers managed to excavate down to ninety feet. Every ten feet, they would find an oak platform, embedded in the clay-lined walls of the pit shaft. A few of the platforms had been sealed with a mixture of coconut fibre and putty at the log joints. At a depth of ninety feet, they found a large flagstone, allegedly inscribed with a coded message in English. It was not until 1843 that a professor from Halifax decoded the message, which read, "Forty feet below two million pounds are buried." However, there is a suspicion that the syndicate, in an attempt to attract new investment, deliberately planted the flagstone and its simple code.

Why would the men who built the shaft have left a code that is decipherable in modern English, rather than in terms of medieval grammar and spelling? The professor in Halifax used a simple substitution method to crack the code. The most commonly used letter in the English alphabet is "e," therefore if "e" were substituted for the most used symbol on the stone, it might be possible to break the code. There was a slight problem because there were two symbols on the stone that appeared five times each, but by subsituting "e" in both cases, the professor was able to discover which symbol represented "e," and thereby crack the code.

Below the flagstone floor the subsoil was waterlogged, with a soil-to-water ratio of 2:1. The excavation continued down another eight feet to a depth of about 98 feet, where another wooden platform was discovered. Without the benefit of modern lighting, as darkness fell, the dig was abandoned for the day. When the workers returned to the pit the following day, they found it filled with water. All attempts to bail out the water failed, so the syndicate decided to sink another shaft adjacent to the original one. The new shaft was dug to a depth of 110 feet before an attempt was made to drive a tunnel through to the original shaft. The workers managed to get within two feet of the first shaft before the pressure of water in the original shaft burst through and flooded the new shaft. At that stage, the syndicate gave up and the pits lay abandoned for over forty years. Although Smith and McInnis continued to live on the island, they both eventually died without having got to the bottom of the mystery of Oak Island. Then, in 1849, a new syndicate, the Truro Company, was formed in an attempt to recover whatever was hidden in the pit. Anthony Vaughan, the only survivor of the three boys who had initially discovered the pit, who was then in his late sixties, was still able to make the trip to the island to indicate the spot where the original shaft had been sunk. Dr Lynds, by then an old man, also bought a stake in the new company. The Truro Company sank a shaft to 86 feet before they hit water, which again flooded the workings. Without the benefit of modern pumps, the company hired a coal prospector who had a pod auger, a hand-powered drill bit on the end of a free shaft. The syndicate used the auger to extract core samples from the original, flooded shaft. At a depth of 98 feet they encountered the same platform that the first syndicate had discovered, but had failed to remove on the evening when the shaft had originally flooded. The platform was constructed from five-inch thick spruce logs. Eventually, the auger drilled through the spruce platform, before again biting into wood, four inches of oak, before entering a twelve-inch deep cavity. Once the auger had reached beyond the cavity, excitement mounted when the team realized the auger was now moving through approximately twenty-two inches of loose pieces of metal, which the workers thought might be loose coins inside an oak chest. Once the auger had passed through the metal, the bit encountered another four inches of oak, which the diggers assumed was the base of an oak chest. This was followed by what was thought to be the top of another oak chest, also filled with twenty-two inches of loose pieces of metal. Once the auger had passed through that metal, and through what seemed to be the base of another oak chest, it bit into another spruce platform, five inches thick. The team continued drilling with the auger and encountered a seven-foot-thick layer of clay. When the auger was withdrawn to the surface, the core samples were examined. Dr Lynds, who was on site, had the auger removed, and, when he cleaned the point, he found three links of a thin, gold chain. During the excitement of this discovery, the site foreman John Pitbaldo, carefully examined the core sample. It was later alleged that he had pocketed something from the core, but had refused to disclose to his colleagues what it was. The reason he gave for his refusal was that it was only for the eyes of the directors of the syndicate, and all would be revealed at the next board meeting. In fact, Pitbaldo failed to attend the next board meeting, and simply disappeared. During the following winter, he was killed in a mining accident, taking to the grave what might have been a valuable clue to what the treasure might be.

The problem facing the Truro Company was how to gain access to the two money chests. Another shaft was sunk and a tunnel dug towards the original shaft, but again water burst through. No one seems to have asked where all the water was coming from. It was only when one of the workers fell into the pit and discovered that the water was salty, that investigations and excavations began on the beach. Someone then noticed that at low tide, water was erupting from the sandy shore at Smith's Cove on the south-eastern end of the island. An excavation on the sandy beach revealed rounded boulders which had been laid on top of a two-foot-thick layer of eelgrass. This man-made filter extended from the low- to the high-tide marks on the beach. When the eel grass was removed, tons of coconut fibre were uncovered, which, when removed, revealed five sink drains located approximately three feet beneath the sand. The drains collected seawater and fed it into a manifold located above a funnel-shaped sump near the shore. The sump fed the seawater into a long tunnel, thirty-inches wide and fifty-four-inches high. Further investigation revealed that the tunnel walls were dressed with limestone blocks, but were without a dam, or sluice gates, or any other method to prevent water entering the tunnel. The tunnel seemed to head for about a quarter of a mile towards the area of the original excavations. The ingenuity of the men who had built the Money Pit was extraordinary. They had created a booby trap which would flood the shafts with seawater if robbers attempted to reach the treasure. Each sink drain had been lined with stone and covered with the coconut fibre and eel grass to act as a filter to prevent a sudden rush of water into the drains at each high tide, thus preventing the drains from filling with sand. The coconut fibre also acted as a reservoir, soaking up and holding vast quantities of seawater between tides. Thus, if the Money Pit was breached below the level of the input flood tunnel at low tide, seawater would be released to flood the workings, and the coconut fibre reservoir would be automatically replenished at the next high tide. How to shut off the ingress of water to the sump and to the flood channel had become the Truro Company's major problem. To the engineers, the problem seemed simple: all that was required was to block off the flow of water from the beach.

The engineers began to build a dam inland from Smith's Cove. Their plan was to then block, or dismantle, the flood tunnel and the five sink drains, but it was not to be. A storm blew up and destroyed the dam before it could be completed. With funds running low, the Truro Company made one last attempt to reach the treasure, by digging a new shaft to the hundred-foot level in an attempt to intercept and plug the flood drain before it entered the money pit. The attempt failed, however, and the Truro Company went into liquidation.

The next attempt to reach the treasure was launched in 1861, when the Halifax Treasure Company was formed. A team of sixty-three men and thirty-three horses were brought to the island. They worked in shifts to keep a bailing plant in continuous operation. This reduced the water level to about eighty-eight feet and maintained it at that level. The team then attempted to tunnel sideways to reach the two chests located at the 110-foot level, but due to disturbance and water action, the wooden platform at that level collapsed into a cavern at a depth of 120 feet.

The chests were now even further out of reach. Undaunted by this setback, the team installed steam pumps to provide a more efficient method of controlling the floodwater, but on starting one of the pumps, the boiler burst, scalding a worker, who later died from his injuries. At this point, the Halifax Company, too, went into liquidation and was forced to give up. The shaft and site lay abandoned once again until 1893, when Mr Frederick L. Blair took an interest in the island and formed a new company. Blair invested his entire inheritance and savings in the project and, although unsuccessful, he remained involved in Oak Island until his death in 1950. At the beginning of his involvement with the Money Pit, as it had become known, Blair met James McInnis, a grandson of one of the three boys who had made the initial discovery. McInnis lived on the island and was a great source of information about previous work on the pit. The new company began excavation work in 1895. One of the first tasks performed by the new company was to dig out the original shaft of the Money Pit which had collapsed due to years of neglect. At thirty-five feet the shaft was found to be blocked with debris, so an adjacent shaft and tunnel was sunk to a depth of a 111 feet. This shaft exposed for the first time the lower end, or exit point, of the flood tunnel which ran down from the sump on the beach to the pit. Although the exit was blocked with loose boulders, the ingress of seawater could not be stopped. Blair's company became desperate to halt the ingress of seawater, and a series of five-inch boreholes were sunk in the shore above the high-water mark. Dynamite was lowered into each shaft and a series of underground explosions triggered at a depth of about 108 feet. The only visible effect of the blast was a ripple effect on the water in the Money Pit shafts, but there was no let-up in the flow of water from the flood tunnel. Once again, work ceased for the winter and, in

1897, a new set of pumps was commissioned, which succeeded in lowering the water level in the Money Pit shaft to a depth of ninety feet. Blair's Company also commissioned a new drilling rig. On the first drilling attempt, they hit another wooden platform at 126 feet. The bit bored through the wood, but was then halted by a metal object of some kind. Withdrawing the drill, the team fitted a new drill with a smaller diameter. Again it hit the metal object, but then the drill seemed to move the object. At 154 feet the drill struck what at first seemed to be a stone slab, through which the men bored into a chamber with a floor area of twenty-five square feet and a height of seven feet. The drill bit was removed and a sample of the roof and floor despatched to a company in London for analysis. It turned out that the "stone" was, in fact, an artificial substance with the same properties as concrete. We tend to think of concrete as a modern invention, but over two thousand years ago, the Romans were using a type of hardened cement or concrete made from mixture of crushed volcanic pozzolan ash mixed with an aggregate of hydrated (slaked) lime and pebbles. This Roman "concrete" was then poured into a shuttered structure to set. The men who built the Money Pit were probably familiar with this Roman technology.

While the sample was being analysed, drilling continued, and, each time the bit was removed from the shaft, core samples were carefully removed and stored in readiness to be presented at the next meeting of the board of directors. The board finally met in Truro and examined the samples which had been packed in a large open-topped receptacle with the result that the heavier debris had sunk to the bottom, while the lighter material floated on the surface. One of the directors retrieved a small, round object and carefully unrolled it. It was a fragment of sheepskin parchment, approximately half an inch by a quarter of an inch, containing the letters "ui," "vi," or "wi," of unknown significance.

Having made further attempts to prevent water from flooding the Money Pit, Blair's company came to the conclusion that there was a second flood tunnel. This was confirmed when Blair's men put dye into the money pit and traces of it appeared in the sea off the south coast of the island, and not at Smith's Cove. This discovery came too late, however, as Blair had run out of money. He protected his interest, though, by making a successful claim for title to the land, and, in 1905, the Canadian government granted Blair a claim of treasure trove to the Oak Island Money Pit.

At the beginning of the twentieth century, a future president of the United States became involved in an exploration project on Oak Island. In 1909, at the age of twenty-seven, Franklin D. Roosevelt became part of an exploration team, and, although the team failed to make any progress in retrieving the treasure, Roosevelt maintained a lifelong interest in Oak Island. There were numerous attempts during the 1930s and right up to the 1960s which achieved very little, though at the cost of several more lives. Then, in 1970, a new investment group, Triton Alliance, commissioned a geological study of the island by Golder Associates of Toronto. The cost of this survey, which was carried out during the summer of 1970, was estimated to be in the region of $100,000. The survey tested soil and obtained core samples from deep drillings, which were used to produce a detailed analysis of the geological structure of the island, which was combined with the production of a set of cross-sectional maps of the underground terrain. The Golder Report has remained confidential, obviously, and is not available for public scrutiny, but a small amount of information to do with the discovery of worthless artefacts in the course of previous excavations has leaked into the public domain. In 1971, a borehole, 10-X, was sunk about ten metres to the north of the original Money Pit, and core samples were taken at a depth of 212 feet. The samples contained fragments of china, brass, and wood cribbing. The borehole was enlarged to allow a camera to be lowered into what turned out to be a water-filled cavern with a roof at the 212-foot level. While the camera was being operated, Dan Blankenship, one of the treasure seekers, was monitoring the television screen and, as the lights on the camera attempted to penetrate the murky water, he observed what appeared to be a severed human hand suspended in the water. There were other witnesses to this revelation, some of whom managed to take photos of the television screen as the camera then picked out what appeared to be a couple of chests, but, before an in-depth investigation of the cavern could be completed, borehole 10-X imploded, crushing the cribbing and almost killing Blankenship.

Since its discovery in the late eighteenth century, the Money Pit on Oak Island has yielded only a few worthless artefacts, gained at the cost of a few fortunes and several lives. For the time being Oak Island remains an elusive mystery, but, if there is a treasure hoard hidden deep below the ground, and if it is the lost treasure of the Templars, not only did the Knights Templar have some treasure worth taking great pains to hide, but they also had the engineering expertise and wealth to hide it on Oak Island. Secrets that threatened the authority and very existence of the Church would have warranted such efforts to conceal them.

The Peasants' Revolt and the Hospitallers

The Peasants' Revolt of 1381 was one of the most serious acts of civil disobedience and unrest that has ever occurred in Britain. What could have led to such a spontaneous uprising right across southern England at a time when communications infrastructure was so poor? The illiterate peasants were serfs, yoked to the land-owning gentry. They worked hard, but had no civil rights, and just about everything they produced belonged either to their liege lord or to the Church. Poverty and malnutrition were their lot under the existing legal system. A peasant caught poaching rabbits or other game for food to supplement his meagre diet would be subjected, at the very least, to a beating, and might quite possibly be executed. Peasants were not even well treated by the Church; any serf heard criticizing the affluent Church was in danger of having his lower lip cut off. Between 1315 and 1318, to compound the problem of malnutrition, there were crop failures, followed by widespread famine in 1340. Then, in 1348, as if the people had not already suffered enough, there was an outbreak of plague, the Black Death, which decimated the population and led to a severe shortage of labour. Between 1310 and

1350, the population declined from around four million to only two-and-a-half million. Due to the shortage of labour, the peasants began to demand their freedom and payment, for their work, but the authorities issued a statute limiting labourers' rights to the pre-plague status quo. However, many estates were suffering from a shortage of labour, and, to encourage peasants to remain on their estates, a number of lords began to offer inducements to retain their labourers. These inducements included granting the serfs their freedom and offering them wages, but thirty years after these concessions had been granted, some unscrupulous lords were employing lawyers to research the genealogy of peasants in an attempt to revoke the privileges of free men and to re-impose the status of serf on those freemen descended from serfs. Peasants were also required to work on Church land for two days each week in return for nothing; this made the Church rich, while keeping the peasantry poor. Peasants did not have enough time to work on their own crops, so their families went hungry.

Before the Peasants' Revolt, John Ball, the rebel priest from Kent, petitioned tirelessly to have this imposition by the Church abolished. Instead, yet another hardship befell the peasants: the Crown levied a poll tax three times higher than its predecessor to pay for the Hundred Years' War. The new poll tax was introduced by John O'Gaunt, Duke of Lancaster, and his fellow councillors, leading to John O'Gaunt being targeted during the rebellion. The peasants failed to kill him only because he was out of London on the king's business. Revolutions are rarely spontaneous, and the Peasants' Revolt was no exception. For several years prior to the Peasants' Revolt, disgruntled clergy had sown the seeds of revolution as they travelled from town to town in England. They had preached against injustice and the wealth and corruption of the Church. In the months preceding the uprising, laymen set up a communications network, subsequently known to historians as "The Great Society," or brotherhood of people. Laymen held secret meetings throughout central England and, after the revolution had been suppressed, some laymen who were arrested as rebel leaders admitted to being agents of a London-based "Great Society."

Three quarters of a century earlier on 16 May, 1312, when Pope Clement V had disbanded the Order of Templars, their estates throughout Europe, including those in Greece and Cyprus, had been given to the Hospitallers. After the Peasants' Revolt, it is alleged that one captured rebel leader, when asked for the reasons for the rebellion, replied, "First, and above all else, the destruction of the Hospitallers." Other leaders admitted that the Hospitallers and their property had been singled out for attack during the revolt because the Hospitallers had paid a large sum of money to the King of France in 1312 to help recompense him for his expenses incurred in suppressing the Templars. It seems that there was a more subversive agenda to the Peasants' Revolt than simply redressing injustices to which the serfs were subject. It appears as if a secret society affiliated to the Templars was established in England four centuries before Freemasonry became fashionable. It is likely that disenchanted parish priests would have spread the message of rebellion initially, but in those times a word in the wrong place could quickly lead to the culprit being hanged from a nearby tree. Secrecy was therefore of critical importance and the clergy must have conspired with the "Great Society," to communicate a secret timetable for the revolution. The Society would have been responsible for co-ordinating the uprising in places as far away as Coventry, Nottingham, and the border with Scotland. The Great Society seems to have had a foot in two camps; one foot was certainly in the Templar camp, given that the mob singled out the Hospitaller leadership and its property for attack during the rebellion, and the other foot was in the camp of Freemasonry, based on the name of Wat Tyler.

Very little is known about Wat Tyler, apart from the fact that when he appeared at the head of the Peasants' Revolt, he was overwhelmingly accepted as the leader of the revolt, despite the fact that rebels from the Home Counties were under the leadership of other revolutionaries, all of which seems to hint that Tyler was a member of, or was being used by, the "Great Society," the possible precursor of Freemasonry. Within Freemasonry, each lodge has a Tyler, a sentry guarding the lodge against intruders. The Wat Tyler of the Peasants' Revolt was accustomed to authority and giving orders in the expectation that they would be carried out. He issued an order that all men within thirty-six miles of a coast should stay put during the revolt, to forestall any attempt by the French to take advantage of the unsettled state of England to stage an invasion. Riots began in several parts of England, notably in Kent and Essex, and, on 7 June, 1381, Wat Tyler came to the fore. For eight days, he held centre stage before being killed by the Mayor of London during negotiations at Smithfield, in London, on Saturday 15 June. During that time, news of the uprising spread and peasants marched on London from Surrey, Sussex, Suffolk, Cambridgeshire, Norfolk, Buckinghamshire, and Hertfordshire. Estimates of the number of rebels vary, with the lowest figure being about 30,000, while some sources estimate that Wat Tyler led an army of around 60,000 peasants. Irrespective of how big the army was, it certainly frightened the establishment. The event that ignited the revolt occurred on 30 May when Thomas Bampton, the king's tax collector for Essex, was harassed and pursued out of Brentwood by men from the villages of Stanford, Fobbing, and Corringham. The authorities responded quickly and, on 2 June, Sir Robert Belknap, a local Chief Justice, entered Brentwood under the protection of a small group of military personnel. But they, too, were evicted from the town and a couple of Belknap's men were captured and killed. The rebels had tasted blood and on 6 June, 1381, John Belling, a serf belonging to Sir Simon Burley's estate, was rescued from Rochester Castle. The following day, following the seizure of the castle, the rebels from Essex elected Wat Tyler as their leader. Immediately, they burnt and sacked a Hospitaller *commanderie* at Cressing Temple which had previously belonged to the Templars. The revolution spread into Kent, where John Ball, one of the disgruntled priests and a key player in the revolution, was rescued from the church prison at Maidstone, where the Archbishop of Canterbury had incarcerated him for sedition. Twenty years earlier, John Ball had begun his mission at York, where he had begun to preach in support of justice for the peasants. From York, he moved to Wat Tyler's home town of Colchester, where he continued to preach his seditious sermons. John Ball spent the next twenty years preaching to the people of Kent about the irregularities and injustices of the Church. Over those years, John Ball was imprisoned twice, once on the orders of Cardinal Simon Langham, Archbishop of Canterbury, and once by his successor, Archbishop Sudbury, who became the Lord Chancellor in 1380, an appointment which was to cost him his life during the rebellion. Sudbury was a close friend of the Lancastrian John O'Gaunt, who had imposed the poll tax.

The rebels of Kent, led by John Ball, seized and sacked the city of Canterbury, but they failed to capture Archbishop Sudbury, who was with Richard II and his ministers in the Tower of London, discussing the rebellion. However, the Archbishop had merely postponed his fate by a few days, as the Kent rebels killed him in the end. The rioting spread to attacks on prisons during which prisoners were freed; the rioters also focused on destroying legal records. The rebels from Essex and Kent then advanced in two columns on the city of London. By 12 June, Wat Tyler and the Essex men were camped in fields just beyond Aldgate, at Mile End. On the morning of 13 June the rebels from Kent arrived at Blackheath, where John Ball preached to the massed rebels, opening his sermon with the famous line, "When Adam dug and Eve span, who was then the gentleman?"

The rebels appreciated this reference to the absence of aristocracy and serfs in the Bible's account of the creation, and felt justified in protesting against a system which treated them as the property of landlords. While John Ball was preaching, news arrived that Richard II had left Westminster Palace and gone to the Tower of London for another conference with his ministers about the worsening situation. Attending the conference was Sir Robert Hales, the king's treasurer, Simon Sudbury, Archbishop of Canterbury, and John Legge, the Kent tax collector; also present was fifteen-year-old Henry of Bolingbroke. Luckily for Richard's uncle, John O'Gaunt, the king's senior adviser and the man who had imposed the poll tax, he was in Scotland on state business. As Richard could call on only 520 militia men for protection, in order to avoid further bloodshed, he opted for mediation rather than confrontation with the rebel leaders. To achieve that aim, Richard left the relative safety of the Tower and travelled by royal barge to Rotherhithe, where he agreed to meet Wat Tyler and the Essex rebels at Mile End. The negotiations at Mile End on the morning of 14 June were organized by the fourteen-year-old king, who, despite his youth, showed great courage in facing the revolutionaries.

At the meeting, Wat Tyler appealed to the king for redress of the injustices done to the serfs. The king responded favourably, and managed to calm the rebels with promises that he would ensure that parliament addressed their complaints, which included a demand for an end to the feudal system, a demand for the opportunity to trade goods in the market place, and, finally, a free pardon for all offences committed during the rebellion. Richard acquiesced immediately to the rebels' demands, issuing signed charters to that effect. The charters gave the serfs their freedom and, at that stage of the rebellion, having received these signed documents, the majority of the Essex rebels dispersed, but a few hardliners, led by Wat Tyler claimed that Richard's leading advisers, John O'Gaunt, Simon Sudbury, the Archbishop of Canterbury, Robert Hales, and John Legge, as well as the Crown officials in charge of levying the poll tax were guilty of corruption and should be executed. Despite his youth, Richard responded diplomatically by saying that the law would punish all persons found guilty of corruption.

While the Essex rebels were negotiating with the king at Mile End, the rebels from Kent arrived at London's Southwark Gate. Supporters of the rebels inside the City lowered the drawbridge, opening the way for the rebels to sack the city. One of the first buildings that they attacked was the Savoy Palace of John O'Gaunt. The fourteenth-century *Anonimalle Chronicle*, written by an unknown monk, gives a particularly vivid description of the sacking and burning of the Savoy Palace. It claims that after the rebels broke down the front door, they took all the torches they could find, lit them, and set fire to all the soft furnishings in the dressing rooms and bed chambers. It seems that the rioters were more interested in destroying property than in looting it; when one rebel was later found to have stolen a silver cup from the Savoy Palace, he was summarily executed by the other rebels. Downstairs, the rebels piled furniture and drapes in the reception rooms, and set fire to those, too. It is alleged that the rioters then found three barrels of gunpowder and, thinking it to be silver or gold dust, they threw the barrels onto the fires, where they exploded, setting the Great Hall alight. The rebels then turned their attention to Highbury Manor, given in 1271 to the Priory of St John of Jerusalem, or, as they are more commonly known, the Hospitallers. Ten years later, Highbury Manor was home to the Royal Treasurer, Robert Hales, Lord Prior of the Hospitallers. During the rebellion, Highbury Manor was earmarked for particular attention by the rebels who were "so offended by the wealth and haughtiness" of the Hospitallers that they destroyed much of the property. Meanwhile, the 20,000 rebels from Kent, led by Jack Straw, split into smaller groups. One group had destroyed the Savoy Palace and Highbury Manor, while another marched on the Tower of London, where King Richard had met with his advisers. About 400 rebels, led by John Starling, achieved what had never before and has never since been accomplished: they gained access to the Tower of London. It is alleged that men sympathetic to the rebel cause had left the gates open, allowing the rebels to storm into the citadel, shouting, "Where is the traitor to the kingdom? Where is the spoiler of the commons?" From the entrance to the White Tower it is alleged that Simon Sudbury, the Archbishop of Canterbury, replied, "Neither a traitor, nor despoiler am I, but thy Archbishop." The Archbishop was arrested, along with a Franciscan Friar, William Appleton, who was John O'Gaunt's physician, Sir Robert Hales, a Hospitaller and Treasurer to the King, and John Legge, a sergeant at arms and the Kent tax collector. The rebels dragged their captives up onto Tower Hill, where they were beheaded. They were killed not by a professional executioner with a single blow from an axe, but by having their heads laid on logs and struck off by repeated blows by peasants armed with whatever weapons they could find. Their heads were then displayed on spikes on London Bridge, as a warning to others who misused their powers. The young Henry of Bolingbroke, who was in the Tower with the others, was spared execution by the intervention of a rebel named John Ferrour of Southwark. He made the plea that a fifteen-year-old boy could not be held responsible for the errors and failings of the king's advisers.

In the late afternoon of 15 June, Richard requested another meeting with Wat Tyler, to be held at Smithfield, and, although William Walworth, the Mayor of London, had by then managed to raise a militia of over 5,000 men, the discussions started well for the rebels. Backed by his diminished force of Essex rebels, Tyler made further demands on the king and his councillors. These included the end of tithing, the abolition of bishops, the redistribution of wealth, equality for all men in law, and the right to hunt for food in the forests. The negotiations dragged on, and, in the late afternoon, as the heat became stifling, what should have been a minor event, turned into mayhem. Wat Tyler ordered a drink to rinse the dust of the day from his mouth. When a jug was brought to him, Tyler filled his mouth and swilled the liquid around, before spitting it out at the feet of the king. One of the king's valets was so incensed by what he saw as loutish behaviour in front of the monarch that he shouted out that he knew Tyler to be the greatest thief and robber in Kent. On hearing this slanderous accusation, Tyler dismounted and ran into the royal entourage to attack the valet. The mayor of London, William Walworth, was wearing chain mail under his cloak, a fact which saved his life when he tried to arrest Tyler, and Tyler fought back with his dagger. The mayor struck back at Tyler, slashing him across the neck. Tyler fell to the ground and one of the king's knights drew his sword and ran Tyler through with a couple of sword thrusts. As the rebel leader lay, mortally wounded, a silence hung over the assembled rebels and the royal party. The rebel bowmen bent their bows, ready to send a shower of arrows into Richard's men. The fate of the revolution hung in the balance. For a few moments of complete silence time seemed to stand still. Then, Richard, showing immense courage for a fourteen-year-old, rode out to the rebels, and spoke at the top of his voice, saying, "You do not wish to shoot your King, do you? I am your King, I am your captain, and your leader; follow me into the field at Clerkenwell and you shall have everything it pleases you to ask." The tension lifted as the rebels left the body of Tyler and slowly made their way to Clerkenwell. The rebels had always expressed loyalty to the king and shown hostility only towards the establishment which was enforcing what they saw as unjust laws.

While King Richard was successfully defusing the situation, the mayor of London rode back into the city as quickly as possible. Once within the city, he sent runners to spread the word for every able-bodied man to bring arms and give aid to the king at Clerkenwell. When the king, dressed in his sumptuous garments, reached St John's Fields, he rode among the rebels absolutely defenceless and unguarded. He rode for hours among the rebels, reasoning with them, aware, no doubt, that it would have taken only one person with a grievance against the monarch to assassinate him and thereby rekindle the revolution. Richard, however, kept the crowd mesmerized with his plain speaking, and his aura. During the hours which Richard had spent calming the crowd of rebels, the armed force raised by the mayor joined the king, but the mayor himself did not go immediately to Clerkenwell. Instead, with vengeance in mind, William Walworth hurried back to Smithfield. He made enquiries as to the fate of Wat Tyler, who, as the rebels dispersed, had been left mortally wounded on the ground. On hearing that Tyler was clinging to life and had been taken by some of his companions to a hospital for the poor at St Bartholomew's, the mayor forced his way into the hospital, where he found Tyler still alive and being cared for. Walworth ordered Tyler to be carried out into the centre of Smithfield and had him publicly beheaded. Tyler's head was then taken on a pole to be presented to King Richard at Clerkenwell. Walworth's action took all the fire out of the rebels' cause. They fell to their knees to implore Richard for mercy, which he wisely granted. The revolt was over.

As the peasants drifted away to their homes, the king knighted William Walworth, making him a gift of land worth one hundred pounds. Richard also granted knighthoods, gifts of land, and forty pounds each to three London citizens, John Philipot, Nicholas Brymber, and Robert Launde. He also knighted the squire who had run Tyler through with his sword. Retribution then followed, with Richard II going back on his word and cancelling all the charters that he had issued on 14 June, 1381. He ordered his army to attack the rebels, who were camped at Billericay in Essex. Almost two weeks later, on 28 June, a battle ensued which resulted in the death of five hundred of the rebels. The following week, a contingent of rebels from Fobbing, led by William Gildebourne and Thomas Baker, was executed at Chelmsford. The retribution continued over the next few weeks, during which an estimated 1,500 rebels were hanged or beheaded. John Ball, the rebel preacher, was captured in Coventry and taken for trial at St Albans, where, on 15 July, 1381, he was hanged, drawn, and quartered.

So ended the Peasants' Revolt, which had done nothing to improve the living standards of the peasants. In fact, it seemed that the only achievement of the revolt lay in the settling of old scores between the Templars and the Hospitallers, inspired and led by the Templar-affiliated Great Society, a precursor of Freemasonry.

Opus Dei

In 1928, Spanish priest Josemaría Escrivá de Balaguer founded a secret organization named Opus Dei ("Work of God," in Latin); since then it has become affiliated to the Roman Catholic Church. It is a relatively small organization, certainly compared with the Freemasons or the Catholic Church, having just over 80,000 members in 80 countries. Escrivá, who died in 1975, has since been fast-tracked towards canonization, the process beginning just seventeen years after his death. In 1992, he was beatified, then elevated, after an unusually brief delay, to sainthood in 2002. Because of some controversial – some might even suggest "unsaintly" – aspects of Escrivá's life, there has been opposition to this process within the Church. Among those who dissented are former members of Opus Dei, who wrote to the Pope before Escrivá's canonization on 6 October, 2002. In their letter, they claim to speak "not only from deep and wounding personal experience but on behalf of other people from a great many nations who have been deceived, mistreated, and dehumanized as members of Opus Dei." The letter goes on to claim that members of Opus Dei do not live and work "in the joyful spirit St Paul calls 'the glorious liberty of the children of God,' but in a mind-controlled parody of Christianity and in the shadow of an idol whom they call 'the Father' and 'our Father.'" While acknowledging Opus Dei's "zeal and efficiency . . . its help in combating communism in Poland and its contribution to countering pro-abortion propaganda in the developing nations," the writers of the letter accuse Escrivá of "dividing families" and seeking "prestige and honors, even as he fosters a cult of personality and promotes his own canonization." They also accuse the organization of doing "moral damage" to its members "through its culture of secrecy and dishonesty, and by the psychological damage it inflicts through depersonalization and emotional deprivation." And they attack Escrivá for his "arrogance and malevolent temper, his unseemly quest for a title (Marquis of Peralta), his dishonesty, his indifference to the poor, his love of luxury and ostentation, his lack of compassion, and his idolatrous devotion to Opus Dei."

No one can apply to join Opus Dei; its membership is by invitation only, leading its critics to accuse it of being secretive and elitist. Some have voiced disapproval of its methods of recruitment, which they liken to those of a cult. Opus Dei recruits most of its members from universities, where young men and women, away from home for the first time in their lives, are vulnerable to brain-washing techniques. Opus Dei has put into practice and made full use of the old Jesuit adage "Give us a boy and we will return you the man, a citizen of his country and a child of God for life." Some members, recruited in the 1980s, are now senior bankers, lawyers, military leaders, and politicians. As in any organization, some members reach great heights in their careers, while others remain on a lower level. The majority of Opus Dei's members have normal jobs, and, although they are not priests, they swear an oath of poverty and some members choose to remain celibate. Obligations to Opus Dei mean that some members live an almost monastic existence: accommodation for men and

women is segregated; the diet is frugal; and most of
members' incomes is donated to charity. Members of Opus
Dei are also expected to indulge in self-mortification as a
way of reminding themselves of how Christ suffered.
Practices include fasting, self-flagellation with a five-tailed
whip, and the wearing of cilices, spiked chains worn
around the thigh, which penetrate more or less deeply into
the flesh depending on the amount of pressure applied.

Opus Dei achieved new prominence when one of its
mentors was elected as Pope John Paul II. The new Pope
quickly granted to Opus Dei a special status in the
hierarchy of the Catholic Church, giving it an unusual
degree of independence under the umbrella of Catholicism.
Opus Dei has come a long way since its foundation in 1928,
but has entered a less certain phase following Pope John
Paul II's death in 2005 and the election of Pope Benedict
XVI. The Church may choose to continue to nurture Opus
Dei, perhaps valuing its political role – as ever, politics and
religion are never far from each other.

The End Times

While this book has attempted to find explanations for some of the mysteries which it describes, it has also raised many more questions, the answers to which could well remain locked away in Church archives and libraries. It has covered much ground, from the Pharaohs and the Essenes to the Dead Sea Scrolls and the various editions of the Gospels, which seem to have passed on a distorted impression of the life of Jesus. It has questioned whether the Church of Rome under the influence of the Pauline doctrines used the story of Jesus to promote its own ends, suppressing the Gnostic message of the early Christian Church of Jerusalem. Certainly, the Gospels have been edited; some of the changes made may have resulted from ignorance of the customs and lifestyles of Jewish communities at the time of Jesus, but others seem to have been made deliberately, for various motives. It seems that the Essenes evolved from an Egyptian priesthood, which fell from favour, leaving Egypt to settle at Qumran. Later, they hid much of their treasure, recording the hiding places on a copper scroll, which was discovered at Qumran in 1952. It is possible that the Essenes, associated with ancient Egypt and the goddess Isis, trained Jesus and John, and there is evidence that the bloodline of the House of David continued through the Magdalene, who, as the wife or consort of Jesus, brought that royal bloodline into French history. There is also evidence that the priest at Rennes-le-Château, Bérenger Saunière, was receiving money from the Hapsburgs for his support for the Priory of Sion's plan to restore a European monarchy under the auspices of the Rex Deus families. The lost treasure of the Templars may have travelled from France to Roslin, and from there to a final hiding place on Oak Island, Nova Scotia. During the Peasants' Revolt in England, peasants were seen to take revenge on individuals associated with the Hospitallers and their property. That hatred suggests a link between the leaders of the revolt and the disbanded Templars, who may well have been affiliated to the "Great Society," which is thought to have given rise to Freemasonry. There is evidence that the Masons lay behind Wat Tyler and the co-ordination of the Peasant's Revolt. A handful of the enlightened, such as Botticelli and Da Vinci, have attempted, through their art, to send messages down through the centuries. Finally, the links between the Rex Deus family, the Templars, and the modern families of the clan have been uncovered.

Today, it seems as if there is a three-way power struggle being waged for the hearts and minds of humanity. Firstly, the Vatican, it has been suggested, is trying to keep the Jews from regaining the Temple Mount. Some have claimed that the Holy See supported the Palestine Liberation Organization (PLO), while, at the same time, attempting to restore unquestioning obedience on the part of the Catholic faithful through organizations such as Opus Dei. As time passes more Opus Dei members may rise to top political and military posts, and thus be able to project Vatican thinking at the highest levels. Secondly, Rex Deus, in the person of King Juan Carlos of Spain, for one, may be in a position to exert influence in high places. Thirdly, the Arab world continues to support the Palestinians in their control of the Temple

Mount. There is also a fourth participant in the power struggle: Israel, which desires to control the Temple Mount, but missed its opportunity in 1967, when Jerusalem became a city under Israeli control. Since then, however, each Israeli president and prime minister, while expressing devotion to that holiest of places, which is so revered by Christians, Jews, and Muslims, has delegated nearly all control of the Temple Mount to Islamic religious authorities. Supposedly, this is to show Israeli commitment to Muslim rights, but it is more likely that Israel fears that any attempt to take control of the Golden Dome Mosque on the Temple Mount would provoke the Islamic world into a jihad which would result in the annihilation of Israel. In such a scenario, Israel is likely to resort to nuclear weapons, resulting in the "end times" forecast by so many religious commentators.

In the year 2000, the Muslim religious authorities – aided by an unlikely ally, the Vatican – raised the stakes by announcing that they would begin extensive excavations beneath the Temple Mount. Originally, it was claimed that the aim was to expand a mosque under Solomon's stables, but the large quantities of rubble and artefacts excavated from the Second Temple and dumped in the Kidron Valley, along with the scale of the operation, makes that claim unlikely. On 26 January, 2001, Israeli TV Channel One broadcast a video clip, which had been secretly filmed, showing a massive, new tunnel under the Temple Mount. This tunnel is directed into the heart of Solomon's Temple, located beneath the seventh-century Islamic building known as the Shrine of Omar, which is constructed over the Holy of Holies. It has been claimed that the purpose of the tunneling project is to recover any remaining treasures. Israelis are concerned that their cultural heritage and religious artefacts are being destroyed, while the Vatican is perhaps afraid that if the Israelis gain control of the Temple Mount, they may recover records which could damage the

Church of Rome. It is for this reason that the Vatican supported the PLO, and is supported, in turn, by its old protégés, the Knights Templar. In January 2001, a spokesman for Militi Templi Scotia, the Scottish Knights Templar admitted to the Glasgow Sunday Post, "We are currently involved in an attempt to remove control of the holy sites from the Israeli government. We believe they should be administered by the United Nations and are working with the UN and NATO to achieve that goal."

All this activity and subterfuge points to a secret struggle for control of the Temple Mount, which, unless it can be defused, has the potential to bring about a global conflict. All the world's religions have one thing in common: each one has a code of moral principles for living life in harmony with others. Some religious teachings also provide rules for good health, but what the religions seem to lack is the teaching of tolerance and respect for other faiths, and also for agnostics and atheists. If these faiths accept the principle of living in harmony with others, why do Protestants fight with Catholics? Why do Muslims fight against Jews and Christians? The answer seems to lie in the power that one faith can wield to subjugate the faithful of another religion; the power of a religion to control its believers is the fundamental corruption behind the political aspirations of all the religions of the world. If we accept that Elijah, Jesus, and Mohammed were all prophets and leaders, we have a basis for humanity to live together, without different faiths railing at each other that their god is better than everyone else's god.

A poet in my home town of Cleveleys, Lancashire, in England, was recently sued for inciting racial hatred because the words of a poem of his were taken out of context by the media. He wrote, "Burn the churches, burn the mosques . . ." before continuing to describe the misery caused by funda-mentalists of all faiths. His poem concluded with the words,

"Build the churches, build the mosques . . . and restore them to the purpose for which they were built" – the creation of a tolerant society, worldwide, free of power-hungry religious fanatics.

What little distance we have come over two millennia.

Select Bibliography

Michael Baigent and Richard Leigh, *The Temple and the Lodge*, New York: Arcade, 1989

Michael Baigent, Richard Leigh, and Henry Lincoln, *The Holy Blood and The Holy Grail*, London: Jonathan Cape, 1982

Michael Baigent, Richard Leigh, and Henry Lincoln, *The Messianic Legacy*, London: Jonathan Cape, 1986

Malcolm Barber, *The New Knighthood: A History of the Order of the Temple*, Cambridge: Cambridge University Press, 1995

E. Raymond Capt, *The Traditions of Glastonbury*, Muskogee: Artisan, 1983

Rev. C. C. Dobson, *Did Our Lord Visit Britain as They Say in Cornwall and Somerset?* London: Avalon Press, 1947

Lionel and Patricia Fanthorpe, *Secrets of Rennes-les-Château*, York Beach: Samuel Weiser Books, 1992

Robert Feather, *The Copper Scroll Decoded*, London: Thorsons, 1999

Laurence Gardner, *Bloodline of the Holy Grail: The Hidden Lineage of Jesus Revealed*, Beverly: Fair Winds Press, 2002

Fida Hassnain, *A Search for the Historical Jesus*, Ashfield: Down-to-Earth Books, 2004

Donovan Joyce, *The Jesus Scroll*, New York: Doubleday, 1973

Christopher Knight and Robert Lomas, *The Second Messiah: Templars, the Turin Shroud and the Great Secret of Freemasonry*, London: Century, 1997

Rev. Jovian P. Lang, *Dictionary of the Liturgy*, Totowa: Catholic Book Publishing Co., 1989

Rev. Lionel Smithett Lewis, *St Joseph of Aramathea at Glastonbury*, London: James Clarke & Co., 1955

Henry Lincoln, *The Holy Place: Discovering the Eighth Wonder of the Ancient World*, New York: Arcade, 1991

William F. Mann, *The Labyrinth of the Grail*, Grand Bay: Laughing Owl Publishing, Inc., 1999

Graham Phillips, *The Marian Conspiracy: The Hidden Truth About the Holy Grail, the Real Father of Christ, and the Tomb of the Virgin Mary*, London: PanMacmillan, 2001

William Smith, *Smith's Bible Dictionary*, Edinburgh: Hendrickson, 1990

Margaret Starbird, *The Woman with the Alabaster Jar: Mary Magdalen and the Holy Grail*, Rochester: Bear & Company, 1993

Andrew Tomas, *We Are Not the First*, London: Souvenir Press, 1971

M. J. Vermaseren, *Mithras, The Secret God*, New York: Barnes & Noble, Inc., 1963

Tim Wallace-Murphy, Graham Simmans, Marilyn Hopkins, *Rex Deus: the True Mystery of Rennes-le-Château and the Dynasty of Jesus*, Shaftesbury: Element, 2000